Educating the "Right" Way

Educating the "Right" Way

MARKETS, STANDARDS, GOD, AND INEQUALITY

Michael W. Apple

RoutledgeFalmer
New York & London

Published in 2001 by
RoutledgeFalmer
29 West 35th Street
New York, NY 10001

Published in Great Britain by
RoutledgeFalmer
11 New Fetter Lane
London EC4P 4EE

RoutledgeFalmer is an imprint of the Taylor & Francis Group.

Copyright © 2001 RoutledgeFalmer

Printed in the United States of America on acid-free paper.

10 9 8 7 6 5 4 3 2 1

Library of Congress Cataloging-in Publication Data is available from the Library
of Congress.

Apple, Michael W.
Educating the "right" way: markets, standards, and inequality / Michael W. Apple
        p. cm
Includes bibliographical references (p.) and index.
ISBN: 0-415-92460-X (hbk.)—ISBN: 0-415-92462-6 (pbk.)

Contents

Acknowledgments

Over the past ten years, I have devoted a number of books to the conservative movements that are continuing to reconstruct education in damaging ways. In *Official Knowledge* and *Cultural Politics and Education,* I combined historical, empirical, and conceptual investigations and sought to demonstrate some of the major dangers associated with such "reforms." The hold that such positions now have on society in general and on educational policy and practice in particular has not lessened. If anything, it has deepened and has become even more of a part of the common-sense of this and many other societies. This situation requires critical analyses that themselves are even deeper and wider. Hence, this book. *Educating the "Right" Way* stands on the shoulders of the volumes that preceded it, but it extends their critical analysis in what I hope are even more compelling directions.

I need to be honest at the very outset here. My arguments in this book are generated out of a number of things: a considerable amount of national and international evidence of what the effects of current policies in education actually are; my participation in movements against the radically conservative restructuring of education in many nations, experiences that provide evidence of the most compelling nature about the lives and hopes that will be lost if we do not continue the battle against these policies; and last but not least, my own anger at the arrogance of those who are such true believers in market logics that they can't see the damage that this arrogance actually creates in the real world.

Thus, my concerns here are grounded not only in the world of academic debate, but also in a considerable number of personal experiences here and abroad. As I say at greater length in my recent book, *Power, Meaning, and Identity*, the years I spent as a teacher in inner-city and rural schools made it absolutely clear to me that high-sounding words about efficiency and accountability and excellence and higher standards all too often fly above the realities of real schools and real classrooms filled with real teachers and real students and are often hopelessly naive about the economic and social conditions of parents and communities. The fact that I have seen close up what such conservative policies and practices, and the cuts in services that they entail, actually have done to close members of my own family also provides another motivation.

As with any book, this volume is something of a collective accomplishment. There are many individuals inside and outside of education whose wisdom has been important in enabling me to see what I might not have seen. Given the nature of this particular book, however, my debts are even more far ranging and international than usual. The list is long; but my debts are large. Among the people who have helped me think through a number of the arguments in this book are Petter Aasen, Jill Adler, Peter Apple, Shigeru Asanuma, Bernadette Baker, Stephen Ball, Len Barton, Basil Bernstein, Jo Boaler, Barbara Brodhagen, Kristen Buras, Dennis Carlson, Wilfred Carr, Roger Dale, Ann DeVaney, Debbie Epstein, Manuel Fabrega, Stephen Fain, Nilton Fischer, Regina Leite Garcia, David Gillborn, Carl Grant, Beth Graue, Maxine Greene, Richard Hatcher, Diana Hess, Allen Hunter, Michael James, Jonathan Jansen, Knud Jensen, Daniel Kallos, Ki Seok Kim, Herbert Kliebard, Jae-Ho Ko, Julia Koza, Gloria Ladson-Billings, Theodore Lewis, Lisbeth Lindahl, Alan Lockwood, Allan Luke, Eric Margonis, Fernando Marhuenda, James Marshall, Cameron McCarthy, Robert McChesney, Mary Metz, Alex Molnar, Antonio Flavio Moreira, Akio Nagao, Antonio Novoa, Michael Olneck, Jose Pacheco, Stefan Palma, Joao Paraskeva, Bu-Kwon Park, Daniel Pekarsky, Michael Peters, Gary Price, Susan Robertson, Judyth Sachs, Fran Schrag, Simone Schweber, Mi Ock Shim, Tomaz Tadeu da Silva, Parlo Singh, Graham Hingangaroa Smith, Linda Tuhiwai Smith, Richard Smith, Amy Stambach, Gita Steiner-Kamsi, William Tate, Carlos Alberto Torres, Jurjo Santome Torres, Renuka Vital, Amy Stuart Wells, Dylan Wiliam, Anna Zantiotis, and Kenneth Zeichner.

I particularly want to recognize the contributions of Steven Selden, Geoff Whitty, and James Beane. Their friendship and the intense discussions we have had over the years have been significant for this volume.

I have had the opportunity to work with many editors over the years at Routledge and other publishers. No one has been more talented than Heidi Freund. Her friendship and advice are deeply appreciated. Thanks also need to be given to Karita Dos Santos who took over from Heidi at RoutledgeFalmer.

It may be getting monotonous, but in each book I have written I thank the Friday Seminar. For the past three decades, I have met every Friday afternoon both with my graduate students and with the visiting faculty members who have come to work with me. These seminars are truly international and often equally intense. They combine political and cultural criticism; reading each others' work; mobilizing around political and educational issues of local, national, or international significance; and at times working with teachers among the group's members in their schools and classrooms. Of just as much import, these Friday meetings are a nice blend of seriousness and humor, the latter being one of the things that is too often missing in critically oriented groups. Almost everything that is found in this book has been written and rewritten with the help of past and current members of the Friday Seminar. Each and every one of them has my sincere thanks.

Bekisizwe Ndimande worked as a research assistant on portions of this volume. Not only are his efforts appreciated, but his experiences in the struggles over education in South Africa constantly served as a reminder of why the issues I deal with here are crucial.

The arguments in this book have been tried out at many universities, political meetings, and working groups throughout the world. A few specific places need to be given special mention, however. First, the University of Wisconsin, Madison continues to be the home of serious intellectual, political, and educational debate. It provides a special space where socially and culturally critical positions are located at the center not the periphery. Three other institutions deserve mention. Portions of this book were written when I was in residence at the Department of Education in the Norges Teknisk-Naturvitenskapelige Universitet in Trondheim, Norway, the Institute of Education at the University of London, and at the International Research Institute for Maori and Indigenous Education at the University of Auckland. Each of these institutions was characterized by that rare combination of stimulating discussion and friendship.

Finally, this book is dedicated to Rima D. Apple. Over the years we have lived and worked together, her own dedication to progressive causes and her commitment to excellence in teaching and scholarship have sustained my own commitments in crucial ways.

Chapter 1

Markets, Standards, God, and Inequality

INTRODUCTION

Open season on education continues. The media, candidates for public office, conservative pundits, corporate leaders, nearly everyone it seems, has an opinion on what's wrong with schools. I have mixed emotions about all this attention. On the one hand, what could be wrong with placing issues of what education does and should do front and center? As someone deeply involved in thinking about and acting upon schools, it's rather pleasing to see that conversations about teaching, curricula, evaluation, funding, and so much more are not seen as the logical equivalent of conversations about the weather. The fact that these discussions often are heated is also something to be welcomed. After all, what our children are to know and the values this should embody is serious business.

On the other hand, all of this attention creates some disquietude. One word in the last sentence of the previous paragraph explains one reason for this—business. For all too many of the pundits, politicians, corporate leaders, and others, education *is* a business and should be treated no differently than any other business. The fact that this position is now becoming increasingly widespread is evidence of some worrisome tendencies. Of the many voices now talking about education, only the most powerful tend to be heard. While there is no one unitary position that organizes those with political, economic, and cultural power, the central tendencies around which they are found tend to be more conservative than not.

What are these voices saying? Over the past decades, conservative groups in particular have been pressing for public funding for private and religious schools. Voucher plans have been at the forefront of this movement. In the eyes of voucher proponents, only by forcing schools onto a competitive market will there be any improvement. These pressures are complemented by other kinds of attacks, such as the following argument. "Facts" are missing in the curriculum. Traditional content and methods have been jettisoned as our schools move toward trendy (and overly multicultural) subjects that ignore the knowledge that made us such a great nation. Raise standards. Get more tests in schools, based on "real" knowledge. Raise the stakes for teachers and students who fail them. This will guarantee that our schools return to time-honored content and more traditional methods. If tests are not enough, mandate and legislate traditional methods and content at a state level.

Vouchers are in the air—and in the courts. High stakes testing is also in the air—and in news reports that document the damaging bureaucratic and technical problems that have occurred when such tests were instituted all too quickly in a number of cities. Other evidence for some of the latter pressures on traditional content and methods is not hard to find either. In several states, hotly contested bills have been introduced, and in some instances passed, that mandate the use of phonics in literacy instruction. The stereotype that what are called "whole-language" methods—that is, methods that are grounded in the lived experience of students' actual language and literacy use—have totally replaced phonics is widespread. There is actually little evidence that this is the case, since most teachers seem to use a "briccolage" of multiple approaches depending on the needs that have to be met.[1] However, this has not interrupted the agenda of those who are deeply committed to the politics of conservative restoration in education. The same groups sponsoring legislative mandates of this type also often stand behind the attacks on the teaching of evolution and the supposed loss of God's guiding word in schools.

All these movements are swirling around simultaneously. Every time one begins to understand one set of pressures, another one enters from a different direction. Each has "the" answer, if only we would become true believers and follow them. Each and every one of these pressures is situated within larger dynamics. I want to stop the swirl for a little while in order to make sense of them both in education and in their relation to larger ideological and economic forces in societies like our own. Because these pressures and forces are complicated, let me begin this sense-making process in a straightforward way—with a story about a child, a teacher, and a school in a particular community.

JOSEPH'S STORY

Joseph sobbed at my desk. He was a tough kid, a hard case, someone who often made life difficult for his teachers. He was all of nine years old and here he was sobbing, holding on to me in public. He had been in my fourth-grade class all year, a classroom situated in a decaying building in an East Coast city that was among the most impoverished in the nation. At times I wondered, seriously, whether I would make it through that year. There were many Josephs in that classroom, and I was constantly drained by the demands, the bureaucratic rules, the daily lessons that bounced off the kids' armor. Yet somehow that year was satisfying, compelling, and important, even though the prescribed curriculum and the textbooks that were meant to teach it were often beside the point. They were boring to the kids and boring to me.

I should have realized the first day what it would be like when I opened that city's "Getting Started" suggested lessons for the first few days and it began with the suggestion that "as a new teacher" I should circle the students' desks and have them introduce each other and tell something about themselves. It's not that I was against this activity; it's just that I didn't have enough unbroken desks (or even chairs) for all the students. A number of the kids had nowhere to sit. This was my first lesson—but certainly not my last—in understanding that the curriculum and those who planned it lived in an unreal world, a world *fundamentally* disconnected from my life with those children in that inner-city classroom.

But here's Joseph. He's still crying. I've worked extremely hard with him all year long. We've eaten lunch together; we've read stories; we've gotten to know each other. There are times when he drives me to despair and other times when I find him to be among the most sensitive children in my class. I just can't give up on this kid. He's just received his report card and it says that he is to repeat fourth grade. The school system has a policy that states that failure in any two subjects (including the "behavior" side of the report card) requires that the student be left back. Joseph was failing "gym" and arithmetic. Even though he had shown improvement, he had trouble staying awake during arithmetic, had done poorly on the mandatory citywide tests, and hated gym. One of his parents worked a late shift and Joseph would often stay up, hoping to spend some time with her. And the things that students were asked to do in gym were, to him, "lame."

The thing is, he had made real progress during the year. But I was instructed to keep him back. I knew that things would be worse next year. There would still not be enough desks. The poverty in that community would still be horrible, and health care and sufficient funding for job training and other services would be diminished. I knew that the available jobs in this former mill town paid deplorable wages and that even with both of his parents working for pay, Joseph's family income was simply insufficient. I also knew that, given all that I already had to do each day in that classroom and each night at home in preparation for the next day, it would be nearly impossible for me to work any harder than I had already done with Joseph. And there were another five children in that class whom I was supposed to leave back.

So Joseph sobbed. Both he and I understood what this meant. There would be no additional help for me—or for children such as Joseph—next year. The promises would remain simply rhetorical. Words would be thrown at the problems. Teachers and parents and children would be blamed. But the school system would look like it believed in and enforced higher standards. The structuring of economic and political power in that community and that state would again go on as "business as usual."

The next year Joseph basically stopped trying. The last time I heard anything about him was that he was in prison.

This story is not apocryphal. While the incident took place a while ago, the conditions in that community and that school are much worse today. And the intense pressure that teachers, administrators, and local communities are under is equally worse. It reminds me of why I mistrust our incessant focus on standards, increased testing, marketization and vouchers, and other kinds of educational "reforms" that may sound good in the abstract but often work in exactly the opposite way when they reach the classroom level. It is exactly this sensibility of the contradictions between proposals for reform and the realities and complexities of education on the ground that provides the impetus for this book.

We face what in the next chapter I call *conservative modernization*. This is a powerful, yet odd, combination of forces that is in play in education, a combination that many educators, community activists, critical researchers, and others believe poses substantial threats to the vitality of our nation, our schools, our teachers, and our children. As I noted, we are told to "free" our schools by placing them into the competitive market, restore "our" traditional common culture and stress discipline and character, return God to our classrooms as a guide to all our conduct inside and outside the school, and tighten central control through more rigorous and tough-minded standards and tests. This is all supposed to be done at the same time. It also is all supposed to guarantee an education that benefits everyone. Well, maybe not.

Education is too often thought of as simply the delivery of neutral knowledge to students. In this discourse, the fundamental role of schooling is to fill students with the knowledge that is necessary to compete in today's rapidly changing world. To this is often added an additional caveat: Do it as cost-effectively and as efficiently as possible. The ultimate arbiter of whether we have been successful at this is students' mean gains on achievement tests. A neutral curriculum is linked to a neutral system of accountability, which in turn is linked to a system of school finance. Supposedly, when it works well, these linkages guarantee rewards for merit. "Good" students will learn "good" knowledge and will get "good" jobs.

This construction of good schooling, good management, and good results suffers from more than a few defects. Its foundational claims about neutral knowledge are simply wrong. If we have learned anything from the intense and continuing conflicts over what and whose knowledge should be declared "official" that have raged throughout the history of the curriculum in so many nations, it should have been one lesson. There is an intricate set of connections between knowledge and power.[2] Questions of whose knowledge, who chooses, how this is justified—these are *constitutive* issues, not "add-ons" that have the status of afterthoughts. This construction of good education not only marginalizes the politics of knowledge but also offers little agency to students, teachers, and community members. In some ways, it represents what Ball has characterized as "the curriculum of the dead."[3]

Further, it is unfortunate but true that most of our existing models of education tend to ratify or at least not actively interrupt many of the inequalities that so deeply characterize this society. Much of this has to do with the relations between schooling and the economy, with gender, class, and race divisions in the larger society, with the intricate politics of popular culture, and with the ways we finance and support (or don't) education.[4] The connections between schooling and good jobs are weakened even more when we closely examine what the paid labor market actually looks like. Rosy statistics of stock market gains and wealth creation obscure the fact that in the real existing economy, all too many jobs require low levels of skills and low levels of formal education. A decided mismatch exists between the promises of schooling and actual job creation in our supposedly glorious free market economy, a mismatch that is distinctly related to the exacerbation of race, gender, and class divisions in this society.[5]

Of course, there are those who see a much different connection between the market and education, one that is much more positive. For them, markets may offer hope for children, but even more so for the entrepreneurs who invest in marketized schooling. In their minds, the $700 billion education sector in the United States is ripe for transformation. It is seen as the "next health care"—that is, as a sphere that can be mined for huge profits. The goal is to transform large portions of publicly controlled nonprofit educational institutions into a "consolidated, professionally managed, money-making set of businesses that include all levels of education."[6] Even though comparatively little money is being made now, for-profit companies are establishing law schools; creating and/or managing elementary, middle, and secondary schools; and engaging in education on factory floors and in businesses. Billions of dollars from corporations, investment funds, and even your pension funds (if you are lucky enough to have one) are pouring into for-profit educational ventures. In essence, in the words of Arthur Levine, the president of Teachers College at Columbia University, capital has said, "You guys are in trouble and we're going to eat your lunch."[7] The motives of the private companies involved are clear. At the same time as they will eliminate the waste that putatively always comes from public schooling, they will turn education into "an efficiently run and profitable machine–using investors' money instead of tax dollars."[8] I wonder what Joseph would say as he sits in his perhaps soon-to-be for-profit prison, having come from a city whose economic base was destroyed as owners and investors closed the factories there and moved them to nonunionized areas so that they wouldn't have to pay a livable wage, or for decent schooling, health care, or pensions.

CONSERVATIVE AGENDAS

From my comments so far, you may have guessed that this book is situated in a specific place on the political/educational spectrum. While there may occasionally be problems with the traditional categories of "left" and "right" in sorting through the complexities of politics on the ground in all of our nations, I consciously and without apology position myself on the left. In my mind, the United States remains a vast experiment, one in which both right and left argue about what it is an experiment *in*. The debate over this is vital and undoubtedly will continue. Indeed, it is part of the political lifeblood of the nation. However, like Richard Rorty, I also believe that it is the left which keeps it going.

> For the Right never thinks that anything much needs to be changed: it thinks the country is basically in good shape, and may well have been in better shape in the past. It sees the Left's struggle for social justice as mere trouble making, as utopian foolishness. [Yet] the Left, by definition is the party of hope. It insists that our nation remains unachieved.[9]

Rorty is insightful about the role of progressive criticism in keeping this nation moving. After all, almost all of the social programs that many of us now take as "natural"—social security, for example—came about because of progressive mobilizations against the denial of basic human rights. However, Rorty is on less secure grounds when he claims that "the Right never thinks anything much needs to be changed," for a good deal of the right is very much involved in radical transformations. Over the past two to three decades, the right has mounted a concerted attack on what many of us took as natural. The entire public sphere has been brought into question. While these attacks on public institutions are broader than education, educational institutions have been centrally located in rightist criticisms. For this very reason, I want to devote this book to an analysis of rightist educational beliefs, proposals, and programs—and to their effects in the real world.

My reason for doing this is grounded in a particular political claim. Not only are rightist social movements exceptionally powerful now, but one of the most important elements of learning how to interrupt them is to understand what they did and do. Rightist movements have engaged in a vast social and ideological project. Examining how this has worked and why it has been successful can tell those of us who oppose it how it might best be countered. In my mind, if you want to stop the right, it is absolutely crucial to study what it did. This is what this book is about.

We need to be careful about essentializing here. The right is not a unitary movement. It is a coalition of forces with many different emphases; some overlap and others conflict with each other. Thus, one of the goals of this book is to examine the contradictions within this movement, demonstrating how these tensions are creatively solved so that this society *does* in fact change—but in particular directions. In none of these directions, however, will children such as Joseph be helped in the long run. Yet it is important to realize that while I disagree profoundly with many of the conservative proposals for education, it would be foolish to mindlessly support schools as they exist today. One of the reasons some people listen carefully to rightist criticisms is because there *are* problems in these institutions. Indeed, this is one of the reasons behind the popularity as well of a number of more critical and democratic school reforms.[10] Recognizing problems, however, does not mean that conservative "solutions" are correct.

One of the most important objects of the rightist agendas is changing our common-sense, altering the meanings of the most basic categories, the key words, we employ to understand the social and educational world and our place in it. In many ways, a core aspect of these agendas is about what has been called identity politics. The task is to radically alter who we think we are and how our major institutions are to respond to this changed identity. Let me say more about this, especially since who we are and how we think about our institutions are closely connected to who has the power to produce and circulate new ways of understanding our identities. Both the politics of education and of the construction of common-sense have played large parts here.

MAPPING THE RIGHT

The concepts we use to try to understand and act on the world in which we live do not by themselves determine the answers we may find. Answers are not determined by words, but by the power relations that impose their interpretations of these concepts.[11] Yet there are key words that continually surface in the debates over education. These key words have complicated histories, histories that are connected to the social movements out of which they arose and in which they are struggled over today.[12] These words have their own histories, but they are increasingly interrelated. The concepts are simple to list. In fact, they form the subtitle for this book: markets, standards, God, and inequality. Behind each of these topics is an assemblage of other words that have an emotional valence and that provide the support for the ways in which differential power works in our daily lives. These concepts include democracy, freedom, choice, morality, family, culture, and a number of other key concepts. And each of these in turn is intertextual. Each and every one of these is connected to an entire set of assumptions about "appropriate" institutions, values, social relationships, and policies.

Think of this situation as something of a road map. Using one key word—*markets*—sends you onto a highway that is going in one direction and that has exits in some places but not others. If you are on a highway labeled market, your general direction is toward a section of the country named *the economy*. You take the exit named *individualism* that goes by way of another road called *consumer choice*. Exits with words such as *unions, collective freedom, the common good, politics,* and similar destinations are to be avoided if they are on the map at all. The first road is a simple route with one goal—deciding where one wants to go without a lot of time-wasting discussion and getting there by the fastest and cheapest method possible. There is a second route, however, and this one involves a good deal of collective deliberation about where we might want to go. It assumes that there may be some continuing deliberation about not only the goal, but even the route itself. Its exits are the ones that were avoided on the first route.

As we shall see, powerful interests have created the road map and the roads. Some want only the road labeled market, because this supposedly leads to individual choice. Others will go down that road, but only if the exits are those that have a long history of "real culture" and "real knowledge." Still others will take the market road because for them God has said that this is "his" road. And finally, another group will sign on to this tour because they have skills in mapmaking and in determining how far we are from our goal. There's some discussion and some compromise—and perhaps even some lingering tension—among these various groups about which exits will ultimately be stopped at, but by and large they all head off in that direction.

This exercise in storytelling maps on to reality in important ways. While I develop this in much greater detail in the next chapter, the first group is what I call *neoliberals.* They are deeply committed to markets and to freedom as "individual choice." The second group, *neoconservatives,* has a vision of an Edenic past and wants a return to discipline and traditional knowledge. The third is what I call *authoritarian populists*— religious fundamentalists and conservative evangelicals who want a return to (their) God in all of our institutions. And finally, the mapmakers and experts on whether we got there are members of a particular fraction of the managerial and professional *new middle class.*

In analyzing this complex configuration of interests on the right, I want to act in a way similar to what Eric Hobsbawm described as the historian's and social critic's duty. For Hobsbawm (and for me), the task is to be the "professional remembrancers of what [our] fellow citizens wish to forget."[13] That is, I want to detail the absent presences, the "there that is not there," in most rightist policies in education. How does their language work to highlight certain things as "real" problems while marginalizing others? What are the effects of the policies that they have promoted? How do the seemingly contradictory policies that have emerged from the various fractions of the right—such as the marketization of education through voucher plans, the pressure to "return" to the Western tradition and to a supposedly common culture, the commitment to get God back into the schools and classrooms of America, and the growth of national and state curriculum and national and state (and often "high stakes") testing—actually get put together in creative ways to push many of the aspects of these rightist agendas forward? These are the questions that guide this book.

CONTESTED FREEDOM

One of the key concepts that is at stake in the discussions over who we are and how our institutions should respond to us is the idea of freedom. Many of the ideological positions that are currently embattled in the arena of education have different presuppositions about this key word. Some of the history of the dominant uses of this concept may be useful here, since these varied uses surface continually in the current debates over education.

Some of our earliest intuitions about the meaning of freedom are religious. For example, Christianity had an ideal of freedom. However, by and large it was not a worldly one, but a spiritual one. Ever since "the Fall," "man has been prone to succumb to his lusts and passions."[14] Freedom has a specific meaning here, one involving abandoning this life of sin and in turn embracing the teachings of Christ in all of one's activities. This definition of freedom can seem contradictory since in essence freedom and servitude exist side by side. Yet these are seen as mutually reinforcing. Those who accept the teachings of Christ are at the very same time "free from sin" and "servants of God."[15] This spiritual definition of freedom was planted early on in the history of the United States by the Puritan settlers of Massachusetts. It is clearly in evidence in the distinction between "natural liberty" and "moral liberty" made in 1645 by John Winthrop, the Puritan governor of the Massachusetts Colony. The former was "a liberty to do evil" while the latter was "a liberty to do only what is good." The distinction itself has an interesting history of effects.

This definition of freedom as flowing from self-denial and moral choice was quite compatible with severe restraints on freedom of speech, religion, movement, and personal behavior. Individual desires must give way to the needs of the community, and "Christian liberty" meant submission not only to the will of God but to secular authority as well, to a well-understood set of interconnected responsibilities and duties, a submission no less complete for being voluntary. The most common civil offense in the courts of colonial New England was "contempt of authority."[16]

Religious definitions of freedom were partly countered and sometimes supplanted by what might be called "republican" visions. Here, the citizen reached his (and it was quite gender specific) highest fulfillment in pursuing the common good rather than private self-interest. This too had contradictory elements. It could be embodied as a form of "thick" democracy by valorizing the common rights of an entire community. Yet such republicanism could embody a distinctly class-based vision when it was applied to the real world. This is visible in its assumption that only those who owned property "possessed the quality known as virtue."[17] Ordinary men were clearly not virtuous.

The religious and republican visions of freedom were not alone. The freedom of living with God and the freedom of living in a state bound by the consent of the governed through a common will were joined by a particular theory of liberty, which was essentially private and individual, enshrined in eighteenth-century liberalism. For classical liberals, only by shielding the realm of private life and personal concerns (the family, religion, and above all economic activity) from the state's interference could freedom be guaranteed. "The public good was less an ideal to be consciously pursued by government than the outcome of free individuals' pursuit of their myriad private ambitions."[18]

There were positive moments here. It needs to be recognized that such classical liberalism did call into question an entire array of hierarchical privileges and arrangements that made individual advancement extremely difficult. It established rights both of chartered corporations independent of the aristocracy and of religious tolerance. Furthermore, there can be no doubt that its grounding in a belief that "mankind" had natural rights that government could not legitimately violate enabled disenfranchised women, paid workers, and slaves to challenge the social and educational barriers they constantly faced. Yet, having said this, it is equally important to note that both republicanism and classical liberalism were also themselves grounded in a belief that only *certain* kinds of persons were actually capable of exercising the rights of freedom. "Dependents lacked a will of their own and thus were unable to participate in public affairs." Given the central place that self-direction and self-government held in these ideas of freedom, those who were not able to control their own lives should not be given a voice in governance. In this way, economic independence became a defining element in political freedom. Freedom and property became intertwined, and economic independence became the identificatory sign of being worthy.[19]

It is not too difficult to see how this connects with the dynamics of class, gender, and race. Any definition of freedom based on economic independence must by its very nature draw a line between those classes of people who have it (economic independence) and those who do not. The definition is also rooted in gender relations, since this ideal of autonomy has historically been defined as a masculine trait, with woman being seen as dependent.[20] Furthermore, slaves and people of color in general were usually seen as either animalistic or childlike. Freedom cannot be extended to those who by their very nature are dependent, especially since "they are not people, but property."

In opposition to these ways of understanding the meaning of freedom, progressive movements took certain elements of the classical liberal understanding of personal freedom, radicalized them, and mobilized around them. By organizing around issues of free speech, labor rights, economic security, women's rights, birth control and the control of one's body, a socially conscious national and regional state, racial justice, the right to a truly equal education, and many other struggles for social justice, a much more expansive positive definition of freedom has been fought for both inside and outside of education. Because of the long history of sacrifices extending beyond even this extensive list to include the struggles by environmental, gay and lesbian, and disability rights activist groups, major elements of this more expansive definition of freedom have been institutionalized within both the state and civil society. Our very idea of freedom has been deepened and transformed, and extended into realms well beyond the more limited positions I described earlier in this section.[21] However, this more expansive ideal of freedom, and each and every one of the gains associated with it, are now under threat.

For example, as consumer culture has grown, the measure of freedom's success has moved away from issues involving, say, the social relations surrounding paid and unpaid labor and has moved toward the gratification of market desires.[22] While this does have its roots in the notions of personal freedom associated with classical definitions of liberalism, freedom means, as a number of commentators have reminded us, more than satisfying one's market desires and more than doing what one pleases. It requires real chances to "formulate the available choices," something many of our fellow citizens are effectively denied.[23] Educational questions enter here in powerful ways as we shall see.

The turn to freedom as the market is registered in the influential writings of Friedrich von Hayek, in many ways the intellectual progenitor of the neoclassical economist Milton Friedman who delights in voucher plans as *the* solution to educational problems. For Hayek, the problem of freedom is related to the fact that conservatives supposedly have let the left both define the concept and mobilize it in debates over what our institutions should do. Instead of apologizing for capitalism, libertarian conservatives influenced by Hayek and others pressed forward the case that "real" freedom can only come from a combination of decentralized political power, extremely limited government, and unregulated markets. Only in this way can conservatives reclaim the idea of freedom and win the consent of the public. To win this kind of freedom, this meant instilling a belief in what are truly radical policies. The public had to be convinced that the unregulated marketplace of the neoliberals was not only the truest expression of individual freedom, but the marketplace must be expanded into every sphere of life. Only through market competition can "people [get] what they want."[24] Why should a marketized society keep schools out of such a market? They must be "freed" as well.

Yet the idea of freedom as a market was too libertarian for some conservatives. It placed individual choice as the arbiter of freedom. This ignored the need for "transcendental" values, for absolute truths. Only in reasserting a definition of freedom grounded in "tradition" and in the primacy of a return to Christian moral values and the values and traditions of the "West" could "virtue" be restored. For without virtue, there could be no freedom. For them, Von Hayek's and Friedman's vision of freedom did not lay the foundation for a moral community whose members shared a common heritage. Naked self-interest, in Marx's apposite phrase, was hardly an appropriate starting point for the defense of "timeless" values. The bottom-line individualism of neoliberals conflicts with the organic society united by the strong moral authority of tradition envisioned by neoconservatives such as William Bennett, who decries the loss of virtues, character, and "real" knowledge in schools.[25] This is one of the defining tensions of conservative movements today, a tension that must be resolved if conservative movements are to move society in the directions they ardently desire to go.[26] How this tension is resolved in practice in education is a focal point of this book.

Part of the problem of moving a society in conservative directions has been the association of neoconservative arguments with elitism. How could people be won to a position that seemed so committed to abstract ideas of truth and virtue? Some of this was accomplished through the development of an antigovernment populism, a stress on law and order, on the evils of welfare and on the breakdown of morality and the family, and on the sanctity of property. Virtue was being lost because of government interference not only into the market, but also into one's home and schools. Morality was lost when government entered, especially liberal government.

Part of this dilemma was also solved through the growth, and then integration within the larger conservative cause, of conservative evangelical movements. Estranged from a culture "that seemed to trivialize religion and exalt immorality," conservative Christians embraced not only the free market but also the need for strong moral authority. Freedom here was the combination of capitalism and what they perceived as the moral life as ordained by God.[27] Authoritarian populist religious conservatives had found a home under the conservative umbrella.

As we shall see later on, much of this movement was and is organized around both conscious and unconscious racial dynamics.[28] It has at its basis as well specific histories and dynamics surrounding gender relations. It also occurred at exactly the same time as the transfer of wealth upward in the United States and from the "Third World" to the "First World" reached almost obscene levels. And it was successful in part because the concept of freedom that became dominant, and that looked forward both to a modernized economy of stimulating desire and giving individual choice, was itself combined with a set of backward-looking visions that brought us closer to supposedly traditional Western values and to the God that established them. Let me preview many of my arguments in this book by saying somewhat more about each of these visions.

MARKETIZING THE WORLD

If we were to point to one specific defining political/economic paradigm of the age in which we live, it would be neoliberalism. This term may be less visible in the United States, but it is definitely known throughout the rest of the world. Although we here in the United States may be less familiar with the term itself, we are not unfamiliar with its tendencies and effects. Robert McChesney defines it in the following way:

> Neoliberal initiatives are characterized as free market policies that encourage private enterprise and consumer choice, reward personal responsibility and entrepreneurial initiative, and undermine the dead hand of the incompetent, bureaucratic and parasitic government, that can never do good even if well intended, which it rarely is.[29]

Such policies almost never require justification any more. They have become the common-sense of an emerging international consensus. Indeed, even with the recent powerful and one would hope lasting protests in Seattle, in Washington, D.C., and elsewhere against the arrogant policies of the World Trade Organization, neoliberal policies still have something of a sacred aura now, especially since we are repeatedly told that there are *no* alternatives worth considering. It may be imperfect, but it is the only system that is even feasible in a world governed by global markets and intense competition. While we are constantly told that nothing else is possible, it is important to realize that neoliberalism is in essence "capitalism with the gloves off."[30]

As I have argued elsewhere and as I demonstrate in the chapters that follow, neoliberalism transforms our very idea of democracy, making it only an economic concept, not a political one.[31] One of its effects is the destruction of what might best be seen as "thick democracy," substituting a much "thinner" version of possessive individualism. Once again, McChesney puts it well in his usual biting way:

> To be effective, democracy requires that people feel a connection to their fellow citizens, and that this connection manifests itself through a variety of nonmarket organizations and institutions. A vibrant political culture needs community groups, libraries, public schools, neighborhood organizations, cooperatives, public meeting places, voluntary associations, and trade unions to provide ways for citizens to meet, communicate, and interact with their fellow citizens. Neoliberal democracy, with its notion of the market *uber alles,* takes dead aim at this sector. Instead of communities, it produces shopping malls. The net result is an atomized society of disengaged individuals who feel demoralized and socially powerless.[32]

Even with these effects, it is still possible to argue on the grounds of efficiency that corporate models should dominate our societies. After all, they do allow for choice. Yet to valorize this vision of democracy as the correct one is to neglect one simple but crucial point. Most major corporations are anything but democratic. In many ways, they are more totalitarian than is admitted openly. Thus, jobs are cut ruthlessly. Profits are much more important than the lives, hopes, and well-being of employees who have given their working lives to these organizations. In general, no level of profit ever makes these jobs secure; profit must be constantly increased, no matter what the cost to families and employees. One must question if this is the ethic we should be introducing as *the* model for our public institutions and our children.

While the marketizers and privatizers feel free to hearken back to Adam Smith for justification of their policies, they are being more than a little selective. Yes, Smith sang the praises of the division of labor. But he also was more than a little clear in his denunciation of many of its inhuman effects. Government action was to be constantly promoted to overcome the destructive effects of the "invisible hand." For Smith, government "regulation in favour of the workmen is always just and equitable," but not "when in favour of the masters." Indeed, underpinning much of his argument was a call for equality of outcome, a position that was at the heart of his argument for markets.[33] It is easy to forget that it was not Karl Marx but Adam Smith who recognized that for every one rich person there must be five hundred poor ones.[34]

Of course, there are multiple ways of understanding this. Grasping what this means is made harder in daily life for all of us because of the dominant forms of interpretation that are now made available or *not* made easily available in education and in the media. As I noted earlier, the very concepts we employ to make sense out of the social relations that organize our lives not only reflect these relations but produce them. For example, our system of economic production and exchange can be understood within very different ideological frameworks using very different systems of representation. The discourse of the "market" brings distinctly different visions front and center than, say, the discourse of production. The language of "consumer" creates a reality that is not the same as the language of worker, capitalist, owner, or producer. Each term posits one of those road maps I discussed earlier; each term situates us as social actors in particular relations in economic and social processes. Each has attached to it an identity that positions us in relation to the account of the process as depicted in the discourse itself. In the words of Stuart Hall:

> The worker who relates to his or her condition of existence in the capitalist process as "consumer"... participates in the process by way of a different practice from those who are inscribed in the system as "skilled laborer"—or

not inscribed in it at all as "housewife." All of these inscriptions have effects which are real. They make a material difference, since how we act in certain situations depends on what our definitions of the situation are.[35]

For these very reasons, in this book I displace our usual understanding of concepts such as the "consumer" and the "market" in which we see these things as good. I place them in a different and much more socially critical framework, one that interrogates their actual functioning in the real world of education. Unless this is done, the use of market categories and concepts prevents us from seeing the process as a whole. Looking at education as part of a mechanism of market exchange makes crucial aspects literally invisible, thereby preventing critique before it even starts.[36] There are no exits to such a critique on its map.

RESTORING CULTURAL ORDER

As I demonstrate in the chapters that follow, the economic focus on flexible accumulation, economic insecurity, and the marketization of social life does not stand alone. An ideology of market freedom and equality based on "choice" is not sufficient to deal with the contradictions and conditions that emerge from such economic, social, and educational policies. Impoverishment, the loss of job security and benefits, racial and gender disparities in the ways "fast capitalism" trickles down to those on the bottom, and so much more—all of these also require a much stronger state to complement the weak state supposedly favored by neoliberals. This smaller strong state, however, is often a repressive one. It is involved in rigorously policing the population of those left out by the economy. Thus, in state after state, a huge amount of money is being spent on prison construction and maintenance. In many states, this is even more than similar expenditures on higher education. As I have argued in *Cultural Politics and Education,* the United States has found a way to deal with many of the effects of poverty; we jail poor people, and especially poor persons of color.[37]

However, as I hinted at before, these things are also accompanied by other ideological movements that are connected, but not reducible, to neoliberal economic policies and their associated small but strong state. It should come as no surprise that in times of insecurity and fragmentation, there is a concomitant rise in longings for social and cultural stability and an increased emphasis on the authority of basic institutions. Against the fears of moral decay and social and cultural disintegration, there is a sense of a need for a "return." In conditions such as these, a romantic past is often constructed, a past that glorifies (particular versions of) family and tradition, patriotism, Victorian values, hard work, and the maintenance of cultural order.[38] Barbarians are at the gates. And unless we restore "our" knowledge, values, and traditions to the central place they once had, civilization will be lost. It should not be surprising that here, too, schools and the curricula, teaching, and testing that are found or not found in them become prime areas of attack.

Again, we should not be too surprised by the rather checkered history these concerns have had both inside and outside of education. Let me give an example.

Manufacturing baron Abram Hewitt said it best when, in the latter part of the nineteenth century, he claimed that the task of social science and education was to find ways of making "men who are equal in liberty [content with the] inequality in distribution inevitable in modern society."[39] Not only the rich, but the middle class in general as well, believed that one's inability to advance in society was simply evidence of a lack of "character." A failure to advance bespoke a moral incapacity, the absence of those characteristics that guaranteed mobility—self-reliance and perseverance. Unions were not the answer, nor was government help. The only way to advance was to demonstrate the force of character to do it oneself, "to practice personal economy, keep out of debt, and educate their children in the principles of the marketplace."[40]

Thus, the suturing together of the needs and norms of the market and conservative views of appropriate character has a long history. Fears of economic decline, of the loss of "genteel" culture, of the loss of a common language and culture have constantly surfaced, often in times of market crisis and surges in immigration. Hybrid cultures are in essence bad cultures. They exacerbate our fears of cultural decline and economic uncertainty. The nature of this is indicated in the invention of (compulsory) common rituals. As Foner writes:

> Wracked by fears that the economic and ethnic unity of American society were in danger of disintegrating, government and private organizations in the 1890s promoted a unifying, coercive patriotism. These were the years when rituals like the Pledge of Allegiance and the practice of standing for the playing of "The Star-Spangled Banner" came into existence, Americans had long honored the Stars and Stripes, but the "cult of the flag," including an official Flag Day, dates to the 1890s.[41]

The current emphasis on "character education," on patriotism, and on restoring "our" culture must be understood in relation to this history. It is not an accident that it has occurred at this time. Nor is it a mere coincidence that those who promote these educational and social answers are also less than critical about both this history and the ways in which dominant economic dynamics may produce the ideological conditions they so lament.

CHURCH AND STATE

Markets and the restoration of character and "real" knowledge in education do not stand alone today. For a rapidly growing segment of the conservative population, God's message to all of us is to turn to both capitalism and tradition. Hence, in a tense but still complementary way, much of this emphasis on a "return" is supported by major elements of the Christian right currently. They believe that only by turning one's entire life over to *their* particular religious beliefs will this society and its schools be saved. Because of this, I shall need to pay a good deal of attention to them in this volume.

As odd as it seems, given my own political and educational beliefs, let me state that the Christian right is correct to the extent that in much of the colonial United States there was no firm separation between church and state. While they would see this positively, as ratification of the status of the United States as a Christian nation, the reality was often rather less positive. In Pennsylvania, while offering "Christian Liberty" to all of those who acknowledged "one Almighty God," all officeholders had to swear to an oath affirming their belief in Jesus Christ. Discrimination against Catholics, Jews, and even dissenting Protestants was rife. Indeed, up until the Revolutionary War, those Baptists who refused to pay taxes to support Congregational ministers were jailed in Massachusetts.[42]

The drive to separate church and state, to build a "wall of separation" as the deist Thomas Jefferson would say, was based on an attempt both by people such as Jefferson and others to free politics and "reason" from theological control and by a number of evangelical movements that wanted to protect religion from the "corrupting embrace of government." Only through such toleration would people be able to lead "truly Christian lives." In the process, many powerful churches lost their supply of public revenue and their special privileges. Yet, in many states, church and state were still closely wedded. Non-Christians were barred from public office; blasphemy and breaches of the Sabbath were rigorously prosecuted.[43] Any current reminder that the United States is and was a Christian nation also needs itself to be reminded that this is what it meant to be a Christian nation as well.

In saying this and in pursuing my arguments throughout this book, I do not wish to imply that religion has no place in schools. I have some sympathy with Warren Nord's position when he argues on secular and liberal grounds that "all students should receive a liberal education that takes seriously a variety of ways of making sense of the world, religious ways included, if they are to be informed, reasonable, and responsible individuals."[44] For Nord, America's public schools are illiberal in their refusal to take religion seriously enough. In the world of elite academic and educational life, religious sensibilities play little or no role. In the process, educational institutions have "disenfranchised large segments of the American people."[45] Nord may be overstating his case a bit here, but clearly religion plays a central role in the lives of a considerable number of people—and they do feel disenfranchised by the absence of religion in schools. Of course, for many of them it is not the study of religion as one of the aforementioned multiple perspectives that they wish to promote. Rather, it is a particular vision of religious truth, of biblical authority in all realms of life, that guides them. And there is a world of difference here.

ECONOMICS AND RELIGION

There is nothing new about movements that try to put all of these elements—capitalist markets, a romantic cultural past, and God—together. Take Christianity and its historical connection to capitalism as an example.

The great economist John Maynard Keynes once wrote that modern capitalism is "absolutely irreligious." The love of money, and the accumulation of capital, had led to the steady decay of religion. Religion had lost its moral significance because it did not touch on matters economic, except in the most tangential ways. The "creative destructiveness" of capitalism and the marketization of all aspects of our lives disrupted families, communities, traditions, paid and unpaid work, the "natural rhythms" of daily life, indeed all of our life.[46] In what is perhaps one of the most famous quotes about this process of creative destruction, Marx and Engels wrote that all "ancient and venerable prejudices and opinions are swept away, all new-formed ones become antiquated before they can ossify. All that is solid melts into air, all that is sacred is profaned."[47]

Yet there has been a powerful sociological and historical tradition that, while admitting the profaning of the sacred under capitalism, argues that capitalism and, say, particular forms of Protestantism have formed a symbiotic relation, each informing and shaping the other. The emphasis in

Calvinism on hard work, saving, and asceticism, for example, closely paralleled the needs of an emerging capitalist economy.[48]

This set of tensions—capitalism destroys traditional religions and uproots any sense of tradition, on the one hand, and capitalism and particular religions form a couplet that support each other, on the other—is creatively solved in the conservative evangelical movement. Capitalism is "God's economy." "Economic freedom" and market economies in education and the larger society are given biblical warrant. As we shall see, this is done quite creatively in schools and the larger society in such a way that the individual choice to be "born again" is mirrored in a market that allows for personal accumulation of wealth and choice.

Yet choice has its limits. For conservative evangelicals, one cannot choose without firm and foundational knowledge of what is right. And there is but one way, one place, to find this out. That is the Bible—and the Bible says what it means and means what it says. This inerrantist position is best exemplified and codified in the Chicago Statement on Biblical Inerrancy. "Holy Scripture, being God's own Word, written by men prepared and superintended by His Spirit, is of infallible divine authority in all matters upon which it touches. . . . Being wholly and verbally God-given, Scripture is without error or fault in its teaching."[49] The Bible, then, is not "man's truth" but God's truth. Its truth does not change; it was given *fully* in biblical times.[50]

Such "truth" is not new to education, by any means. Even a brief examination would show the ways in which biblical forms were powerfully influential in early schooling in the United States. Take as one example the ways in which children were to be instructed in literacy in the New England colonies. The most commonly used schoolbook in the later part of the seventeenth century, the *New England Primer,* instructed children in the alphabet in the following way:

A wise son makes a glad Father, but a foolish son is the heaviness of his mother.
B etter is little with the fear of the Lord, than great treasure and trouble therewith.

C ome unto Christ all ye that labour and are heavy laden, and He will give you rest.[51]

The *Primer* did not stop there. Lessons followed on "The Dutiful Child's Promises" in which one vowed that "I will fear GOD, and honour the KING." It included the Lord's Prayer, the Apostle's Creed, and a listing of the books of the Bible. Numbers were to be learned in order to "serve for the ready finding of any Chapter, Psalm, and Verse in the Bible." It ended with the Westminster Assembly's Shorter Catechism, including questions such as "What is the chief end of Man?" The answer is "Man's chief end is to glorify God, and to enjoy him forever." Another question asks, "What rule hath God given to direct us how we may glorify and enjoy him?" This is answered by, "The word of God which is contained in the Scriptures of the Old and New Testament, is the only rule to direct us how we may glorify and enjoy him."[52] Thus, there is no doubt that religion was central to the founding of schooling in America.

Later texts showed this continued influence. The McGuffey Readers, of which over 120 million were printed and used in the nineteenth and early twentieth centuries, read as much like a text in theology as in literacy. God was omnipresent within it, just but stern. The truths of the Bible were unquestioned; nor did one question their relevance to everyday life. Life was "God-conscious and God-centered." Students are to "live for salvation." All elements of the natural world can only be understood as "the expression of God's order." Indeed, as Nord reminds us, there are more references to God in the *Annotated McGuffey* than any other subject. Interestingly, the subject of death has the second largest number.[53]

These are not the only possibilities of understanding religion and its relations to the larger society, of course. The ways we think socially about religion have been varied. For some commentators, religion symbolizes the "felt whole" of a society and involves the deployment of symbols of social identity. Thus, religious meanings and institutions provide integrative forms that keep societies together and promote harmony. For others, such as Emile Durkheim, religion's very action in dividing the sacred from the profane is a positive response that celebrates sociality. It "sacralizes the fact and manner of human bonding as a prerequisite of any particular form of society."[54] For still others, such as some versions of Marx and Engels, religion played a less positive symbolic and material role. Beliefs in the supernatural and in divine powers represented ways in which social relations and inequalities were masked. Their social function was to obscure or distort the prevailing distribution of power and wealth and the social relations that supported them.[55] For those such as Weber and Simmel, religion is a vast symbolic resource in which meanings are able to be produced, transmitted, and contested. It is separated from other symbolic resources by the fact that it provides a warrant for claims to ultimate significance, but it could be adapted to suit the interests of particular sections of the society.[56] Thus, for Weber, there were close connections between particular kinds of Protestantism and the rationalization of the modern world.

Closer in time to us, those observers such as Peter Berger argue that religion plays another crucial role in "modern" societies. It keeps the existential nightmare away. For him, culture today is unstable, as are people's identities. Religious beliefs enable one to better withstand the corrosive effects of bureaucratic rationality and the development of *homo economicus,* the person who is defined only by her or his place as an economic being.[57] Finally, Michel Foucault traces out the ways in which the "pastoral power" that had been fostered by the major Christian churches spread out throughout society. It was assimilated into the state and used as an "individualizing tactic which characterized a series of powers: those of the family, medicine, psychiatry, education, and employers."[58] Yet, no matter what the differences in each of these perspectives on religion, each sees religion fundamentally *socially,* not as apart from society in some otherworldly realm but as integral to society. It has power—individually and collectively, positively and negatively. This is exactly what I wish to explore in the latter parts of this book when I discuss the growing influence of authoritarian populist religious conservatism on education as well.

However, I want to do this in a particular way. Following the leadership of Antonio Gramsci, I believe that the social meaning of religion has to be decoded in terms of the real-life experiences of people at particular times and places. He urged us to examine the ways in which churches worked to prevent a gap from forming between its formalized institutions and rituals and "the people"—that is, how at specific times and places religion connected to popular culture and the meanings of daily life. Gramsci's interest was in making organic connections between working-class and poor people and progressive movements for social justice.[59] My own interest is grounded in a similar politics; but I want to explore how organic connections are now made between people's daily lives and *conservative* religious movements, since these are the one's increasingly dominant today and these are the ones that seem to be exceptionally powerful in polarizing our beliefs about schooling currently. At the same time, I want to show connections that have been made between such religious tendencies and the growing belief that only through markets and a return to an Edenic past can schools, our children, and our nation itself be "saved." In doing this, I want to be absolutely clear that I am not taking a position that religious meanings and institutions must by their very nature be conservative. Popular religious meanings, movements, and institutions are not a priori radical or conservative. Much depends on the uses to which they are put and on the balance of social and ideological forces at a given time.[60] (Actually, from my own personal experiences working outside the United States, I tend to believe that in many nations it would be impossible to develop larger liberatory movements without religious mediations as one of the major dynamics. I take this position not only for empirical reasons—that is, because of the power of religion in these nations—but because I believe that utopian hopes are important for envisioning a better future. And religious yearnings often embody such dreams.)

MANAGERIALISM

The three previous elements of the radical restructuring of education and other institutions that I've just described—neoliberalism, neoconservatism, and authoritarian populism—do not cover all of the tendencies currently in motion on the conservative side of the spectrum. A final one concerns the impulses driving the restructuring of the role of government and the ways in which a relatively autonomous fraction of the managerial and professional middle class has taken on even more power in directing social and educational policies in directions that actually give this particular group of people more power and new identities as well. I pointed out earlier that the role of the state has been altered along the lines of a radical redefinition of the boundaries between public and private. We can think of this as involving three strategic transformations. First, many public assets have been privatized. Public utilities are sold off to the highest bidder; schools are given to corporations to run. Second, rigorous competition between institutions is sponsored so that public institutions are constantly compared with supposedly more efficient private ones. Hence, even if schools and other institutions are still state funded, their internal procedures increasingly mirror those of the corporate sector. Third, public responsibilities have been shifted onto the informal sector, under the argument that the government can no longer afford the expense of such services. In practice this has meant that a good deal of child care, caring for the elderly and the infirm, and so much more has been "dumped" onto the local community and the family. This is one of the reasons that it is crucial to realize that behind a good deal of the new managerialism and the importation of business models into the state is a specifically patriarchal set of assumptions and effects, since it is largely the unpaid labor of women in the family and in local communities that will be exploited to deal with the state's shedding of its previous responsibilities.[61] At the same time, while some aspects of the state are indeed dumped onto local communities, other aspects of state control are enhanced and made even stronger, especially its control over knowledge and values in schools and over the mechanisms of evaluating institutional success or failure in such cultural reproduction.

However, managerialism is not only about altering what the state does and how much power it has. It also offers new and powerful roles for the individuals and groups who occupy positions within the state. In technical terms, we might say that managerial discourse provides "subject positions" through which people can imagine themselves and their institutions in different ways. Thus, one of the key characteristics of managerial discourse is in the positions it offers to managers. They are not passive, but active agents—mobilizers of change, dynamic entrepreneurs, shapers of their own destinies.[62] No longer are the organizations they inhabit ploddingly bureaucratic and subjected to old-fashioned statism. Instead, they and the people who run them are dynamic, efficient, productive, "lean and mean."[63]

By importing business models and tighter systems of accountability into education and other forms of public services, managerialism doesn't just offer state managers new ways of thinking about their lives and their organizations. Aside from giving new meaning to the lives of managers within the new middle class, it promises—in the words of new managerialism—transparency, at the same time as it supposedly empowers the individual consumer. It is an ideal project, merging the language of empowerment, rational choice, efficient organization, and new roles for managers all at the same time. While the "spartan language" of efficiency does have its attractiveness to certain business groups, it has only limited appeal to many others. By reappropriating the discourse of antipaternalism and user-centeredness, it offers metaphors for a range of people to see their place in the new more responsive future. One can modernize the machinery of schools and of the government in general, be an efficient and business-like manager, and help people by ensuring "quality" at the same time.[64] What could be wrong with that? As I show later, however, this is not the rolling back of state power, nor is it really "empowering" for the least-advantaged members of our communities. Furthermore, its vision of managers organized around an efficient and revitalized professionalism in the service of consumers is partly a fiction. Active professionals are free to follow their entrepreneurial urges—as long as they "do the right thing."[65] As we shall see, Foucault's panopticon is everywhere.

ANALYZING CONSERVATIVE MODERNIZATION

In the chapters that follow, I provide a picture of how the odd combination of markets, return to lost traditions and values, a godly education, and the managerialism of tightened standards and guaranteeing "quality" are pulled together. In the process, I want to demonstrate which groups of people will wind up winning and losing as this constellation of "reforms" goes forward. In pursuit of this, I must bring to the attention of people in the United States not only research and arguments about what is happening here, but also evidence of similar reforms that have appeared in other nations. There are several reasons for approaching these issues with an international perspective. All too many discussions of education in the United States are characterized by a particular form of arrogance. "We" have nothing to learn from other nations. Or such discussions are unaware that many of the things in which we are engaged here have a history elsewhere, a history whose effects should make us rather cautious about engaging in the same policies. Or, finally, there is an assumption that our motives are pure and our traditions democratic. Hence, whatever has occurred in educational reforms in other nations (say, an increase in social inequalities in education when a particular change is instituted) simply couldn't happen here. It can and it is.

Chapter 2 goes into more detail about the assumptions that underpin the forces of conservative modernization specifically in education today and gives a clearer sense of the tensions and contradictions in the conservative movements. Chapter 3 deals with the actual effects that "reforms" such as establishing a competitive market in schooling, national and state curricula, ever-rising standards, and the increasing mandates of testing have had in schools in a number of countries. Its focus is on the neoliberal and neoconservative proposals that are having such a profound effect on educational policy and practice. This chapter also critically examines the ways in which the supposed alternative to these proposals— that is, ones that center around the literature on "critical pedagogy"—are weak in crucial ways, and thus will have a hard time interrupting rightist transformations. Chapters 4 and 5 deal directly with the growing power of conservative religious groups in debates over the ends and means of schooling. Chapter 4 discusses some of their recent effects and traces out the history of such movements, while Chapter 5 critically illuminates the ways in which their beliefs about curricula and pedagogy cohere with their larger positions on the economy, government, the family, gender relations, and the politics of class and race. Chapter 6 examines the ways in which the home schooling movement provides a mechanism for many of these emphases to come together. In Chapter 7, I assess the possibilities of interrupting the movement toward the right and suggest some strategies for doing so.

As you will see, a good deal of time is spent on conservative religious critics of schooling in the later sections of this book. I do this for a number of reasons. First, although it is crucial to pay close attention to the criticism of markets, standards, and testing (and I do), too often the creative ways in which many other groups have been brought under the umbrella of neoliberal leadership have been largely ignored. Second, such religious groups have been very powerful in putting pressure on schools in states and municipalities throughout the country, often making educators think twice (or three or four times) about what they will and will not teach and how they will and will not teach it. These groups have also been growing rapidly in influence so that many more people now consider themselves to be conservative evangelicals and are willing to take a public position on education based on this identification than ever before in recent history. Third, perhaps unlike many other people on the left, I believe that there are elements of insight in the position of the populist religious critics and that they have been stereotyped and ignored. Not only do I think that this is intellectually suspect, but it is also dangerous strategically if we do wish to counter the rightist turn in education in serious ways.

Because of this, while I am deeply concerned about what their implications are, throughout the chapters on conservative religious impulses I also want to be fair to the concerns they express—many of which cannot be easily dismissed. Thus, I will be at pains to show the elements of "good sense" as well as "bad sense" in their criticisms of some aspects of formal education.

These are the complicated tendencies I focus on in *Educating the "Right" Way*. I wish that it could be simpler. That certainly would make the story I need to tell much easier. However, when reality itself is complex and contradictory, so too must be our critical analyses. Throughout this book I combine the theoretical and the empirical. I must admit to being deeply worried that we have played the theoretical card so often at such a level of abstraction that we have vacated the empirical space and left it open for neoliberals and neoconservatives to occupy—which they predictably have done. Yet at times we positively *need* the distance that theory gives us in order to think through difficult issues.

Because of this, I fully recognize that there are tensions in what I do here. I criticize the kinds of theories that underpin many of the current educational reforms; and sometimes I do this theoretically as well as empirically. However, having done this I tend to take the position that "the only theory worth having is that which you fight off, not that which you speak with profound fluency."[66] This is a bit of an overstatement of course, since we do need to be "fluent" in any theory we propose to use. But it does point out that one's theoretical success should not be measured by whether there is an exact "fit." Rather, the efficacy of our theories needs to be measured by our ability to work productively with theories that are almost always inadequate in some ways but push us "further down the road" and enable us to see things that were hidden before.[67] The road I want us to travel on has exits that are not visible on the maps about education, culture, government, and the economy provided to us by dominant groups. Let us now look at these maps in more detail.

Chapter 2

Whose Markets,
Whose Knowledge?

INTRODUCTION

In the first chapter, I described the general directions this society has taken. I employed key concepts such as freedom to analyze the ideological dynamics that underpin these directions. In this and the next chapter, our attention will be more specifically on education—on the educational positions of each of the elements within the groups I identified and on a number of their largely negative effects on schooling here and elsewhere.

As I noted, we have entered a period of reaction in education. Our educational institutions are seen as total failures. High dropout rates, a decline in "functional literacy," a loss of standards and discipline, the failure to teach "real knowledge" and economically useful skills, poor scores on standardized tests, and more—all these are charges leveled at schools. And all of these, we are told, have led to declining economic productivity, unemployment, poverty, a loss of international competitiveness, and so on. Return to a "common culture," make schools more efficient, more responsive to the private sector. Do this and our problems will be solved.

Behind all of these charges is an attack on egalitarian norms and values. Though hidden in the rhetorical flourishes of the critics, in essence "too much democracy"—culturally and politically—is seen as one of the major causes of "our" declining economy and culture. Similar tendencies are quite visible in other countries as well. The extent of the reaction is captured in the words of Kenneth Baker, former British Secretary of Education and Science in the Thatcher government, who evaluated nearly a decade of rightist efforts in education by saying, "The age of egalitarianism is over."[1] He was speaking decidedly positively, not negatively.

The threat to egalitarian ideals that these attacks represent is not usually made quite this explicitly, since they are often couched in the discourse of "improving" competitiveness, jobs, standards, and quality in an educational system that is seen as in total crisis. This discourse is clearly present today in "New Labour" in the United Kingdom and in similar policies in the United States. In all too many ways, both nations' educational policies continue trends established under earlier conservative governments.

It would be simplistic, however, to interpret what is happening as only the result of efforts by dominant economic elites to impose their will on education. Many of these attacks do represent attempts to reintegrate education into an economic agenda. Yet they cannot be fully reduced to that, nor can they be reduced to being only about the economy. Cultural struggles and struggles over race, gender, and sexuality coincide with class alliances and class power.

Education is a site of struggle and compromise. It serves as a proxy as well for larger battles over what our institutions should do, who they should serve, and who should make these decisions. And, yet, by itself it is one of the major arenas in which resources, power, and ideology specific to policy, finance, curriculum, pedagogy, and evaluation in education are worked through. Thus, education is both cause and effect, determining and determined. Because of this, no one chapter could hope to give a complete picture of this complexity. What I hope to do instead is to provide an outline of some of the major tensions surrounding education in the United States as it moves in conservative directions. A key word here is direction*s*. The plural is crucial to my arguments, since, as I showed, there are multiple and at times contradictory tendencies within the rightist turn.

Although my focus in this chapter is largely internal, it is impossible to understand current educational policy in the United States without placing it in its international context. Thus, behind the stress on higher standards, more rigorous testing, education for employment and a much closer relationship between education and the economy in general, and so on was the fear of losing in international competition and the loss of jobs and money to Japan and increasingly the "Asian Tiger" economies, to Mexico, and elsewhere (although this has been mediated by the economic upheavals still being experienced in Asia).[2] In the same way, the equally evident pressure in the United States to reinstall a (selective) vision of a common culture, to place more emphasis on the "Western tradition," on religion, on the English language, and similar emphases are deeply connected to cultural fears about Latin America, Africa, and Asia. This context provides a backdrop for my discussion.

The rightward turn has been the result of the successful struggle by the right to form a broad-based alliance. This new alliance has been so successful in part because it has been able to win the battle over common-sense.[3] That is, it has creatively stitched together different social tendencies and commitments and has organized them under its own general leadership in issues dealing with social welfare, culture, the economy, and as we shall see in this chapter, education. Its aim in educational and social policy is what I called "conservative modernization."[4]

As I noted in my introductory chapter, this alliance contains four major elements. Each has its own relatively autonomous history and dynamics, but each has also been sutured into the more general conservative movement. These elements include neoliberals, neoconservatives, authoritarian populists, and a particular fraction of the upwardly mobile professional and managerial new middle class. I pay particular attention to the first two of these groups here since they—especially neoliberals—are currently in leadership in this alliance to "reform" education. However, in no way do I want to dismiss the power of the latter two groups, and I return to them in later chapters.

NEOLIBERALISM: SCHOOLING, CHOICE, AND DEMOCRACY

I made the point in Chapter 1 that neoliberals are the most powerful element within the alliance supporting conservative modernization. They are guided by a vision of the weak state. Thus, what is private is necessarily good and what is public is necessarily bad. Public institutions such as schools are "black holes" into which money is poured—and then seemingly disappears—but which do not provide anywhere near adequate results. For neoliberals, one form of rationality is more powerful than any other—economic rationality. Efficiency and an "ethic" of cost-benefit analysis are the dominant norms. All people are to act in ways that maximize their own personal benefits. Indeed, behind this position is an empirical claim that this is how *all* rational actors act. Yet, rather than being a neutral description of the world of social motivation, this is actually a construction of the world around the valuative characteristics of an efficiently acquisitive class type.[5]

Underpinning this position is a vision of students as human capital. The world is intensely competitive economically, and students—as future workers—must be given the requisite skills and dispositions to compete efficiently and effectively.[6] Further, any money spent on schools that is not directly related to these economic goals is suspect. In fact, as "black holes," schools and other public services as they are currently organized and controlled waste economic resources that should go into private enterprise. Thus, for neoliberals, not only are public schools failing our children as future workers, but like nearly all public institutions they are sucking the financial life out of this society. Partly this is the result of "producer capture." Schools are built for teachers and state bureaucrats, not "consumers." They respond to the demands of professionals and other selfish state workers, not the consumers who rely on them.

The idea of the "consumer" is crucial here. For neoliberals, the world in essence is a vast supermarket. "Consumer choice" is the guarantor of democracy. In effect, education is seen as simply one more product like bread, cars, and television.[7] By turning it over to the market through voucher and choice plans, education will be largely self-regulating. Thus, democracy is turned into consumption practices. In these plans, the ideal of the citizen is that of the purchaser. The ideological effects of this position are momentous. Rather than democracy being a *political* concept, it is transformed into a wholly *economic* concept. The message of such policies is what might best be called "arithmetical particularism," in which the unattached individual—as a consumer—is deraced, declassed, and degendered.[8]

The metaphors of the consumer and the supermarket are actually quite apposite here. For just as in real life, there are individuals who indeed can go into supermarkets and choose among a vast array of similar or diverse products. And there are those who can only engage in what can best be called "postmodern" consumption. They stand outside the supermarket and can only consume the image.

The entire project of neoliberalism is connected to a larger process of exporting the blame from the decisions of dominant groups onto the state and onto poor people. After all, it was not the government that made the decisions to engage in capital flight and to move factories to those nations that have weak or no unions, fewer environmental regulations, and repressive governments. And it was not working-class and poor communities (such as those in which Joseph and his parents lived) that chose to lose those jobs and factories, with the loss of hope and schools and communities in crisis that were among the results of these decisions. And it was neither of them who chose to lay off millions of workers—many of whom had done rather well in school—due to mergers and leveraged buyouts.

With their emphasis on the consumer rather than the producer, neoliberal policies need also to be seen as part of a more extensive attack on government employees. In education in particular, they constitute an offensive against teacher unions that are seen to be much too powerful and much too costly. Neoliberal policies, although they may not have been created as a conscious attack on women, need to be interpreted as part of a longer history of attacks on women's labor, since the vast majority of teachers in the United States—as in so many other nations— are women.[9]

Varied policy initiatives have emerged from the neoliberal segments of the new hegemonic alliance. Most have centered around either creating closer linkages between education and the economy or placing schools themselves into the market. The former is represented by widespread proposals for "school to work" and "education for employment" programs, and by vigorous cost-cutting attacks on the "bloated state." The latter initiative is no less widespread and is becoming increasingly powerful. It is represented by both national and state-by-state proposals for voucher and choice programs.[10] These include providing public money for private and religious schools (although these are highly contested proposals). Behind this is a plan to subject schools to the discipline of market competition. Such "quasi-market solutions" are among the most divisive and hotly debated policy issues in the entire nation, with important court cases concerning funding for private and/or religious schools through voucher mechanisms having been decided or now being closely watched.[11]

Some proponents of "choice" argue that only enhanced parental "voice" and choice will provide a chance for "educational salvation" for minority parents and children.[12] Moe, for instance, claims that the best hope for the poor to gain the right "to leave bad schools and seek out good ones" is through an "unorthodox alliance."[13] Only by allying themselves with Republicans and business—the most powerful groups supposedly willing to transform the system—can the poor succeed.

As I show in more detail in Chapter 3, growing empirical evidence indicates that the development of "quasi-markets" in education has led to the exacerbation of existing social divisions surrounding class and race.[14] There are now increasingly convincing arguments that while the supposed overt goal of voucher and choice plans is to give poor people the right to exit public schools, among the ultimate long-term effects may be the increase of "white flight" from public schools into private and religious schools and the creation of the conditions where affluent white parents may refuse to pay taxes to support public schools that are more and more suffering from the debilitating effects of the fiscal crisis of the state. The result is even more educational apartheid, not less.[15]

In his own review of evidence from the U.S. experience, Whitty argues that while advocates of choice assume that competition will enhance the efficiency and responsiveness of schools, as well as give disadvantaged children opportunities that they currently do not have, this may be a false hope. These hopes are not now being realized and are unlikely to be realized in the future "in the context of broader policies that do nothing to challenge deeper social and cultural inequalities." As he goes on to say, "Atomized decision-making in a highly stratified society may appear to give everyone equal opportunities but transforming responsibility for decision-making from the public to the private sphere can actually reduce the scope for collective action to improve the quality of education for all."[16]

This position is ratified by Henig who states that "the sad irony of the current education-reform movement is that, through over-identification with school choice proposals, the healthy impulse to consider radical reforms to address social problems may be channeled into initiatives that further erode the potential for collective deliberation and collective response."[17] When this effect is coupled with the fact that such neoliberal policies in practice may reproduce traditional hierarchies of class, race, and gender, these proposals should give us serious pause.[18]

There is a second variant of neoliberalism. This one *is* willing to spend more state and/or private money on schools, if and only if schools meet the needs expressed by capital. Thus, resources are made available for "reforms" and policies that further connect the education system to the project of making our economy more competitive. Two examples can provide a glimpse of this position. In a number of states, legislation has been passed that directs schools and universities to make closer links between education and the business community. In the state of Wisconsin, for instance, all teacher education programs have had to include identifiable experiences on "education for employment" for all of its future teachers; and all teaching in the public elementary, middle, and secondary schools of the state have had to include elements of education for employment in its formal curricula.[19]

The second example is seemingly less consequential, but in reality it is a powerful statement of the reintegration of educational policy and practice into the ideological agenda of neoliberalism. I am referring here to Channel One, a for-profit television network that is now being broadcast into schools enrolling over 40 percent of all middle and secondary school students in the nation (many of these schools are financially hard-pressed given the fiscal crisis, even though many states are currently experiencing budget surpluses). In this "reform," schools are offered a "free" satellite dish, two VCRs, and television monitors for each of their classrooms by a private media corporation. They are also offered a free news broadcast for these students. In return for the equipment and the news, all participating schools must sign a three- to five-year contract guaranteeing that their students will watch Channel One every day.

This agreement sounds relatively benign. However, not only is the technology "hardwired" so that *only* Channel One can be received, but also *mandatory advertisements* for major fast food, athletic wear, and other corporations are broadcast along with the news, which students—by contract—must also watch. Students, in essence, are sold as a captive audience to corporations. Since, by law, these students must be in schools, the United States is one of the first nations in the world to consciously allow its youth to be sold as commodities to those many corporations willing to pay the high price of advertising on Channel One to get a guaranteed (captive) audience. Thus, under a number of variants of neoliberalism not only are schools transformed into market commodities, but so too now are our children.[20]

As I noted, the attractiveness of conservative policies in education rests in large part on major shifts in our common-sense—about what democracy is, about whether we see ourselves as possessive individuals ("consumers"), and ultimately about how we see the market working. Underlying neoliberal policies in education and their social policies in general is a faith in the essential fairness and justice of markets. Markets ultimately will distribute resources efficiently and fairly according to effort. They ultimately will create jobs for all who want them. They are the best possible mechanism to ensure a better future for all citizens (consumers).

Because of this, we of course must ask what the economy that reigns supreme in neoliberal positions actually looks like. Far from the positive picture painted by neoliberals in which technologically advanced jobs will replace the drudgery and the under- and unemployment so many people now experience if we were to only set the market loose on our schools and children, the reality is something else again. Unfortunately, markets clearly are as powerfully destructive as they are productive in people's lives.[21]

Let us take as a case in point the paid labor market to which neoliberals want us to attach so much of the education system. Even with the growth in proportion in high-tech-related jobs, the kinds of work that are and will be increasingly available to a large portion of the American population will not be highly skilled, technically elegant positions. Just the opposite will be the case. The paid labor market will increasingly be dominated by low-paying, repetitive work in the retail, trade, and service sectors. This is made strikingly clear by one fact. More cashier jobs will be created by the year 2005 than jobs for computer scientists, systems analysts, physical therapists, operations analysts, and radiologic technicians *combined*. In fact, it is projected that 95 percent of all new positions will be found in the service sector. This sector broadly includes personal care, home health aides; social workers (many of whom are now losing or have lost their jobs because of cutbacks in social spending); hotel and lodging workers; restaurant employees; transportation workers; and business and clerical personnel. Further, eight of the top ten individual occupations that will account for the most job growth in the next ten years include the following: retail salespersons, cashiers, office clerks, truck drivers, waitresses/waiters, nursing aides/orderlies, food preparation workers, and janitors. The majority of these positions obviously do not require high levels of education. Many of them are low-paid, nonunionized, temporary, and part-time, with low or no benefits. And many are dramatically linked to, and often exacerbate, the existing race, gender, and class divisions of labor.[22] This is the emerging economy we face, not the overly romantic picture painted by neoliberals who urge us to trust the market.

Neoliberals argue that making the market the ultimate arbiter of social worthiness will eliminate politics and its accompanying irrationality from our educational and social decisions. Efficiency and cost-benefit analysis will be the engines of social and educational transformation. Yet among the ultimate effects of such "economizing" and "depoliticizing" strategies is actually to make it ever harder to interrupt the growing inequalities in resources and power that so deeply characterize this society. Nancy Fraser illuminates the process in the following way:

> In male dominated capitalist societies, what is "political" is normally defined contrastively against what is "economic" and what is "domestic" or "personal." Here, then, we can identify two principal sets of institutions that depoliticize social discourses: they are, first, domestic institutions, especially the normative domestic form, namely the modern restricted male-headed nuclear family; and, second, official economic capitalist system institutions, especially paid workplaces, markets, credit mechanisms, and "private" enterprises and corporations. Domestic institutions depoliticize certain matters by personalizing and/or familializing them; they cast these as private-domestic or personal-familial matters in contradistinction to public, political matters. Official economic capitalist system institutions, on the other hand, depoliticize certain matters by economizing them; the issues in question here are cast as impersonal market imperatives, or as "private" ownership prerogatives, or as technical problems for managers and planners, all in contradistinction to political matters. In both cases, the result is a foreshortening of chains of in-order-to relations for interpreting people's needs; interpretive chains are truncated and prevented from spilling across the boundaries separating the "domestic" and the "economic" from the political.[23]

This very process of depoliticization makes it very difficult for the needs of those with less economic, political, and cultural power to be accurately heard and acted upon in ways that deal with the true depth of the problem. For Fraser, this outcome occurs because of what happens when "needs discourses" get retranslated into both market talk and "privately" driven policies.

For our purposes here, we can talk about two major kinds of needs discourses: oppositional and reprivatization discourses. *Oppositional* forms of needs talk arise when needs are politicized from below and are part of the crystallization of new oppositional identities on the part of subordinated social groups. What was once seen as largely a "private" matter is now placed into the larger political arena. Sexual harassment, race and sex segregation in paid labor, and affirmative action policies in educational and economic institutions provide examples of "private" issues that have now spilled over and can no longer be confined to the "domestic" sphere.[24]

Reprivatization discourses emerge as a response to the newly emergent oppositional forms and try to press these forms back into the "private" or the "domestic" arena. They are often aimed at dismantling or cutting back social services, deregulating "private" enterprise, or stopping what are seen as "runaway needs." Thus, reprivatizers may attempt to keep issues such as, say, domestic battery from spilling over into overt political discourse and will seek to define it as purely a family matter. Or they will argue that the closing of a factory is not a political question, but instead is an "unimpeachable prerogative of private ownership or an unassailable imperative of an impersonal market mechanism."[25] In each of these cases, the task is to contest both the possible breakout of runaway needs and to depoliticize the issues.

In educational policy in the United States, there are a number of clear examples of these processes. The state of California provides a well-known instance. A binding referendum that prohibited the use of affirmative action policies in state government, in university admission policies, and so on was passed overwhelmingly as reprivatizers spent an exceptional amount of money on an advertising campaign that labeled such policies as "out of control" and as improper government intervention into decisions involving "individual merit." The California referendum has spawned similar, and quite controversial, initiatives in other states. Voucher plans in education—where contentious issues surrounding whose knowledge should be taught, who should control school policy and practice, and how schools should be financed are left to the market to decide—offer another prime example of such attempts at "depoliticizing" educational needs. Finally, giving primary responsibility over the definition of important "work skills" to the private sector—an act that evacuates the possibility of criticism of the ways work is actually constructed, controlled, and paid—enables a definition of work both as a "private" matter and as purely a technical choice to go unchallenged. All these examples show the emerging power of reprivatizing discourses.

A distinction that is useful here in understanding what is happening in these cases is that between "value" and "sense" legitimation.[26] Each signifies a different strategy by which powerful groups or states legitimate their authority. In the first (value) strategy, legitimation is accomplished by actually giving people what may have been promised. Thus, the social democratic state may provide social services for the population in return for continued support. That the state will do this is often the result of oppositional discourses gaining more power in the social arena and having more power to redefine the border between public and private.

In the second (sense) strategy, rather than providing people with policies that meet the needs they have expressed, states and/or dominant groups attempt to *change the very meaning* of the sense of social need into something that is very different. Thus, if less powerful people call for "more democracy" and for a more responsive state, the task is not to give "value" that meets this demand, especially when it may lead to runaway needs. Rather, the task is to change what actually *counts* as democracy. In the case of neoliberal policies, democracy is now redefined as guaranteeing choice in an unfettered market. In essence, the state withdraws. The extent of acceptance of such transformations of needs and needs discourses shows the success of the reprivatizers in redefining the borders between public and private again and demonstrates how a people's common-sense can be shifted in conservative directions during a time of economic and ideological crisis.

NEOCONSERVATISM: TEACHING "REAL" KNOWLEDGE

While neoliberals largely are in leadership in the conservative alliance, I noted that the second major element within the new alliance is neoconservatism. Unlike the neoliberal emphasis on the weak state, neoconservatives are usually guided by a vision of the strong state. This is especially true surrounding issues of knowledge, values, and the body. Whereas neoliberalism may be seen as being based in what Raymond Williams would call an "emergent" ideological assemblage, neoconservatism is grounded in "residual" forms.[27] It is largely, though not totally, based in a romantic appraisal of the past, a past in which "real knowledge" and morality reigned supreme, where people "knew their place," and where stable communities guided by a natural order protected us from the ravages of society.[28]

Among the policies being proposed under this ideological position are mandatory national and statewide curricula, national and statewide testing, a "return" to higher standards, a revivification of the "Western tradition," patriotism, and conservative variants of character education. Yet underlying some of the neoconservative thrust in education and in social policy in general is not only a call for "return." Behind it as well— and this is essential—is a fear of the "Other." This is expressed in its support for a standardized national curriculum, its attacks on bilingualism and multiculturalism, and its insistent call for raising standards.[29]

That the neoconservative emphasis on a return to traditional values and "morality" has struck a responsive chord can be seen in the fact that among the best-selling books in the nation during the past decade was William Bennett's *The Book of Virtues.*[30] Bennett, a former Secretary of Education in a conservative Republican administration, has argued that for too long a period of time, "We have stopped doing the right things

[and] allowed an assault on intellectual and moral standards." In opposition to this, we need "a renewed commitment to excellence, character, and fundamentals."[31] Bennett's book aims at providing "moral tales" for children to "restore" a commitment to "traditional virtues" such as patriotism, honesty, moral character, and entrepreneurial spirit. Such positions not only have entered the common-sense of society in quite influential ways, but also have provided part of the driving force behind the movement toward charter schools. These schools have individual charters that allow them to opt out of most state requirements and develop curricula based on the wishes of their clientele. While in theory there is much to commend such policies, as I demonstrate later all too many charter schools have become ways through which conservative religious activists and others gain public funding for schools that would otherwise be prohibited such support.[32]

Behind much of the neoconservative position is a clear sense of loss—a loss of faith, of imagined communities, of a nearly pastoral vision of like-minded people who shared norms and values and in which the "Western tradition" reigned supreme. It is more than a little similar to Mary Douglas's discussion of purity and danger, in which what was imagined to exist is sacred and "pollution" is feared above all else.[33] We/they binary oppositions dominate this discourse and the culture of the "Other" is to be feared.

This sense of cultural pollution can be seen in the increasingly virulent attacks on multiculturalism (which is itself a very broad category that combines multiple political and cultural positions),[34] on the offering of schooling or any other social benefits to the children of "illegal" immigrants and even in some cases to the children of legal immigrants, in the conservative English-only movement, and in the equally conservative attempts to reorient curricula and textbooks toward a particular construction of the Western tradition.

In this regard, neoconservatives lament the "decline" of the traditional curriculum and of the history, literature, and values it is said to have represented. Behind this worry is a set of historical assumptions about "tradition," about the existence of a social consensus over what should count as legitimate knowledge, and about cultural superiority.[35] Yet it is crucial to remember that the "traditional" curriculum whose decline is lamented so fervently by neoconservative critics "ignored most of the groups that compose the American population whether they were from Africa, Europe, Asia, Central and South America, or from indigenous North American peoples."[36] Its primary and often exclusive focus was typically only on quite a narrow spectrum of those people who came from a small number of northern and western European nations, in spite of the fact that the cultures and histories represented in the United States were "forged out of a much larger and more diverse complex of peoples and societies." The mores and cultures of this narrow spectrum were seen as archetypes of "tradition" for everyone. They were not simply taught, but taught as superior to every other set of mores and culture.[37]

As Lawrence Levine reminds us, a selective and faulty sense of history fuels the nostalgic yearnings of neoconservatives. The canon and the curriculum have never been static. They have always been in a constant process of revision, "with irate defenders insisting, as they still do, that change would bring with it instant decline."[38] Indeed, even the inclusion of such "classics" as Shakespeare within the curriculum of schools in the United States came about only after prolonged and intense battles, ones that were the equal of the divisive debates over whose knowledge should be taught today. Thus, Levine notes that when neoconservative cultural critics ask for a "return" to a "common culture" and "tradition," they are oversimplifying to the point of distortion. What is happening in terms of the expansion and alteration of official knowledge in schools and universities today "is by no means out of the ordinary; certainly it is not a radical departure from the patterns that have marked the history of [education]—constant and often controversial expansion and alteration of curricula and canons and incessant struggle over the nature of that expansion and alteration."[39]

Of course, such conservative positions have been forced into a kind of compromise in order to maintain their cultural and ideological leadership as a movement to "reform" educational policy and practice. A prime example is the emerging discourse over the history curriculum—

in particular the construction of the United States as a "nation of immigrants."[40] In this hegemonic discourse, everyone in the history of the nation was an immigrant, from the first Native American population who supposedly trekked across the Bering Strait and ultimately populated North, Central, and South America, to the later waves of populations who came from Africa, Mexico, Ireland, Germany, Scandinavia, Italy, Russia, Poland, and elsewhere, to finally the recent populations from Asia, Latin America, Africa, and other regions. Although it is true that the United States is constituted by people from all over the world—and that is one of the things that makes it so culturally rich and vital—such a perspective constitutes an erasure of historical memory. For some groups came *in chains* and were subjected to state-sanctioned slavery and apartheid for hundreds of years. Others suffered what can only be called bodily, linguistic, and cultural destruction.[41]

This said, however, it does point to the fact that while the neoconservative goals of national curricula and national testing are pressed for, they are strongly mediated by the necessity of compromise. Because of this, even the strongest supporters of neoconservative educational programs and policies have had to also support the creation of curricula that at least partly recognize "the contributions of the Other."[42] This is partly due to the fact that there is an absence of an overt and strong national department of education and a tradition of state and local control of schooling. The "solution" has been to have national standards developed "voluntarily" in each subject area.[43] Indeed, the example I gave above about history is one of the results of such voluntary standards.

Since it is the national professional organizations in these subject areas—such as the National Council of Teachers of Mathematics (NCTM)—that are developing such national standards, the standards themselves are compromises and thus are often more flexible than those wished for by neoconservatives. This very process does act to provide a check on conservative policies over knowledge. However, this should not lead to an overly romantic picture of the overall tendencies emerging in educational policy. Leadership in school "reform" is increasingly dominated by conservative discourses surrounding "standards," "excellence," "accountability," and so on. Since the more flexible parts of the standards have proven to be too expensive to actually implement and have generated considerable conservative backlash,[44] standards talk ultimately functions to give more rhetorical weight to the neoconservative movement to enhance central control over "official knowledge" and to "raise the bar" for achievement. The social implications of this in terms of creating even more differential school results are increasingly worrisome.[45]

Yet it is not only in such things as the control over legitimate knowledge where neoconservative impulses are seen. The idea of a strong state is also visible in the growth of the regulatory state as it concerns teachers. There has been a steadily growing change from "licensed autonomy" to "regulated autonomy" as teachers' work is more highly standardized, rationalized, and "policed."[46] Under conditions of licensed autonomy, once teachers are given the appropriate professional certification they are basically free—within limits—to act in their classrooms according to their judgment. Such a regime is based on trust in "professional discretion." Under the growing conditions of regulated autonomy, teachers' actions are now subject to much greater scrutiny in terms of process and outcomes.[47] Indeed, some states in the United States not only have specified the content that teachers are to teach, but also have regulated the only appropriate methods of teaching. Not following these specified "appropriate" methods puts the teacher at risk of administrative sanctions. Such a regime of control is based not on trust, but on a deep suspicion of the motives and competence of teachers. For neoconservatives it is the equivalent of the notion of "producer capture" that is so powerful among neoliberals. For the former, however, it is not the market that will solve this problem, but a strong and interventionist state that will see to it that only "legitimate" content and methods are taught. And this will be policed by statewide and national tests of both students and teachers.

I have claimed elsewhere that such policies lead to the "deskilling" of teachers, the "intensification" of their work, and the loss of autonomy and respect. This is not surprising, since behind much of this conservative impulse is a clear distrust of teachers and an attack both on teachers' claims to competence and especially on teachers' unions.[48]

The mistrust of teachers, the concern over a supposed loss of cultural control, and the sense of dangerous "pollution" are among the many cultural and social fears that drive neoconservative policies. However, as I noted earlier, underpinning these positions as well is often an ethnocentric, and even racialized, understanding of the world. Perhaps this can be best illuminated through the example of Herrnstein and Murray's volume, *The Bell Curve*.[49] In a book that sold hundreds of thousands of copies, the authors argue for a genetic determinism based on race (and to some extent gender). For them, it is romantic to assume that educational and social policies can ultimately lead to more equal results, since differences in intelligence and achievement are basically genetically driven. The wisest thing policymakers can do would be to accept this and plan for a society that recognizes these biological differences and does not provide "false hopes" to the poor and the less intelligent, most of whom will be black. Obviously, this book has reinforced racist stereotypes that have long played a considerable part in educational and social policies in the United States.[50]

Rather than seeing race as it is—as a fully *social* category that is mobilized and used in different ways by different groups at different times[51]—positions such as those argued by Herrnstein and Murray provide a veneer of seeming scientific legitimacy for policy discourses that have been discredited intellectually many times before. The sponsored mobility given to this book, in which it is reported that the authors received large sums of money from neoconservative foundations to write and publicize the volume, speaks clearly not only to the racial underpinnings of important parts of the neoconservative agenda but also to the power of conservative groups to bring their case before the public.

The consequences of such positions are not only found in educational policies, but in the intersection of such policies with broader social and economic policies, where they have been quite influential. Here too we can find claims that what the poor lack is not money, but both an "appropriate" biological inheritance and a decided lack of values regarding discipline, hard work, and morality.[52] Prime examples here include programs such as "Learnfare" and "Workfare" where parents lose a portion of their welfare benefits if their children miss a significant number of school days or where no benefits are paid if a person does not accept low paid work, no matter how demeaning or even if child care or health care are not provided by the state. Such policies reinstall earlier "workhouse" policies that were so popular—and so utterly damaging—in the United States, Britain, and elsewhere.[53]

I have spent much of my time in this section documenting the growing power of neoconservative positions in educational and social policy in the United States. Neoconservatives have forged a creative coalition with neoliberals, a coalition that—in concert with other groups—is effectively changing the landscape on which policies are argued out. Yet, even given the growing influence of neoliberal and neoconservative policies, they would be considerably less successful if they had not also brought authoritarian populist religious fundamentalists and conservative evangelicals under the umbrella of the conservative alliance. It is to this group that we now turn.

AUTHORITARIAN POPULISM: SCHOOLING AS GOD WANTED IT

Perhaps more than in any other major industrialized nation, it is not possible to fully understand educational politics in the United States without paying a good deal of attention to the "Christian Right." It is exceptionally powerful and influential, beyond its numbers, in debates over public policy in the media, education, social welfare, the politics of sexuality and the body, religion, and so on. Its influence comes from the immense commitment by activists within it, its large financial base, its populist rhetorical positions, and its aggressiveness in pursuing its agenda. As I showed in Chapter 1, "New Right" authoritarian populists ground their positions on education and social policy in general in particular visions of biblical authority, "Christian morality," gender roles, and the family. The New Right sees gender and the family, for instance, as an organic and divine unity that resolves "male egoism and female selflessness."

As Hunter puts it:

Since gender is divine and natural . . . there is [no] room for legitimate political conflict. . . . Within the family women and men—stability and dynamism—are harmoniously fused when undisturbed by modernism, liberalism, feminism, and humanism which not only threaten masculinity and femininity directly, but also [do so] through their effects on children and youth. . . ."Real women," i.e., women who know themselves as wives *and* mothers, will not threaten the sanctity of the home by striving for self. When men or women challenge these gender roles they break with God and nature; when liberals, feminists, and secular humanists prevent them from fulfilling these roles they undermine the divine and natural supports upon which society rests.[54]

In the minds of such groups, public schooling thus is *itself* a site of immense danger, a point I develop in considerably more detail in Chapters 4, 5, and 6. In the words of conservative activist Tim LaHaye, "Modern public education is the most dangerous force in a child's life: religiously, sexually, economically, patriotically, and physically."[55] This is connected to the New Right's sense of loss surrounding schooling and the family.

Until recently, as the New Right sees it, schools were extensions of home and traditional morality. Parents could entrust their children to public schools because they were locally controlled and reflected Biblical and parental values. However, taken over by alien, elitist forces, schools now interpose themselves between parents and children. Many people experience fragmentation of the unity between family, church, and school as a loss of control of daily life, one's children, and America. Indeed, [the New Right] argues that parental control of education is Biblical, for in God's plan, the primary responsibility for educating the young lies in the home and directly in the father.[56]

It is exactly this sense of "alien and elite control," the loss of biblical connections, and the destruction of "God-given" family and moral structures that drives the authoritarian populist agenda. It is an agenda that is increasingly powerful, not only rhetorically, but in terms of funding and in conflicts over what schools should do, how they should be financed, and who should control them. This agenda includes, but goes beyond, issues of gender, sexuality, and the family. It extends as well to a much larger array of questions about what is to count as "legitimate" knowledge in schools. And in this larger arena of concern about the entire corpus of school knowledge, conservative activists have had no small measure of success in pressuring textbook publishers to change what they include and in altering important aspects of state educational policy on teaching, curriculum, and evaluation. This is crucial, since in the absence of an overt national curriculum, the commercially produced *textbook*—regulated by individual state's purchases and authority—remains the dominant definition of the curriculum in the United States,[57] a point to which I return in Chapter 4.

The power of these groups is visible, for example, in the "self-censorship" in which publishers engage. For instance, under conservative pressure a number of publishers of high school literature anthologies have chosen to include Martin Luther King's "I Have a Dream" speech, but *only* after all references to the intense racism of the United States have been removed.[58] At the level of state curriculum policy, this is very visible in the textbook legislation in, say, Texas, which mandates texts that stress patriotism, obedience to authority, and the discouragement of "deviance."[59] Since most textbook publishers aim the content and organization of their textbooks at what will be approved by a small number of populous states that in essence approve and purchase their textbooks *statewide,* this gives states like Texas (and California) immense power in determining what will count as "official knowledge" throughout the entire country.[60]

Thus, in concert with neoconservative elements within the conservative alliance, authoritarian populist religious activists have had a substantial influence on curriculum policy and practice. For them, only by recentering issues of authority, morality, family, church, and "decency" can schools overcome the "moral decay" so evident all around us. Only by returning to inerrantist understandings of biblical teachings and fostering (or mandating) a climate in schools where such teachings are given renewed emphasis can our culture be saved.[61]

As I showed in *Cultural Politics and Education,* although a number of states and school systems have been able to create mechanisms that deflect some of these pressures, the bureaucratic nature of many school systems and of the local and regional state in general has actually produced the conditions where parents and other community members who might otherwise disagree with the New Right ideologically are convinced to join them in their attacks on the content and organization of schooling.[62]

While authoritarian populist struggles over curriculum and texts have been growing rapidly, this mistrust of public schools has also fueled considerable and intense support among them for neoliberal policies such as voucher and choice plans. The New Right, as a largely populist assemblage, has some very real mistrust of the motives and economic plans of capital. After all, such rightist populists have themselves experienced the effects of downsizing, layoffs, and economic restructuring. However, even given their partial insights into the differential effects of global competition and economic restructuring, they see in proposals for educational marketization and privatization a way in which they can use such "reforms" for their own purposes. Either through reduced school taxes, through tax credits, or through the allocation of public money to private and religious schools, they can create a set of schools organized around the more moral "imagined communities" they believe have been lost.[63] I take this up in more detail later on.

This search for the reconstitution of imagined communities points to one of the effects of reprivatization talk on the politics surrounding educational policy. In the process of denying the legitimacy of oppositional claims, reprivatization discourses may actually tend to politicize the issues even more. These issues become even more a part of public, not "domestic," contestation. This paradox—reprivatization talk may actually lead to further public discussion of breakaway needs—does *not* always lead to victories by oppositional groups such as feminists, racially subjected peoples, or other disempowered groups, however. Rather, such politicization can in fact lead to the growth of new social movements and new social identities whose fundamental aim is to push breakaway needs back into the economic, domestic, and private spheres. New, and quite conservative, coalitions can be formed.

This is exactly what has happened in the United States, where a set of reprivatizing discourses "in the accents of authoritarian populism" has made creative connections with the hopes and especially the fears of a range of disaffected constituencies and has united them into a tense but very effective alliance supporting positions behind reprivatization.[64] And this could not have been done if rightist groups had not succeeded in changing the very meaning of key concepts of democracy in such a way that the Christian Right could comfortably find a place under the larger umbrella of the conservative alliance.

THE PROFESSIONAL AND MANAGERIAL NEW MIDDLE CLASS: MORE TESTING, MORE OFTEN

Although I speak somewhat more briefly about them here because of their relatively limited—but rapidly growing—power, as I argued in Chapter 1 there is a final group that provides some of the support for the policies of conservative modernization. This is a fraction of the professional new middle class that gains its own mobility within the state and within the economy based on the use of technical expertise. These are people with backgrounds in management and efficiency techniques who provide the technical and "professional" support for accountability, measurement, "product control," and assessment that is required by the proponents of neoliberal policies of marketization and neoconservative policies of tighter central control in education.

Members of this fraction of the upwardly mobile professional and managerial new middle class do not necessarily believe in the ideological positions that underpin the conservative alliance. In fact, in other aspects of their lives they may be considerably more moderate and even "liberal" politically. However, as experts in efficiency, management, testing, and accountability, they provide the technical expertise to put in place the policies of conservative modernization. Their own mobility *depends* on the expansion of both such expertise and the professional ideologies of control, measurement, and efficiency that accompany it. Thus, they often support such policies as "neutral instrumentalities," even when these policies may be used for purposes other than the supposedly neutral ends this class fraction is committed to.[65]

Because of this situation, it is important to realize that a good deal of the current emphasis in schools on high-stakes testing, on more rigorous forms of accountability, and on tighter control is not totally reducible to the needs of neoliberals and neoconservatives. Rather, part of the pressure for these policies comes from educational managers and bureaucratic offices who fully believe that such control is warranted and "good." Not only do these forms of control have an extremely long history in education, but tighter control, high-stakes testing, and (reductive) accountability methods provide more dynamic roles for such managers, a point I noted earlier. These policies enable such actors to engage in a moral crusade and enhance the status of their own expertise.

Yet, in a time when competition for credentials and cultural capital is intense, the increasing power of mechanisms of restratification such as the return of high levels of mandatory standardization also provides mechanisms that enhance the chances that the children of the professional and managerial new middle class will have *less competition* from other children. Thus, the introduction of devices to restratify a population enhances the value of the credentials that the new middle class is more likely to accumulate, given the stock of cultural capital it already possesses.[66] I am not claiming that this is necessarily intentional, but creating such devices does *function* to increase the chances for mobility by middle-class children who depend not on economic capital but on cultural capital for advancement.

In such a situation, I believe that this group is not immune to ideological shifts to the right. Given the fear generated by the attacks on the state and on the public sphere by both neoliberals and neoconservatives, this class fraction is decidedly worried about the future mobility of its children in an uncertain economic world. Thus, they may be drawn more overtly to parts of the conservative alliance's positions, especially those coming from the neoconservative elements that stress greater attention to traditional "high-status" content, greater attention to testing, and a greater emphasis on schooling as a stratifying mechanism. This can be seen in a number of states where parents of this class fraction are supporting charter schools that will stress academic achievement in traditional subjects and traditional teaching practices. Where the majority of members of this class grouping will align in the future in the debates over policy remains to be seen. Given their contradictory ideological tendencies, it is possible that the right will be able to mobilize them under conditions of fear for the future of their jobs and children.[67]

CONCLUSION

Because of the complexity of educational politics in the United States, I have devoted most of this chapter to an analysis of the conservative social movements that are having a powerful impact on debates over policy and practice in education and in the larger social arena. I have suggested that conservative modernization in education is guided by a tense coalition of forces, some of whose aims partly contradict others.

The very nature of this coalition is crucial. It is more than a little possible that the alliance underpinning conservative modernization can overcome its own internal contradictions and can succeed in radically transforming educational policy and practice. Thus, while neoliberals call for a weak state and neoconservatives demand a strong state, these very evident contradictory impulses can come together in creative ways. The emerging focus on centralized standards, content, and tighter control paradoxically can be the first and most essential step on the path to marketization through voucher and choice plans.

Once statewide and/or national curricula and tests are put in place, comparative school-by-school data will be available and will be published in a manner similar to the "league tables" on school achievement published in England. Only when there is standardized content and assessment can the market be set free, since the "consumer" can then have "objective" data on which schools are "succeeding" and which schools are not. Market rationality, based on "consumer choice," will ensure that the supposedly good schools will gain students and the bad schools will disappear.

In my next chapter, I focus on the effects of this and similar kinds of policies on real schools. But let me say here that one of these effects is that when the poor "choose" to keep their children in underfunded and decaying schools in the inner cities or in rural areas (given the decline and expense of urban mass transportation, poor information, the absence of time, and their decaying economic conditions, to name but a few of the realities), *they* (the poor) will be blamed individually and collectively for making bad "consumer choices." Reprivatizing discourses and arithmetical particularism will justify the structural inequalities that will be (re)produced here. In this way, as odd as it may seem, neoliberal and neoconservative policies, ones ultimately supported by authoritarian populists and even by many members of the professional middle class, that are seemingly contradictory may mutually reinforce each other in the long run,[68] a point I also take up in the next chapter.

Yet, while I have argued that the overall leadership in educational policy is exercised by this alliance, I do not want to give the impression that these four elements under the hegemonic umbrella of this coalition are uncontested or are always victorious. This is simply not the case. As a number of people have demonstrated, scores of counterhegemonic programs and possibilities exist at the local level throughout the United States. Many institutions of higher education, schools, and even entire school districts have shown remarkable resiliency in the face of the concerted ideological attacks and pressures from conservative restorational groups. And many teachers, academics, community activists, and others have created and defended educational programs that are both pedagogically and politically emancipatory.[69]

Indeed, we are beginning to see cracks in the alliance's power in unanticipated ways. For example, a growing number of students in elementary, middle, and secondary schools are actively refusing to take the mandatory tests that many states have introduced. This action has been supported by groups of teachers, administrators, parents, and activists.[70] Clearly, things are bubbling up from below the surface whose effects will be "interesting" to say the least.

Having said this, however, it is important to note the obstacles in creating the conditions for large-scale movements to defend and build progressive policies. We need to remember that there is no powerful central ministry of education in the United States. Teachers' unions are relatively weak at a national level (nor is there any guarantee that teachers' unions always act progressively). There is no consensus about an "appropriate" progressive agenda in educational policy here, since there is a vast multiplicity of compelling (and unfortunately at times competing) agendas involving race/ethnicity, gender, sexuality, class, religion, "ability," and so on. Thus, it is structurally difficult to sustain long-term national movements for more progressive policies and practices.

Because of this, most counterhegemonic work is organized locally or regionally. However, there currently are growing attempts at building national coalitions around what might best be called a "decentered unity." Organizations such as the National Coalition of Educational Activists and those centered around "Rethinking Schools" are becoming more visible nationally.[71] None of these movements have the financial and organizational backing that stands behind the neoliberal, neoconservative, and authoritarian populist groups. None have the ability to bring their case before the "public" through the media and through foundations in the ways that conservative groups have been able to do. And none have the capacity or the resources to quickly mobilize a large base of nationally directed membership to challenge or promote specific policies in the ways that the members of the alliance can.

Yet, in the face of all of these structural, financial, and political dilemmas, the fact that so many groups of people have not been integrated under the alliance's hegemonic umbrella and have created scores of local examples of the very possibility of difference shows us in the most eloquent and lived ways that educational policies and practices do not go in any one unidimensional direction. Even more important, these multiple examples demonstrate that the success of conservative policies is never guaranteed. This is crucial in a time when it is easy to lose sight of what is necessary for an education worthy of its name.

Why taking a position that might be called "optimism, but without illusions" is important will become clearer in the next chapter where I discuss in much greater depth not only the effects of the forces of conservative modernization on the policies and practices of schools, but also weaknesses of many of the ways the supposed alternative—"critical pedagogy"—deals with them.

Chapter 3

Producing Inequalities: Conservative Modernization in Policy and Practice

GRITTY MATERIALITIES

For the past two or more decades, even before the new hegemonic bloc I have been describing assumed power, a body of literature in education has grown that has sought to help us think politically about curriculum, teaching, and evaluation. I myself have participated in the building of these critical perspectives. Much of the literature on "critical pedagogies" has been politically and theoretically important and has helped us make a number of gains. However, given what I said in the past two chapters, this literature has some characteristics that limit its effectiveness in mounting serious challenges to what is happening all around us. It too often has not been sufficiently connected to the ways in which the current movement toward conservative modernization both has altered common-sense and has transformed the material and ideological conditions surrounding schooling. It, thereby, sometimes becomes a form of what best be called "romantic possibilitarian" rhetoric, in which the language of possibility substitutes for a consistent tactical analysis of what the balance of forces actually is and what is necessary to change it.[1]

In this chapter, I examine in even more detail the ways in which the social and cultural terrain of educational policy and discourse has been altered "on the ground" so to speak. I argue that we need to make closer connections between our theoretical and critical discourses on the one hand and the real transformations that are currently shifting educational policies and practices in fundamentally rightist directions on the other. Thus, part of my discussion is conceptual, but part of it appropriately is more empirical than in Chapter 2 in order for me to pull together what is known about the real and material effects of the shift to the right in education.

My focus on the "gritty materialities" of these effects is not meant to dismiss the importance of theoretical interventions. Nor is it meant to suggest that dominant discourses should not be constantly interrupted by the creative gains that have emerged from various neo-Marxist, feminist, postmodern, poststructural, postcolonial, queer, and other communities. Indeed, critical pedagogies *require* the fundamental interruption of common-sense. However, while the construction of new theories and utopian visions is important, it is equally crucial to base these theories and visions in an unromantic appraisal of the material and discursive terrain that now exists. Common-sense is already being radically altered, but not in directions that any of us on the left would find comforting. Without an analysis of such transformations and of the balance of forces that have created such discomforting alterations, without an analysis of the tensions, differential relations of power, and contradictions within it, we are left with increasingly elegant new theoretical formulations, but with a less than elegant understanding of the field of social power on which they operate.[2]

RIGHT TURN

In his influential history of curriculum debates, Herbert Kliebard has documented that educational issues have consistently involved major conflicts and compromises among groups with competing visions of "legitimate" knowledge, what counts as "good" teaching and learning, and what is a "just" society.[3] That such conflicts have deep roots in conflicting views of racial, class, and gender justice in education and the larger society is ratified in even more critical recent work as well.[4] These competing visions have never had equal holds on the imagination of educators or the general citizenry nor have they ever had equal power to effect their visions. Because of this, no analysis of education can be fully serious without placing at its very core a sensitivity to the ongoing struggles that constantly shape the terrain on which education operates.

Today is no different from the past. As I argued in Chapter 2, a "new" set of compromises, a new alliance, and new power bloc have been formed that have increasing influence in education and all things social. This power bloc combines multiple fractions of capital who are committed to neoliberal marketized solutions to educational problems, neoconservative intellectuals who want a "return" to higher standards and a "common culture," authoritarian populist religious fundamentalists who are deeply worried about secularity and the preservation of their own traditions, and particular fractions of the professionally oriented new middle class who are committed to the ideology and techniques of accountability, measurement, and "management." Although clear tensions and conflicts exist within this alliance, in general its overall aims are to provide the educational conditions believed necessary both for increasing international competitiveness, profit, and discipline and for returning us to a romanticized past of the "ideal" home, family, and school.[5]

In essence, the new alliance has integrated education into a wider set of ideological commitments. The objectives in education are the same as those which guide its economic and social welfare goals. They include the dramatic expansion of that eloquent fiction, the free market; the drastic reduction of government responsibility for social needs; the reinforcement of intensely competitive structures of mobility both inside and outside the school; the lowering of people's expectations for economic security; the "disciplining" of culture and the body; and the popularization of what is clearly a form of Social Darwinist thinking, as the recent popularity of *The Bell Curve* so obviously and distressingly indicates.[6]

The seemingly contradictory discourse of competition, markets, and choice on the one hand and accountability, performance objectives, standards, national testing, and national curriculum on the other has created such a din that it is hard to hear anything else. Even though these seem to embody different tendencies, they actually oddly reinforce each other and help cement conservative educational positions into our daily lives.[7]

While lamentable, the changes that are occurring present an exceptional opportunity for serious critical reflection. In a time of radical social and educational change, it is crucial to document the processes and effects of the various and sometimes contradictory elements of the conservative restoration and of the ways in which they are mediated, compromised with, accepted, used in different ways by different groups for their own purposes, and/or struggled over in the policies and practices of people's daily educational lives.[8] I give a more detailed sense of how this might be happening in current "reforms" such as marketization and national curricula and national testing in this chapter. For those interested in critical educational policies and practices, not to do this means that we act without understanding the shifting relations of power that are constructing and reconstructing the social field of power. While Gramsci's saying "Pessimism of the intellect, optimism of the will" has a powerful resonance to it and is useful for mobilization and for not losing hope, it would be foolish to substitute rhetorical slogans for the fuller analysis that is undoubtedly required if we are to be successful.

NEW MARKETS, OLD TRADITIONS

Historically, behind a good deal of the New Right's emerging discursive ensemble was a position that emphasized "a culturalist construction of the nation as a (threatened) haven for white (Christian) traditions and values."[9] This involved the construction of an imagined national past that is at least partly mythologized, and then employing it to castigate the present. Gary McCulloch argues that the nature of the historical images of schooling has changed. Dominant imagery of education as being "safe, domesticated, and progressive" (that is, as leading toward progress and social/personal improvement) has shifted to become "threatening, estranged, and regressive."[10] The past is no longer the source of stability, but a mark of failure, disappointment, and loss. This is seen most vividly in the attacks on the "progressive orthodoxy" that supposedly now reigns supreme in classrooms in many nations.[11]

For example, in England—though much the same is echoed in the United States, Australia, and elsewhere—Michael Jones, the political editor of *The Sunday Times,* recalls the primary school of his day:

> Primary school was a happy time for me. About 40 of us sat at fixed wooden desks with ink wells and moved from them only with grudging permission. Teacher sat in a higher desk in front of us and moved only to the blackboard. She smelled of scent and inspired awe.[12]

The mix of metaphors invoking discipline, scent (visceral and almost "natural"), and awe is fascinating. But he goes on, lamenting the past thirty years of "reform" that transformed primary schools. Speaking of his own children's experience, Jones says:

> My children spent their primary years in a showplace school where they were allowed to wander around at will, develop their real individuality and dodge the 3Rs. It was all for the best, we were assured. But it was not.[13]

For Jones, the "dogmatic orthodoxy" of progressive education "had led directly to educational and social decline." Only the rightist reforms instituted in the 1980s and 1990s could halt and then reverse this decline.[14] Only then could the imagined past return.

Much the same is being said on this side of the Atlantic. These sentiments are echoed in the public pronouncements of such figures as William Bennett, E. D. Hirsch Jr., and others, all of whom seem to believe that progressivism is now in the dominant position in educational policy and practice and has destroyed a valued past. All of them believe that only by tightening control over curriculum and teaching (and students, of course), restoring "our" lost traditions, making education more disciplined and competitive as they are certain it was in the past—only then can we have effective schools. These figures are joined by others who have similar criticisms, but who instead turn to a different past for a different future. Their past is less that of scent and awe and authority, but one of market "freedom." For them, nothing can be accomplished—even the restoration of awe and authority—without setting the market loose on schools so as to ensure that only "good" ones survive.

We should understand that these policies are radical transformations. If they had come from the other side of the political spectrum, they would have been ridiculed in many ways, given the ideological tendencies in our nations. Further, not only are these policies based on a romanticized pastoral past, these reforms have not been notable for their grounding in research findings. Indeed, when research has been used, it has often either served as a rhetoric of justification for preconceived beliefs about the supposed efficacy of markets or regimes of tight accountability or they have been based—as in the case of Chubb and Moe's much publicized work on marketization—on quite flawed research.[15]

Yet, no matter how radical some of these proposed "reforms" are and no matter how weak the empirical basis of their support, they have now redefined the terrain of debate of all things educational. After years of conservative attacks and mobilizations, it has become clear that "ideas that were once deemed fanciful, unworkable—or just plain extreme" are now increasingly being seen as common-sense.[16]

Tactically, the reconstruction of common-sense that has been accomplished has proven to be extremely effective. For example, clear discursive strategies are being employed here, ones that are characterized by "plain speaking" and speaking in a language that "everyone can understand." (I do not wish to be wholly negative about this. The importance of these things is something many "progressive" educators, including many writers on critical pedagogy, have yet to understand.)[17] These strategies also involve not only presenting one's own position as "common-sense," but also usually tacitly implying that there is something of a conspiracy among one's opponents to deny the truth or to say only that which is "fashionable."[18] As Gillborn notes,

> This is a powerful technique. First, it assumes that there are no *genuine* arguments against the chosen position; any opposing views are thereby positioned as false, insincere or self-serving. Second, the technique presents the speaker as someone brave or honest enough to speak the (previously) unspeakable. Hence, the moral high ground is assumed and opponents are further denigrated.[19]

It is hard to miss these characteristics in some of the conservative literature such as Herrnstein and Murray's publicizing of the unthinkable "truth" about genetics and intelligence or E. D. Hirsch's latest "tough" discussion of the destruction of "serious" schooling by progressive educators.[20]

MARKETS AND PERFORMANCE

Let us take as an example of the ways in which all of these arguments operate one element of conservative modernization—the neoliberal claim that the invisible hand of the market will inexorably lead to better schools. As Roger Dale reminds us, "the market" acts as a metaphor rather than an explicit guide for action. It is not denotative, but connotative. Thus, it must itself be "marketed" to those who will exist in it and live with its effects.[21] Markets are marketed, are made legitimate, by a depoliticizing strategy. They are said to be natural and neutral, and governed by effort and merit. And those opposed to them are by definition, hence, also opposed to effort and merit. Markets, as well, are supposedly less subject to political interference and the weight of bureaucratic procedures. Plus, they are grounded in the rational choices of individual actors.[22] Thus, markets and the guarantee of rewards for effort and merit are to be coupled together to produce "neutral," yet positive, results. Mechanisms, hence, must be put into place that give evidence of entrepreneurial efficiency and effectiveness. This coupling of markets and mechanisms for the generation of evidence of performance is exactly what has occurred. Whether it works is open to question. Indeed, as I shall show shortly, in practice neoliberal policies involving market "solutions" may actually serve to reproduce—not subvert—traditional hierarchies of class and race. Perhaps this should give us reason to pause?[23]

Thus, rather than taking neoliberal claims at face value, we should want to ask about their hidden effects that are too often invisible in the rhetoric and metaphors of their proponents. I shall select a number of issues that have been given less attention than they deserve, but on which there is now significant research.

The English experience is apposite here, especially since proponents of the market such as Chubb and Moe rely so heavily on it[24] and because that is where the tendencies I analyze are most advanced. In England, the 1993 Education Act documents the state's commitment to marketization. Governing bodies of local educational authorities (LEAs) were mandated to formally consider "going GM" (that is, opting out of the local school system's control and entering into the competitive market) every year.[25] Thus, the weight of the state stood behind the press toward neoliberal reforms there.[26] Yet, rather than leading to curriculum responsiveness and diversification, the competitive market has not created much that is different from the traditional models so firmly entrenched in schools today.[27] Nor has it radically altered the relations of inequality that characterize schooling.

In their own extensive analyses of the effects of marketized reforms "on the ground," Ball and his colleagues point to some of the reasons why we need to be quite cautious here. As they document, in these situations educational principles and values are often compromised such that commercial issues become more important in curriculum design and resource allocation.[28] For instance, the coupling of markets with the demand for and publication of performance indicators such as "examination league tables" in England has meant that schools are increasingly looking for ways to attract "motivated" parents with "able" children. In this way, schools are able to enhance their relative position in local systems of competition. This represents a subtle, but crucial shift in emphasis—one that is not openly discussed as often as it should be—from student needs to student performance and from what the school does for the student to what the student does for the school. This is also accompanied too uncomfortably often by a shift of resources away from students who are labeled as having special needs or learning difficulties, with some of these needed resources now being shifted to marketing and public relations. "Special needs" students not only are expensive, but also deflate test scores on those all important league tables.

Not only does this make it difficult to "manage public impressions," but it also makes it difficult to attract the "best" and most academically talented teachers.[29] The entire enterprise does, however, establish a new metric and a new set of goals based on a constant striving to win the market game. What this means is of considerable import, not only in terms of its effects on daily school life but in the ways all of this signifies a transformation of what counts as a good society and a responsible citizen. Let me say something about this generally.

I noted earlier that behind all educational proposals are visions of a just society and a good student. The neoliberal reforms I have been discussing construct this in a particular way. While the defining characteristic of neoliberalism is largely based on the central tenets of classical liberalism, in particular classic economic liberalism, there are crucial differences between classical liberalism and neoliberalism. These differences are absolutely essential in understanding the politics of education and the transformations education is currently undergoing. Mark Olssen clearly details these differences in the following passage. It is worth quoting in its entirety.

> Whereas classical liberalism represents a negative conception of state power in that the individual was to be taken as an object to be freed from the interventions of the state, neo-liberalism has come to represent a positive conception of the state's role in creating the appropriate market by providing

the conditions, laws and institutions necessary for its operation. In classical liberalism, the individual is characterized as having an autonomous human nature and can practice freedom. In neo-liberalism the state seeks to create an individual who is an enterprising and competitive entrepreneur. In the classical model the theoretical aim of the state was to limit and minimize its role based on postulates which included universal egoism (the self-interested individual); invisible hand theory which dictated that the interests of the individual were also the interests of the society as a whole; and the political maxim of laissez-faire. In the shift from classical liberalism to neo-liberalism, then, there is a further element added, for such a shift involves a change in subject position from "homo economicus," who naturally behaves out of self-interest and is relatively detached from the state, to "manipulatable man," who is created by the state and who is continually encouraged to be "perpetually responsive." It is not that the conception of the self-interested subject is replaced or done away with by the new ideals of "neo-liberalism," but that in an age of universal welfare, the perceived possibilities of slothful indolence create necessities for new forms of vigilance, surveillance, "performance appraisal" and of forms of control generally. In this model the state has taken it upon itself to keep us all up to the mark. The state will see to it that each one makes a "continual enterprise of ourselves". . . in what seems to be a process of "governing without governing."[30]

The results of Ball and his colleagues' research document how the state does indeed do this, enhancing that odd combination of marketized individualism and control through constant and comparative public assessment. Widely publicized league tables determine one's relative value in the educational marketplace. Only those schools with rising performance indicators are worthy. And only those students who can "make a continual enterprise of themselves" can keep such schools going in the "correct" direction, a discussion to which I return shortly. Yet, while these issues are important, they fail to fully illuminate some of the other mechanisms through which *differential* effects are produced by neoliberal reforms. Here, class issues come to the fore in ways that Ball, Bowe, and Gewirtz make clear.

Middle-class parents are clearly the most advantaged in this kind of cultural assemblage, and not only as we saw because schools seek them out. Middle-class parents have become quite skilled, in general, in exploiting market mechanisms in education and in bringing their social, economic, and cultural capital to bear on them. "Middle class parents are more likely to have the knowledge, skills and contacts to decode and manipulate what are increasingly complex and deregulated systems of choice and recruitment. The more deregulation, the more possibility of informal procedures being employed. The middle class also, on the whole, are more able to move their children around the system."[31] As I argue in more detail later on, both because class and race intersect and interact in complex ways and because marketized systems in education often *expressly* have their conscious and unconscious raison d'être in a fear of "the Other" and these often are hidden expressions of a racialization of educational policy, the differential results will "naturally" be decidedly raced as well as classed.[32]

Economic and social capital can be converted into cultural capital in various ways. In marketized plans, more affluent parents often have more flexible hours and can visit multiple schools. They have cars—often more than one—and can *afford* driving their children across town to attend a "better" school. They can as well provide the hidden cultural resources such as camps and after-school programs (dance, music, computer classes, etc.) that give their children an "ease," a "style," that seems "natural" and acts as a set of cultural resources. Their previous stock of social and cultural capital—who they know, their "comfort" in social encounters with educational officials—is an unseen but powerful storehouse of resources. Thus, more affluent parents are more likely to have the informal knowledge and skill—what Bourdieu would call the habitus[33]—to be able to decode and use marketized forms to their own benefit. This sense of what might be called "confidence"—which is itself the result of past choices that tacitly but no less powerfully depend on the economic resources to actually have had the ability to make economic choices—is the unseen capital that underpins their ability to negotiate marketized forms and "work the system" through sets of informal cultural rules.[34]

Of course, it needs to be said that working-class, poor, and/or immigrant parents are not skill-less in this regard, by any means. (After all, it requires an immense amount of skill, courage, and social and cultural resources to survive under exploitative and depressing material conditions. Thus, collective bonds, informal networks and contacts, and an ability to work the system are developed in quite nuanced, intelligent, and often impressive ways here.)[35] However, the match between the historically grounded habitus expected in schools and in its actors and those of more affluent parents, combined with the material resources available to more affluent parents, usually leads to a successful conversion of economic and social capital into cultural capital.[36] And this is exactly what is happening in England and elsewhere.

These claims both about what is happening inside of schools and about larger sets of power relations are supported by even more recent synthetic analyses of the overall results of marketized models. This research on the effects of the tense but still effective combination of neoliberal and neoconservative policies examines the tendencies internationally by comparing what has happened in a number of nations—for example, the United States, England and Wales, Australia, and New Zealand—where this combination has been increasingly powerful. The results confirm the arguments I have made here. Let me rehearse some of the most significant and disturbing findings of such research.

It is unfortunately all too usual that the most widely used measures of the "success" of school reforms are the results of standardized achievement tests. This simply will not do. We need to constantly ask what reforms do to schools as a whole and to each of their participants, including teachers, students, administrators, community members, local activists, and so on. To take one set of examples, as marketized "self-managing" schools grow in many nations, the role of the school principal is radically transformed. More, not less, power is actually consolidated within an administrative structure. More time and energy is spent on maintaining or enhancing a public image of a "good school" and less time and energy is spent on pedagogic and curricular substance. At the same time, teachers seem to be experiencing not increased autonomy and professionalism, but intensification.[37] And, oddly, as noted before, schools themselves become more *similar,* and more committed, to standard, traditional, whole-class methods of teaching and a standard and traditional (and often monocultural) curriculum.[38] Only directing our attention to test scores would cause us to miss some truly profound transformations, many of which we may find disquieting.

One of the reasons these broader effects are so often produced is that in all too many countries, neoliberal visions of quasi markets are usually accompanied by neoconservative pressure to regulate content and behavior through such things as national curricula, national standards, and national systems of assessment. The combination is historically contingent; that is, it is not absolutely necessary that the two emphases are combined. But neoliberalism has characteristics that make it more likely that an emphasis on the weak state and a faith in markets will cohere with an emphasis on the strong state and a commitment to regulating knowledge, values, and the body.

This is partly the case because of the increasing power of the "evaluative state" and the members of the managerial and professional middle class who tend to populate it. This signifies what initially may seem to be contradictory tendencies. At the same time as the state appears to be devolving power to individuals and autonomous institutions that are themselves increasingly competing in a market, the state remains strong in key areas.[39] As I claimed earlier, one of the key differences between classical liberalism and its faith in "enterprising individuals" in a market and current forms of neoliberalism is the latter's commitment to a regulatory state. Neoliberalism does indeed demand the constant production of evidence that one is in fact "making an enterprise of oneself."[40] Thus, under these conditions not only does education become a marketable commodity like bread and cars in which the values, procedures, and metaphors of business dominate, but its results must be reducible to standardized "performance indicators."[41] This is ideally suited to the task of providing a mechanism for the neoconservative attempts to specify what knowledge, values, and behaviors should be standardized and officially defined as "legitimate," a point I expand upon in the next section of this chapter.

In essence, we are witnessing a process in which the state shifts the blame for the very evident inequalities in access and outcome it has promised to reduce, from itself onto individual schools, parents, and children. This is, of course, also part of a larger process in which dominant economic groups shift the blame for the massive and unequal effects of their own misguided decisions from themselves onto the state. The state is then faced with a very real crisis in legitimacy. Given this, we should not be at all surprised that the state will then seek to export this crisis outside itself.[42]

Of course, the state is not only classed but inherently *sex/gendered* and *raced* as well.[43] This is evident in Whitty, Power, and Halpin's arguments. They point to the gendered nature of the ways in which the management of schools is thought about, as "masculinist" business models become increasingly dominant.[44] While there is a danger of these claims degenerating into reductive and essentializing arguments, there is a good deal of insight here. They do cohere with the work of other scholars inside and outside of education who recognize that the ways in which our very definitions of public and private, of what knowledge is of most worth, and of how institutions should be thought about and run are fully implicated in the gendered nature of this society.[45] These broad ideological effects—for example, enabling a coalition between neoliberals and neoconservatives to be formed; expanding the discourses and practices of new middle-class managerialism; the masculinization of theories, policies, and management talk—are of considerable import and make it harder to change common-sense in more critical directions.

Other, more proximate, effects inside schools are equally striking. For instance, even though principals seem to have more local power in these supposedly decentralized schools, because of the cementing in of neoconservative policies principals "are increasingly forced into a position in which they have to demonstrate performance along centrally prescribed curricula in a context in which they have diminishing control."[46] Because of the intensification that I mentioned before, both principals and teachers experience considerably heavier workloads and ever-escalating de-have discussed so far. The case of New Zealand is useful here, especially since a large percentage of the population of New Zealand is multiethnic, and the nation has a history of racial tensions and inequalities. Furthermore, the move toward New Right policies occurred faster there than elsewhere. In essence, New Zealand became the laboratory for many of the policies I am analyzing. In their exceptional study, based in large part on a conceptual apparatus influenced by Pierre Bourdieu, Lauder and Hughes document that educational markets seem to lead to an overall decline in educational standards. Paradoxically, they have a negative, not a positive, effect on the performance of schools with large working-class and minority populations. In essence, they "trade off the opportunities of less privileged children to those already privileged."[51] The combination of neoliberal policies of marketization and the neoconservative emphasis on "tougher standards," about which I say more in the next section, creates an even more dangerous set of conditions. Lauder and Hughes's analysis confirms the conceptual and empirical arguments of Ball, Brown, and others that markets in education are not only responses by capital to reduce both the sphere of the state and of public control. They are also part of an attempt by the middle class to alter the rules of competition in education in light of the increased insecurities their children face. "By changing the process of selection to schools, middle class parents can raise the stakes in creating stronger mechanisms of exclusion for blue collar and post-colonial peoples in their struggle for equality of opportunity."[52]

The results from New Zealand not only mirror what was found elsewhere, but also demonstrate that the further one's practices follow the logics of action embodied in marketizing principles, the worse the situation tends to get. Markets *systematically* privilege families with higher socioeconomic status (SES) through their knowledge and material resources. These are the families who are most likely to exercise choice. Rather than giving large numbers of students who are working class, poor, or of color the ability to exit, it is largely higher SES families who exit from public schools and schools with mixed populations. In a situation of increased competition, this in turn produces a spiral of decline in which schools populated by poorer students and students of color are again systematically disadvantaged and schools with higher SES and higher white populations are able to insulate themselves from the effects of market competition.[53] "White flight" then enhances the relative status of those schools already advantaged by larger economic forces; schooling for the "Other" becomes even more polarized and continues a downward spiral.[54]

Having said this, however, we need to be cautious not to ignore historical specificities. Social movements, existing ideological formations, and institutions in civil society and the state may provide some support for countervailing logics. In some cases, in those nations with stronger and more extensive histories of social democratic policies and visions of collective positive freedoms, the neoliberal emphasis on the market has been significantly mediated. Hence, as Petter Aasen has demonstrated in Norway and Sweden, for instance, privatizing initiatives in education have had to cope with a greater collective commitment than in, say, the United States, England, and New Zealand.[55] However, these commitments partly rest on class relations. They are weakened when racial dynamics enter in. Thus, for example, the sense of "everyone being the same" and hence being all subject to similar collective sensibilities is challenged by the growth of immigrant populations from Africa, Asia, and the Middle East. Greater sympathy for marketized forms may arise once the commonly understood assumptions of what it means to be, say, Norwegian or Swedish are interrupted by populations of color who now claim the status of national citizenship. For this reason, it may be the case that the collective sensibilities that provide support for less market oriented policies are based on an unacknowledged *racial contract* that underpins the ideological foundations of a national "imagined community."[56] This, then, may also generate support for neoconservative policies, not because of neoliberalism's commitment to "perpetual responsiveness," but rather as a form of cultural restoration, as a way of reestablishing an imagined past when "we were all one." Because of this, it is important that any analysis of the current play of forces surrounding conservative modernization is aware of the fact that not only are such movements in constant motion, but once again we need to remember that they have a multitude of intersecting and contradictory dynamics including not only class, but race and gender as well.[57]

Most of the data I have drawn upon come from schools outside the United States, although they should make us stop dead in our tracks and give some very serious thought to whether we want to proceed with similar policies here. Yet the United States still sits at the center of much of the discussion in this literature. For example, charter schools and their equivalents in the United States and England are also put under critical scrutiny. In both places, while we need to be careful not to overstate this, they tend to attract parents who live and work in relatively privileged communities. Here, too, "it would appear that any new opportunities are being colonized by the already advantaged, rather than the 'losers' identified by Chubb and Moe."[58]

In the process, this critical research suggests that there are hidden similarities between advocates of school effectiveness research and those committed to neoliberal "reforms." Both tend to ignore the fact that external characteristics of schools such as poverty, political and economic power, and so on consistently account for much more of the variation in school performance than things like organizational features or those characteristics that supposedly guarantee an "effective school."[59]

The overall conclusions are clear. "[In] current circumstances choice is as likely to reinforce hierarchies as to improve educational opportunities and the overall quality of schooling."[60] As Whitty, Power, and Halpin put it in their arguments against those who believe that what we are witnessing in the emergence of "choice" programs is the postmodern celebration of difference:

> There is a growing body of empirical evidence that, rather than benefiting the disadvantaged, the emphasis on parental choice and school autonomy is further disadvantaging those least able to compete in the market. . . . For most disadvantaged groups, as opposed to the few individuals who escape from schools at the bottom of the status hierarchy, the new arrangements seem to be just a more sophisticated way of reproducing traditional distinctions between different types of school and the people who attend them.[61]

All of this critical information gives us ample reason
Henig's insightful argument I quoted in the previous chapter
sad irony of the current education-reform movement is that,
over-identification with school-choice proposals rooted in market-based
ideas, the healthy impulse to consider radical reforms to address social
problems may be channelled into initiatives that further erode the potential for collective deliberation and collective response."[62]

This is not to dismiss either the possibility or necessity of school reform. However, we need to take seriously the probability that only by
focusing on the exogenous socioeconomic features, not simply the organizational features, of "successful" schools can all schools succeed. Elimi-
nating poverty through greater income parity, establishing effective and
much more equal health and housing programs, and positively refusing to
continue the hidden and not so hidden politics of racial exclusion and
degradation that so clearly still characterize daily life in many nations (and
in which marketized plans need to be seen as partly a structure to avoid
the body and culture of the Other)—only by tackling these issues together
can substantive progress be made. Unless discussions of critical pedagogy
are themselves grounded in a recognition of these realities, they too may
fall into the trap of assuming that schools can do it alone.

These empirical findings are made more understandable in terms of
Pierre Bourdieu's analysis of the relative weight given to cultural capital
as part of mobility strategies today.[63] The rise in importance of cultural
capital infiltrates all institutions in such a way that there is a relative
movement away from the *direct* reproduction of class privilege (where
power is transmitted largely within families through economic property)
to *school-mediated* forms of class privilege. Here, "the bequeathal of privilege is simultaneously effectuated and transfigured by the intercession
of educational institutions."[64] This is *not* a conspiracy; it is not "conscious" in the ways we normally use that concept. Rather it is the result
of a long chain of relatively autonomous connections between differentially accumulated economic, social, and cultural capital operating at the
level of daily events as we make our respective ways in the world, including as we saw in the world of school choice.

Thus, while not taking an unyieldingly determinist position, Bourdieu argues that a class habitus tends to reproduce the conditions of its own reproduction "unconsciously." It does this by producing a relatively coherent and systematically *characteristic* set of seemingly natural and unconscious strategies—in essence, ways of understanding and acting on the world that act as forms of cultural capital that can be and are employed to protect and enhance one's status in a social field of power. He aptly compares this similarity of habitus across class actors to handwriting:

> Just as the acquired disposition we call "handwriting," that is a particular way of forming letters, always produces the same "writing"—that is, graphic lines that despite differences in size, matter, and color related to writing surface (sheet of paper or blackboard) and implement (pencil, pen, or chalk), that is despite differences in vehicles for the action, have an immediately recognizable affinity of style or a family resemblance—the practices of a single agent, or, more broadly, the practices of all agents endowed with similar habitus, owe the affinity of style that makes each a metaphor for the others to the fact that they are the products of the implementation in different fields of the same schemata of perception, thought, and action.[65]

This very connection of habitus across fields of power—the ease of bringing one's economic, social, and cultural resources to bear on "markets"—enables a comfort between markets and self that characterizes the middle-class actor here. This constantly *produces* differential effects. These effects are not neutral, no matter what the advocates of neoliberalism suggest. Rather, they are themselves the results of a particular kind of morality. Unlike the conditions of what might best be called "thick morality" where principles of the common good are the ethical basis for adjudicating policies and practices, markets are grounded in aggregative principles. They are constituted out of the sum of individual goods and choices. "Founded on individual and property rights that enable citizens to address problems of interdependence via exchange," they offer a prime example of "thin morality" by generating both hierarchy and division based on competitive individualism.[66] And in this competition, the general outline of the winners and losers *has* been identified empirically.

NATIONAL STANDARDS, NATIONAL CURRICULUM, AND NATIONAL TESTING

I showed in the previous section that there are connections between at least two dynamics operating in neoliberal reforms, "free" markets and increased surveillance. This can be seen in the fact that in many contexts, marketization has been accompanied by a set of particular policies for "producers," for those professionals working within education. These policies have been strongly regulatory and have been quite instrumental in reconstituting common-sense. As in the case of the linkage between national tests and performance indicators published as league tables, they have been organized around a concern for external supervision, regulation, and external judgment of performance[67] and have increasingly been colonized by parents who possess what is seen as "appropriate" economic, social, and cultural capital. This concern for external supervision and regulation is not only connected with a strong mistrust of "producers" (e.g., teachers) and to the need for ensuring that people continually make enterprises out of themselves. It is also clearly linked both to the neoconservative sense of a need to "return" to a lost past of high standards, discipline, awe, and "real" knowledge and to the professional middle-class' own ability to carve out a sphere of authority within the state for its own commitment to management techniques and efficiency. The focus on efficient management plays a prime role here, one that many neoliberals and neoconservatives alike find useful.

A shift has occurred in the relationship between the state and "professionals." In essence, the move toward a small strong state that is increasingly guided by market needs seems inevitably to bring with it reduced professional power and status.[68] Managerialism takes center stage here. Managerialism is largely charged with "bringing about the cultural transformation that shifts professional identities in order to make them more responsive to client demand and external judgement." It aims to justify and to have people internalize fundamental alterations in professional practices. It both harnesses energy and discourages dissent.[69]

There is no necessary contradiction between a general set of marketizing and deregulating interests and processes—such as voucher and choice plans—and a set of enhanced regulatory processes—such as plans for national or state standards, curricula, and testing.[70] "The regulatory form permits the state to maintain 'steerage' over the aims and processes of education from within the market mechanism."[71] Such "steerage at a distance" has often been vested in such things as national standards, national curricula, and national testing. Forms of all of these are being pushed for in the United States both at national and state levels currently and are the subject of considerable controversy, some of which cuts across ideological lines and shows some of the tensions within the different elements contained under the umbrella of conservative modernization.

I have argued that paradoxically a national curriculum and especially a national testing program are the first and most essential steps toward increased marketization. They actually provide the mechanisms for comparative data that "consumers" need to make markets work as markets.[72] Absent these mechanisms, there is no comparative base of information for "choice." Yet we do not have to argue about these regulatory forms in a vacuum. Like the neoliberal markets I discussed in the previous section, they too have been instituted in England; and, once again, important research is available that can and must make us duly cautious in going down this path.

One might want to claim that a set of national or state standards, national or state curricula, and national or state tests would provide the conditions for thick morality. After all, such regulatory reforms are supposedly based on shared values and common sentiments that also create social spaces in which common issues of concern can be debated and made subject to moral interrogation.[73] Yet what counts as the "common," and how and by whom it is actually determined, is rather more thin than thick.

Although the national curriculum now so solidly in place in England and Wales is clearly prescriptive, it has not always proven to be the kind of straitjacket it has often been made out to be. As several researchers have documented, it is not only possible that policies and legislative mandates are interpreted and adapted, but it seems inevitable. Thus, the national curriculum is "not so much being 'implemented' in schools as being 'recreated,' not so much 'reproduced,' as 'produced'."[74]

In general, it is nearly a truism that there is no simplistic linear model of policy formation, distribution, and implementation. Complex mediations always occur at each level of the process. A complex politics goes on within each group and between these groups and external forces in the formulation of policy, in its being written up as a legislative mandate, in its distribution, and in its reception at the level of practice.[75] Thus, the state may legislate changes in curriculum, evaluation, or policy (which is itself produced through conflict, compromise, and political maneuvering), but policy writers and curriculum writers may be unable to control the meanings and implementations of their texts. All texts are "leaky" documents. They are subject to "recontextualization" at every stage of the process.[76]

However, this general principle may be just a bit too romantic. None of this occurs on a level playing field. As with market plans, there are very real differences in power in one's ability to influence, mediate, transform, or reject a policy or a regulatory process. Granted, it is important to recognize that a "state control model"—with its assumption of top-down linearity—is much too simplistic and that the possibility of human agency and influence is always there. However, having said this, this should not imply that such agency and influence will be powerful.[77]

The case of national curriculum and national testing in England and Wales documents the tensions in these two accounts. The national curriculum that was first legislated and then imposed there was indeed struggled over. It was originally too detailed and too specific and, hence, was subject to major transformations at the national, community, school, and then classroom levels. However, even though the national curriculum was subject to conflict, mediation, and some transformation of its content, organization, and invasive and immensely time consuming forms of evaluation, its utter power is demonstrated in its radical reconfiguration of the very process of knowledge selection, organization, and assessment. It changed the entire terrain of education radically. Its subject divisions "provide more constraint than scope for discretion." The "standard attainment targets" that have been mandated cement these constraints in place. "The imposition of national testing locks the national curriculum in place as the dominant framework of teachers' work whatever opportunities teachers may take to evade or reshape it."[78]

Thus, it is not sufficient to state that the world of education is complex and has multiple influences. The purpose of any serious analysis is to go beyond such overly broad conclusions. Rather, we need to "discriminate degrees of influence in the world," to weigh the relative efficacy of the factors involved. Hence, although it is clear that while the national curriculum and national tests that now exist in England and Wales have come about because of a complex interplay of forces and influences, it is equally clear that "state control has the upper hand."[79]

The national curricula and national tests *did* generate conflict about issues. They did partly lead to the creation of social spaces for moral questions to get asked. (Of course, these moral questions had been asked all along by dispossessed groups.) Thus, it was clear to many people that the creation of mandatory and reductive tests that emphasized memory and decontextualized abstraction pulled the national curriculum in a particular direction—that of encouraging a selective educational market in which elite students and elite schools with a wide range of resources would be well (if narrowly) served.[80] Diverse groups of people argued that such reductive, detailed, and simplistic paper-and-pencil tests "had the potential to do enormous damage," a situation that was made even worse because the tests were so onerous in terms of time and record keeping. Teachers had a good deal of support when as a group they decided to boycott the administration of the test in a remarkable act of public protest. This also led to serious questioning of the arbitrary, inflexible, and overly prescriptive national curriculum. While the curriculum is still inherently problematic and the assessment system does still contain numerous dangerous and onerous elements within it, organized activity against them did have an impact.[81]

Yet, unfortunately, the story does not end there. By the mid-1990s, even with the government's partial retreat on such regulatory forms as its program of constant and reductive testing, it had become clearer by the year that the development of testing and the specification of content had been "hijacked" by those who were ideologically committed to traditional pedagogies and to the idea of more rigorous selection.[82] The residual effects are both material and ideological. They include a continuing emphasis on trying to provide the "rigor [that is] missing in the practice of most teachers, . . . judging progress solely by what is testable in tests of this kind" and the development of a "very hostile view of the accountability of teachers" that was seen as "part of a wider thrust of policy to take away professional control of public services and establish so called consumer control through a market structure."[83]

The authors of an extremely thorough review of recent assessment programs instituted in England and Wales provide a summary of what has happened. Gipps and Murphy argue that it has become increasingly obvious that the national assessment program attached to the national curriculum is more and more dominated by traditional models of testing and the assumptions about teaching and learning that lie behind them. At the same time, equity issues are becoming much less visible. In the calculus of values now in place in the regulatory state, efficiency, speed, and cost control replace more substantive concerns about social and educational justice. The pressure to get tests in place rapidly has meant that "the speed of test development is so great, and the curriculum and assessment changes so regular, that [there is] little time to carry out detailed analyses and trialing to ensure that the tests are as fair as possible to all groups."[84] Echoes of these very same effects are seen throughout major cities in the United States as well. The conditions for "thin morality"—in which the competitive individual of the market dominates and social justice will somehow take care of itself—are reproduced here. The combination of the neoliberal market and the regulatory state, then, does indeed "work." However, it works in ways in which the metaphors of free market, merit, and effort hide the differential reality that is produced. While on the one hand this makes a socially and culturally critical pedagogy even more essential, it also makes it much more difficult to actually accomplish.

Basil Bernstein's discussion of the general principles by which knowledge and policies ("texts") move from one arena to another is useful in understanding this. As Bernstein reminds us, when talking about educational change, we must be concerned with three fields. Each field has its own rules of access, regulation, privilege, and special interests: (1) the field of "production" where new knowledge is constructed; (2) the field of "reproduction" where pedagogy and curriculum are actually enacted in schools; and, between these other two, (3) the "recontextualizing" field where discourses from the field of production are appropriated and then transformed into pedagogic discourse and recommendations.[85] This appropriation and recontextualization of knowledge for educational purposes is itself governed by two sets of principles. The first—delocation—implies that there is always a *selective* appropriation of knowledge and discourse from the field of production. The second—relocation—points to the fact that when knowledge and discourse from the field of production is pulled within the recontextualizing field, it is subject to ideological transformations due to the various specialized and/or political interests whose conflicts structure the recontextualizing field.[86]

A good example of this, one that confirms Gipps and Murphy's analysis of the dynamics of national curricula and national testing during their more recent iterations, is found in the process by which the content and organization of the mandated national curriculum in physical education were struggled over and ultimately formed in England. In this instance, a working group of academics both within and outside the field of physical education, headmasters of private and state-supported schools, well-known athletes, and business leaders (but *no* teachers) was formed.

The original curriculum policies that arose from the group were relatively mixed educationally and ideologically, taking account of the field of production of knowledge within physical education. That is, they contained both critical and progressive elements and elements of the conservative restoration, as well as academic perspectives within the specialized fields from the university. However, as these policies made their way from report to recommendations and then from recommendations to action, they steadily came closer to restorational principles. An emphasis on efficiency, basic skills and performance testing, on the social control of the body, and on competitive norms ultimately won out. Like the middle-class capturing of the market discussed earlier, this too was not a conspiracy. Rather, it was the result of a process of "overdetermination." That is, it was not due to an imposition of these norms, but to a combination of interests in the recontextualizing field—an economic context in which public spending was under severe scrutiny and cost savings had to be sought everywhere; government officials who were opposed to "frills" and consistently intervened to institute only a selection of the recommendations (conservative ones that did *not* come from "professional academics" preferably); ideological attacks on critical, progressive, or child-centered approaches to physical education; and a predominant discourse of "being pragmatic." These came together in the recontextualizing field and helped ensure in practice that conservative principles would be reinscribed in policies and mandates, and that critical forms were seen as too ideological, too costly, or too impractical.[87] "Standards" were upheld; critical voices were heard, but ultimately to little effect; the norms of competitive performance were made central and employed as regulatory devices. Regulatory devices served to privilege specific groups in much the same way as did markets. If this is the case in physical education, it is not hard to predict what is happening and will happen in those curriculum areas that are socially defined as even higher status, and where the stakes seem higher as well.

But it is important not to leave our discussion at such an abstract level or at the level of curriculum planning. What has happened in schools themselves in the United States and elsewhere when such "pragmatic" standards, curricula, and tests are actually instituted?

CREATING EDUCATIONAL TRIAGE

Analyses here in the United States have begun to document similar kinds of effects.[88] However, unfortunately, the predominance of relatively un-reflective and at times almost self-congratulatory policies around markets, standards, testing, and reductive forms of accountability is exactly that here—predominant. Even given the exceptional work that is being done, for example, by Jeannie Oakes, Amy Stuart Wells, and others on the hidden effects of some of these kinds of policies and practices, and even given the fact that there are numerous examples of extremely effective schools in our urban and rural areas that succeed through using much more democratic and critical models of curriculum, teaching, and evaluation,[89] it still feels as if one has to constantly swim against the tide of conservative modernization.

Given this state of affairs, it is now even more important that we pay attention to material that demonstrates what can happen in situations where the stress on higher standards and higher test scores hits both the realities of schools and the different populations they serve. David Gillborn and Deborah Youdell's volume *Rationing Education* is just such a book.[90] It goes into even more detail about the powerful, and often damaging, effects on teachers and students of our seeming fascination with ever-rising standards, mandated curricula, and overemphasis on testing.

The volume is based on in-depth research on the equivalent of middle and secondary schools in England. It details the overt and hidden effects of policies that are currently being undertaken in the United States as well. These include such things as creating a situation where the tail of a high-stakes test "wags the dog" of the teacher, pressuring schools to constantly show increased achievement scores on such standardized tests no matter what the level of support or the impoverished conditions in schools and local communities, to publicly display such results in a process of what might be realistically called shaming, and to threaten schools that do not show "improvement" on these tests with severe sanctions or loss of control.

Of course, there are poor schools and there are ineffective practices in schools. However, the reduction of education to scores on what are often inadequate measures, often used in technically and educationally inappropriate ways for comparative purposes, has some serious consequences. What these consequences are provides the context for the story Gillborn and Youdell tell.

In many ways, *Rationing Education* provides what might be called a microeconomy of school life. It examines the ways in which certain valued commodities are accumulated by schools in a time of intense competition for scarce resources. In this case, the commodities are higher test scores and the resources are both numbers of students and public recognition of being a "good" school. The authors' way of describing this is what they call the "A–C economy."

In England, as in the United States, schools exist in what is really a hierarchical ordering, a market, in prestige and reputation. They are valued by the number of students who get passing scores on particular national tests. The national tests are made public as a form of "league tables" in which schools are rank-ordered according to their relative results. Schools with large numbers of students getting grades A–C are more highly valued than those with students whose rates of passing are less——even though everyone tacitly knows that there is a very strong relationship between school results and poverty. (We need again to remember in the United States, for example, that poverty explains *much* more of the variance in school achievement than any school reform.)

This is straightforward and not surprising. However, this situation creates an economy that has certain characteristics. Students with predicted higher test scores are even more valuable. Students with predicted lower test scores are seen as less useful to the school's place in the market. This too is not surprising. The results of such an economy, however, are powerful. Another key group of students is focused upon and on whom considerable resources, energy, and attention are devoted— students who are on the border between passing grades and failing grades. These students—often seen as middle-class "underachievers"— become objects of great value in the school. After all, if this key group can be pulled across the border into the A–C column, the school's results will be that much more positive.

What could be wrong with an increased focus on students on the border? Here is one of the places where Gillborn and Youdell's results are ominous. In such an A–C economy, specific students are seen as movable. Other students' abilities are seen as increasingly fixed and less worthy of attention. The class and race characteristics of these latter students are striking. Poor and working-class students, students of African descent, and other ethnically "different" children are not valued commodities on this kind of market. Even though gender divisions were less pronounced in the schools that Gillborn and Youdell studied, divisions strongly rooted in racializing and class-based structures were not simply mirrored in the schools. They actually were *produced* in these institutions.

Thus, policies that were put in place to raise standards, to increase test scores, to guarantee public accountability, and to make schools more competitive had results that were more than a little damaging to those students who were already the least advantaged in these same schools. Yet it was not only the students who witnessed these negative effects. The voices of teachers and administrators indicate what happens to them as well. They too begin to harden their sense of which students are "able" and which students are not. Tracking returns in both overt and covert ways. And once again, black students and students in government-subsidized lunch programs are the ones most likely to be placed in those tracks or given academic and career advice that nearly guarantees that they will have limited or no mobility and will confirm their status as students who are "less worthy."

Equally worth noting here is the specific way the A–C economy works to choose those students who are deemed to have worthiness. Often, students whose behavior and test results are quite similar have very different careers in the school. Thus, a black student and a white student may be, say, on the border of the A–C/failing divide, but the black student will not be the beneficiary of the added attention. These situations are all too often characterized by tacitly operating visions of ability, ones that have been hardened by years of discourse on the "problem" of black student achievement and especially by the increased visibility

once again of supposedly scientific (and ultimately racist and empirically problematic) "research" on genetic differences in mean intelligence
between blacks and whites. As I noted, not only would no reputable
population geneticist make such a claim, but these theories have been
discredited multiple times.[91] The fact that they reenter into our common-
sense decision-making in schools in times of scarce resources and increased pressure shows how deeply seated such preconceived notions are
in the sets of assumptions educators may unconsciously mobilize in their
attempt to be pragmatic in dealing with large numbers of students.

As previous research has clearly indicated, students are not passive in
the face of these tendencies. Indeed, as Gillborn and Youdell show, students "interpret, question, and on occasion, resist." However, "the scope
for resistance is severely constrained, and pupils are clearly positioned
as the subject of numerous organizational and disciplinary discourses in
which the young people themselves play little active role."[92] In what is
perhaps one of the most powerful messages of the book, the authors
summarize the effects of this entire process in the following way. "It is
a cruel irony that the processes of selection and monitoring that have
been adopted with the aim of heightening attainment are so frequently
experienced as disempowering and demotivating by the students."[93]
These experiences are turned into feelings of being treated unfairly, of
teachers and schools being organized in ways that privilege the already
privileged in terms of class and race. If this is the case, some of the most
powerful messages "reforms" of this type may send is that not only is the
world deeply unfair but also that schools themselves are prime examples
of institutions that simply respond to those who already possess economic and cultural capital. This is decidedly *not* the message that any
society that is serious about what might be called thick democracy wants
to teach. But it may be what our children, including many like Joseph,
learn in school systems that are so driven by the assumption that putting into place higher standards and higher-stakes testing will somehow
magically solve deep-seated educational and social problems. A close
reading of *Rationing Education* should make us much more cautious
about such unwarranted assumptions.

Unfortunately, recent research on the effects of all the preceding issues in the United States confirms these worries. Linda McNeil's powerful and detailed investigation of what has actually happened in Texas when state-mandated "reforms" involving imposed standards and curricula, reductive and competitive testing, and attacks on teachers' professionalism were instituted demonstrates in no uncertain terms that the very children and schools that these policies and practices are supposed to help are actually hurt in the process.[94] Similar tendencies toward producing inequalities have been documented in the conservative modernization reforms in tax credits, testing, and curricula in Arizona and elsewhere.[95] Thus goeth democracy in education.

THINKING STRATEGICALLY

In this chapter, I have raised serious questions about current educational "reform" efforts now under way in a number of nations. I have used research from England, New Zealand, the United States, and elsewhere to document some of the hidden differential effects of two connected strategies—neoliberal-inspired market proposals and neoliberal-, neoconservative-, and middle-class-managerial-inspired regulatory proposals. Taking a key from Herbert Kliebard's historical analysis, I have described how different interests with different educational and social visions compete for dominion in the social field of power surrounding educational policy and practice. In the process, I have documented some of the complexities and imbalances in this field of power. These complexities and imbalances result in thin rather than thick morality and in the reproduction of both dominant pedagogical and curricular forms and ideologies and the social privileges that accompany them. I have suggested that the rhetorical flourishes of the discourses of critical pedagogy need to come to grips with these changing material and ideological conditions. Critical pedagogy cannot and will not occur in a vacuum. Unless we honestly face these profound rightist transformations and think tactically about them, we will have little effect either on the creation of a counterhegemonic commonsense or on the building of a counterhegemonic alliance. The growth of that odd combination of marketization and regulatory state, the move toward pedagogic similarity and "traditional" academic curricula and teaching, the ability of dominant groups to exert leadership in the struggle over this, and the accompanying shifts in commonsense—all this cannot be wished away. Instead, it needs to be confronted honestly and self-critically.

Having said this, however, I want to point to a hidden paradox in what I have done. Even though much of my own and others' research recently has been on the processes and effects of conservative modernization, we should be aware of the dangers in such a focus. Research on the history, politics, and practices of rightist social and educational movements and "reforms" has enabled us to show the contradictions and unequal effects of such policies and practices. It has enabled the rearticulation of claims to social justice on the basis of solid evidence. This is all to the good. However, in the process, one of the latent effects has been the gradual framing of educational issues largely in terms of the conservative agenda. The very categories themselves—markets, choice, national curricula, national testing, standards—bring the debate onto the terrain established by neoliberals and neoconservatives. The analysis of "what is" has led to a neglect of "what might be." Thus, there has been a withering of substantive large-scale discussions of feasible alternatives to neoliberal and neoconservative visions, policies, and practices, ones that would move well beyond them.[96]

Because of this, at least part of our task may be politically and conceptually complex, but it can be said simply. In the long term, we need to "develop a political project that is both local yet generalizable, systematic without making Eurocentric, masculinist claims to essential and universal truths about human subjects."[97] Another part of our task, though, must be and is more proximate, more appropriately educational. While I say more about this in my final chapter, defensible, articulate, and fully fleshed out alternative critical and progressive policies and practices in curriculum, teaching, and evaluation need to be developed and made widely available. But this too must be done with due recognition

of the changing nature of the social field of power and the importance
of thinking tactically and strategically. Let me be specific here.

For example, in the United States the increasingly popular journal
Rethinking Schools has provided an important forum for social and educational criticism and for descriptions of critical educational practices
in schools and communities. At times influenced directly by the work
of Paulo Freire and by educators who have themselves elaborated and
extended it, and at other times coming out of diverse indigenous radical educational traditions specific to the United States, *Rethinking Schools*
and emerging national organizations such as the National Coalition of
Educational Activists have jointly constructed spaces for critical educators, cultural and political activists, radical scholars, and others to teach
each other, to provide supportive criticism of one another's work, and
to build a more collective set of responses to the destructive educational
and social policies coming from the conservative restoration.[98]

In using the phrase "collective responses," however, I need to stress
that this phrase does not signify anything like "democratic centrism" in
which a small group or a party cadre speaks for the majority and establishes the "appropriate" position. Given that there are diverse emancipatory movements whose voices are heard in publications like *Rethinking
Schools* and in organizations such as the National Coalition of Educational Activists—antiracist and postcolonial positions, radical forms
of multiculturalism, gays and lesbians, multiple feminist voices, neo-
Marxists and democratic socialists, "greens," and so on—a more appropriate way of looking at what is happening is to call it a *decentered unity.*
Multiple progressive projects, multiple "critical pedagogies," are articulated. Like Freire, each of them is related to real struggles in real institutions in real communities. We of course should not be romantic about
this. There are very real differences—political, epistemological, and/or
educational—in these varied voices. But they are united in their opposition to the forces involved in the new conservative hegemonic alliance.
There *are* tensions, but the decentered unity has remained strong enough
for each constituent group to support the struggles of the others.

This is not all. At the same time as these critical movements are being built, critical educators are also attempting to occupy the spaces provided by existing "mainstream" publication outlets to publish books that provide *critical* answers to teachers' questions about "What do I do on Monday?" during a conservative era. This space has too long been ignored by many theorists of critical pedagogy. Some of these attempts have been remarkably successful. Let me give one example. One very large "professional" organization in the United States—the Association for Supervision and Curriculum Development (ASCD)—publishes books that are distributed each year to its more than 150,000 members, most of whom are teachers or administrators in elementary, middle, or secondary schools. ASCD has not been a very progressive organization, preferring to publish largely technicist and overtly depoliticized material. Yet it has been concerned that its publications have not sufficiently represented socially and culturally critical educators. It, thus, has been looking for ways to increase its legitimacy to a wider range of educators. Because of this legitimacy problem and because of its large membership, it became clear to a number of people who were part of the critical educational traditions in the United States that it might be possible to convince ASCD to publish and widely circulate material that would demonstrate the actual practical *successes* of critical models of curriculum, teaching, and evaluation in solving real problems in schools and communities, especially with working-class and poor children and children of color.

After intense negotiations that guaranteed an absence of censorship, a colleague of mine and I agreed to publish a book—*Democratic Schools*[99]—with ASCD that provided clear practical examples of the power of Freirean and similar critical approaches at work in classrooms and communities. *Democratic Schools* was not only distributed to all 150,000 members of the organization, but it has gone on to sell an additional 100,000 copies. Thus, nearly 250,000 copies of a volume that tells the practical stories of the largely successful struggles of critically oriented educators in real schools are now in the hands of educators who daily face similar problems.[100] This is an important intervention. While there is no guarantee that teachers will always be progressive (nor is there any guarantee that those who are progressive around class and union issues will be equally progressive around issues of gender, sexuality, and race), many teachers do have socially and pedagogically critical intuitions. However, they often do not have ways of putting these intuitions into practice because they cannot picture them in action in daily situations. Due to this, critical theoretical and political insights, then, have nowhere to go in terms of their embodiment in concrete pedagogical situations where the politics of curriculum and teaching must be *enacted.* This is a tragic absence and strategically filling it is absolutely essential. Thus, we need to use and expand the spaces in which critical pedagogical "stories" are made available so that these positions do not remain only on the theoretical or rhetorical level. The publication and widespread distribution of *Democratic Schools* provides one instance of using and expanding such spaces in ways that make Freirean and similar critical educational positions seem actually doable in "ordinary" institutions such as schools and local communities.

Although crucial, it is then not enough to deconstruct restorational policies in education. The right has shown how important changes in commonsense are in the struggle for education. It is our task to collectively help rebuild it by reestablishing a sense that thick morality, and a thick democracy, are truly possible today.

This cannot be done without paying considerably more attention to two things. The first—the material and ideological transformations that the right has effected—has been a key topic of this chapter. Yet another element needs to be stressed—the building of large-scale counterhegemonic movements that connect educational struggles to those in other sites and also assist both in creating new struggles and defending existing ones within educational institutions themselves. In the current conservative context, some of the material on critical pedagogy has characteristics that make this an even more difficult act, however.

In the past, I have warned that the stylistic politics of some of our most "advanced" work forces the reader to do all of the work.[101] Neologism after neologism reigns supreme. As Dennis Carlson and I have argued elsewhere,[102] the discourse of critical pedagogy in its Freirean and feminist forms has increasingly been influenced by postmodern theories. While this has proven to be very useful in reconceptualizing the field and its politics, it has also opened up the discourse to the criticism that it has become too theoretical, abstract, esoteric, and out of touch with the conflicts and struggles that teachers, students, and activists act on. Henry Giroux and others have defended these discourses as necessary in critical pedagogy, since to reconstruct the world one must first learn to speak a new language and "new ideas require new terms."[103] This is undoubtedly correct. Indeed, such a position is one I consciously took when I first introduced Gramscian and Habermasian theories into education in the early 1970s.

Yet, having said this, given the very real success of the strategy of "plain speaking" by neoliberals and neoconservatives, some of the criticisms of material on critical pedagogy do have power. Even though a good deal of it is rich and provocative, some of it *is* conceptually and politically confused and confusing. Some of it *is* disconnected from the gritty materialities of daily economic, political, and educational/cultural struggles. Some of it *does* romanticize the cultural at the expense of equally powerful traditions of analysis based in political economy and the state. And some of it *does* place so much emphasis on the "post" that it forgets the structural realities that set limits on real people in real institutions in everyday life.

Thus, as many commentators have argued repeatedly, much more effort must be given to ground the discourse of critical pedagogy in the concrete struggles of multiple and identifiable groups.[104] Much of it needs to be considerably less dismissive of previous critical traditions that— rightly—continue to influence educational and cultural activists. Just as important, as I just noted, what critical pedagogies actually look like when put into practice—not only their theoretical elaborations—needs to made much more visible than we have been apt to do. Unfortunately, when rightist mobilizations have had no small measure of success in creating a reactionary commonsense about education (and even among many educators), the linguistic styles of all too much critical work gets labeled as "arrogant" (sometimes appropriately) and cuts itself off from many of the radical teachers and activists it wants to support.

It is *hard* work not to be sloppy. It is hard work to write in such a way that theoretical and political nuance are not sacrificed on the altar of commonsense, but also in a way that the hard work of reading can actually pay off for the reader her- or himself. And it is hard and time-consuming work to write at multiple levels. But if we don't, neoliberals and neoconservatives will. And we will be much the worse for it. In this time of conservative restoration, the multiple projects of critical education are indeed crucial. A good dose of reality will do no harm, and I believe will actually make them more effective in the long run.

Although populism can and has been a double-edged sword, being effective, then, requires a somewhat more populist set of impulses than those that have dominated critical pedagogy over the past years. However, the terrain out of which such populist forms grow is already being occupied by a very different kind of "popular" consciousness. Nearly all populisms are critical of elitist tendencies. Yet who and what actually counts as elitism is part of a contested terrain. Unfortunately, in part because the left has evacuated that terrain, the kinds of populism that are currently growing most rapidly are authoritarian in nature. While they do cohere around themes that are based on "plain speaking" and "letting the people decide," they are all too often based on assumptions that God has selected "the people" whose voices are more important than anyone else's. As I noted in Chapters 1 and 2, authoritarian populism is an increasingly powerful and persuasive social movement in many nations throughout the world. Its adherents have been integrated under the umbrella of conservative modernization also in part because neoliberals and neoconservatives have been able to tap into the strong undercurrents of populist resentment that exist among many segments of the (especially) white population. The right has understood Gramscian strategies—and has used them for retrogressive purposes. We shall now turn to the structures of the authoritarian populist world. No progressive counterhegemonic strategy, no critical pedagogy, can succeed unless it understands the reality constructed by these groups. I devote the next three chapters to their history; to their economic, political, and cultural arguments; and to their claims about educational policy and practice.

Chapter 4

Endangered Christianity

DARWIN, GOD, AND EVIL

To understand authoritarian populist religious conservatives, we have to go further than was done in my analysis of neoliberalism, neoconservatism, and the managerialism of the new middle class. We also need to think historically both about particular theological impulses and about the importance of how race, class, gender, and religious and regional relations interact over time. But this needs to be in such a way that the intersections and contradictions of these relations are not ignored. In this chapter, I focus largely on the historical genesis of such movements. In Chapter 5, I examine the ways in which all of the major elements within such conservative religious beliefs can make sense to their proponents, even when they seem repressive to an outsider. Then, in Chapter 6, I take one of the most powerful results of their anti-school sentiments—home schooling—and critically analyze its social, ideological, and educational impulses and a number of its hidden costs. However, it is important to remember at the outset of this section of the book Gramsci's admonition that there will be elements of good sense as well as bad sense in such conservative positions. Not to realize this makes authoritarian populists into mere puppets. This is decidedly not the case.

One should never underestimate the power of religion in the United States. While polling data are clearly skewed by the specific construction and wording of questions and by who is doing the asking, the results are often striking in terms of religious leanings. A sense of the nature and extent of religious beliefs in my own state, Wisconsin—historically one of the most progressive states in the nation—is indicative of the situation. When asked by the University of Wisconsin's Survey Research Laboratory about their religious beliefs, 94 percent of respondents said that they believed in God; 67 percent affirmed their belief in the devil; and 80 percent believed in the existence of angels. It is the latter two that may be surprising. That two-thirds of the people asked believe in the existence of the devil is evidence of the power of a sense of evil—real and embodied—in people's psyche. For many people, this very sense of embodied good and evil is rooted in a strict reading of the Bible. This inerrantist (the Bible is without error) position has certainly had an impact on debates over educational policy and practice.

In the 1980s, the Institute for Creation Research created a model piece of legislation, the Balanced Treatment for Creation-Science and Evolution-Science Act. It required that equal time be given in schools for both creationist and evolutionary perspectives. It described creation-science as based on six tenets:

> Creation-science includes the scientific evidences and related inferences that indicate: (1) Sudden creation of the universe, energy, and life from nothing; (2) The insufficiency of mutation and natural selection in bringing about development of all living kinds from a single organism; (3) Changes only within fixed limits of originally created kinds of plants and animals; (4) Separate ancestry for men and apes; (5) Explanation of the earth's geology by catastrophism, including the occurrence of a worldwide flood; and (6) A relatively recent inception of the earth and living kinds.[1]

A decade later, on August 11, 1999, the Kansas Board of Education voted to delete virtually any mention of evolution from the state's science curriculum. While this did not officially prevent the teaching of evolution, it did make it much less likely since questions on evolution will not be included on the statewide assessment tests. Thus, instead of attempting to push creationism into the curriculum—something that historically has not been successful by itself—creationists have found more success in keeping Darwinism out of the curriculum or in having it presented as merely an unproved theory. Even where it is not prohibited, many teachers have decided that teaching evolution is too risky in the face of outcries from conservative parents, school boards, and churches.[2]

Not only did the state's Board of Education delete most references to biological evolution, but it also expunged any mention of such things as the "big bang theory." For creationists, a position that holds that the universe was born out of a vast primordial explosion contradicts the entire premise of the Bible and Genesis. The curriculum that was approved by the state Board went so far as to include a case study that creationists use to debunk evolution.[3]

A sense of what is at stake for creationists in their consistent historical attempt to remove Darwinian evolution from the curriculum of the schools of the nation can be seen in the following quote from the leader of a creationist group, Answers in Genesis:

> Students in the public schools are being taught that evolution is a fact, that they're just products of survival of the fittest. There's not meaning in life if we're just animals in a struggle for survival. It creates a sense of purposeless and hopelessness, which I think leads to pain, murder and suicide.[4]

The Kansas decision is likely to embolden other efforts. It gives support to those who insist that the world can be no more than ten thousand years old (what is called "flood geology" with its vision of a cataclysmic event) even more so than the less strict creationists who believe that the world is too complex to be explained without the intervention of God ("intelligent design"). Even more important, the decision will undoubtedly lead to even greater attempts at local school district levels to adopt creationist textbooks, something that is already occurring.[5]

Thus, the repeated protests and lawsuits stimulated by conservative religious activists have had powerful effects. One of the key effects has been less overt than that in the Kansas decision. It involves the self-censorship by publishers who are more than a little conscious of the "bottom line."[6] In one of the best analyses of the influence of such conservative attacks on textbooks, Joan Delfattore quotes a representative of one of the largest textbook publishers: "When you are publishing a book, if there's something that is controversial, it's better to take it out."[7]

The contentious nature of this dispute and how it works at the level of school knowledge can be seen in the decision by the superintendent of schools of a district in Kentucky to have the pages that discussed evolution in an elementary school textbook glued together. In yet another school district, this time in a suburban area outside of Atlanta, school officials asked that a chapter on "The Birth of the Earth" be removed from a fourth-grade textbook. Using electronic publishing, Macmillan/ McGraw-Hill excised the seventeen offending pages and customized the text specifically for Cobb County, Georgia. The list goes on. In 1995, the state school board of Alabama demanded that all biology textbooks used in the state have a disclaimer that says that evolution is simply one theory among many. It states, "No one was present when life first appeared on earth. Therefore, any statement about life's origins should be considered as theory, not fact." It goes on, raising questions that have their basis in scientific creationism's rejection of much of evolutionary biology. Among the questions are:

> . . . Why did the major groups of animals suddenly appear in the fossil record?
>
> Why have no new major groups of living things appeared in the fossil record for a long time?
>
> Why do major groups of plants and animals have no transitional forms in the fossil record?
>
> How did you and all living things come to possess such a complete and complex set of "Instructions" for building a living body?[8]

Although the text of this pasted-in statement of "A Message from the Alabama State Board of Education" concludes with the words "Study hard and keep an open mind,"[9] the underlying message clearly is one of supporting the tenets of creation-science. The tactic of challenging evolution by having it declared only one theory among many has proven effective and is being given renewed emphasis throughout the nation, especially in struggles over textbooks.

These are not isolated incidents. Past and present politicians such as Ronald Reagan, Pat Buchanan, and many others have insisted that parents have the "right to insist that Godless evolution not be taught to their children." Throughout the nation, Republican parties have made certain that creationist planks are part of their platforms. Creationists run for school boards at state and local levels and often win. Legislatures in some states have proposed laws that would lead to the firing of any teacher who teaches evolution as fact rather than theory.[10]

Perhaps the most telling fact is that recent polls have indicated that 47 percent of the people in the United States believe that "God created man pretty much in his present form at one time within the last 10,000 years." A further 35 percent believe that there was divine guidance behind the process of evolution. The growth of such beliefs has not stopped at the borders of the United States. The active evangelizing of conservative Christians has led to the growing popularity of scientific creationism in Europe, Asia, and the South Pacific as well.[11]

Oddly enough, while most conservative Christians assume that this is what they have always believed, the roots of creation-science are rather complex. They can be traced directly back to the Seventh Day Adventist emphasis on both a literal six-day creation and a fossil-forming flood. This moves from George McCready Price's 1906 work, *Illogical Geology*, to Whitcomb and Morris's 1961 book, *The Genesis Flood*.[12] The popularity of this latter book provided a significant impetus to the revival of creationism in the last decades. What is interesting about this history is the fact that Price's "flood geology" was *not* based on traditional biblical accounts of creation that were most accepted by evangelical churches. Price's account was specifically developed to support

Adventist theology. Many evangelical Christians who see this as "the tradition" are unaware of its actual history.[13]

Yet, having said this, we need to be careful not to assume that all of the antipathy of conservative religious groups toward evolution means that they equally and totally reject it. Historically, there is no doubt that theological conservatives saw Darwinism as both erroneous and dangerous, especially when it was applied to humans. Seeing Darwin as implying that "might makes right," they felt quite strongly that not only would this undermine Christian morality, but that the very act of drawing a line from apes to modern humans would invalidate their belief that human beings were created in the image of God.[14]

However, this general rejection of Darwin did not always take the same form. Those conservative Christians who defended the recent appearance of life on earth (the world was literally created no more than ten thousand years ago in six twenty-four-hour days) were clear that the description of creation and of Noah's flood in the Bible explained all of the fossil record. These positions generally went by the name of "flood geology." Yet other groups were rather less literal. Holders of "day-age theory" interpreted the seven days in Genesis metaphorically as vast geological ages. Others followed what was called "gap theory," believing that an entire series of catastrophes and recreations or ruins and restorations occurred, which they inserted into an imagined gap between the Bible's first two verses.[15] While the positions based on flood geology became stronger over the years, especially within fundamentalist circles, it is important not to stereotype the opposition.

There was little organized opposition to evolution before the 1920s. After that, the opposition picked up considerable intensity when fundamentalist Christians began a state-by-state crusade to make the teaching of evolution in public schools illegal. Although they ultimately only succeeded in outlawing such teaching in three states—Tennessee, Mississippi, and Arkansas[16]—by the end of that decade there can be no doubt that the conflict itself made the teaching of evolution in public schools much more difficult in general for decades to come, including as we saw today.

To understand the more current revival, we need to think beyond the sphere of theological disagreements to see the connections between schooling and larger issues surrounding international relations and the state. The creationist controversy was reignited in the aftermath of the Soviet Union's launching of Sputnik into space in 1957 before an embarrassed America. Cold warriors, conservative critics, academics, and policy experts were quick to place the blame on the inferior teaching of science in schools. The federal government established programs to funnel considerable amounts of money into discipline-based curricula, especially in the sciences. A good deal of money went into biology, as well as physics and chemistry. One of the major results was a spate of new curricular materials, including the Biological Sciences Curriculum Study (BSCS) and "Man: A Course of Study." With many leading biologists proclaiming that "one-hundred years without Darwinism is enough," the study of evolution was turned into one of the centerpieces of biological study in schools.

Predictably, the dissemination of such pro-evolution material that was sponsored and funded by the federal government immediately generated protests from conservative Christians. For them, "Man: A Course of Study" and similar material was an "attempt to ram evolution down the throats of our children."[17] Not only was it ungodly, but it signified a federal government out of control. This suturing together of the themes of ungodliness, government intervention and control, and a major distrust of school texts and curricula was of considerable import since it became a trope in which any of these three themes nearly automatically brought the others to the fore in the same way that when you look into one facet of a diamond or crystal all of the other facets are reflected up into it.

The threat that this perceived constellation posed to conservative Christians led many of them to harden their positions. Retreating ever more to a literal reading of the Bible, they became even stronger in their position that the task was *not* to accommodate the Bible into science, but to fit science into inerrant readings of Genesis. The strict creationism of flood geology became even more dominant as a dramatic shift occurred. "Old-earth" theories lost their adherents to "new-earth" advocates.[18] It is clear through all this that the school and struggles over it cial conditions created these feelings, desires, and intellectual/emotional needs, the theological issues cannot be ignored. But one thing is clear, out of this assemblage, a narrative is created in which books mean what they say, the complexity of texts is made satisfyingly clear, and science itself is given a respected place—under biblical authority. In a world in which "all things solid melt in the air" and "all that is sacred is profaned," the acceptance of such narratives and such a politics of reading is partly understandable.

The 1960s and 1970s witnessed a major tactical shift among strict creationists. Rather than denying the power of evolutionary science as so many religious conservatives had done before, scientific creationists argued for granting creation and evolution equal scientific standing. Unlike the 1920s when conservative religious activists sought to ban the teaching of evolution from the classrooms of public schools, these activists demanded that creation-science be accorded equal time. In their public arguments, creation-science was not primarily a religious belief, "but . . . an alternative scientific explanation of the world in which we live."[21] While this was a change in tactics stimulated in part by the formation of the Creation Research Society in the early 1970s, it did not mark a total break. Even though they were successful in gaining a conviction of Thomas Scopes for illegally teaching evolution in Tennessee in the famous Scopes trial in 1925, conservative religious activists suffered a string of legislative defeats in the next years. This convinced many of them that rather than focusing on statehouses, they would have considerable success if they turned their attention to the local level and to schoolhouses in particular.[22]

Indeed, throughout the nation, and especially in the South, heated debates about evolution took place during the early decades of the twentieth century. The three states mentioned earlier—Tennessee, Mississippi, and Arkansas—prohibited its teaching. Two additional states—Oklahoma and Florida—either prohibited the adoption of textbooks with evolutionary content or condemned Darwinism as "improper and subversive." The South's reputation for antiscientific backwardness was not helped by the national and international attention devoted to the

Scopes trial.[23] Yet it is important to realize that most legislatures in the South did not outlaw such teaching.[24] However, while there was not an overwhelming surge in legal prohibitions to the teaching of Darwinism, at the level of popular culture and local community sentiments antievolutionary positions were more than a little visible.

Once again, this is a complicated situation, and it is wise to be wary of reductive explanations of antievolutionary declarations of faith. For example, most critical commentators miss the class dynamics that may help to explain the growth of antievolutionary sentiments in the South during the early decades of the twentieth century. The popularity of Darwin among the *educated* classes of the South, a region in which not only race but class dynamics had played such a major role in the development of education,[25] would have generated rejection among those who felt that these educated classes looked with disdain upon those with little formal education. A sign of this can be found in the fact that the word *redneck* was not originally a label with negative connotations when applied to the poor and working class of the South. Exactly the opposite was the case. Redneck was a description applied proudly to oneself. It referred to those people who did "real" work, hard work. It was meant to differentiate people who did such labor from the pale and wan elitist and affluent upper classes who lived what were seen as parasitic lives.

The antielitist impulses that have stood behind some of this ferment over God, evolution, and schooling are clear in the ways that the religious right now sees itself as oppressed. It feels that secular humanist "bigots" who do not understand the long struggle by religious people to gain respect in the public arena are not listening to them. Oddly enough, this viewpoint has actually led to a reinterpretation of the Scopes trial.

One of the more interesting current effects of the changes in how the Scopes trial is now seen is the way in which the prosecutors—antievolutionary activists—now use the words of the defense counsel, Clarence Darrow. In defending Thomas Scopes against the charges that he had taught the forbidden subject of evolution, it is claimed that Darrow said that "teaching only one theory of evolution is sheer bigotry." He was, of course, speaking against the insistence upon biblical inerrancy by fundamentalists. Scientific creationists have since reappropriated these words, arguing that it is "sheer bigotry" to not give equal weight to creation-science in textbooks and the curriculum.[26] Such strategic reappropriations demonstrate that political language is something of a floating signifier. It can be used for multiple purposes by decidedly different groups. The authoritarian populist right has been successful in part because they have taken the rhetoric of what they see as hegemonic liberalism and recast it around their own core concerns. As I show in considerably more detail in the next chapter, the language of equal access, discrimination, and rights has provided them with both ideological and linguistic resources[27] and has helped in their integration under the umbrella of conservative modernization.

A number of themes have emerged from my discussion so far. The authoritarian populist religious right believes *they* are under attack. Their traditions are disrespected; the very basis of their understanding of the world is threatened. Evolutionary perspectives are not simply one element among many in the curriculum that wrong them. Such perspectives go to the very core of their universe, even though they may not fully understand their own history in regard to the positions they take. Notice that not only were there and are there ideological and religious differences among these groups, but elements of good sense exist as well. Class dynamics did and *do* count in schools and the larger society. Thus, even when many people may not agree with authoritarian populist conservatives on their position on evolution and much else, there may be elements that demand and deserve a more sympathetic reading. This may be difficult, but I believe that it is essential if we are to avoid arrogance ourselves and to understand how they have creatively worked to build a growing movement that is having no small measure of success.

To more fully understand not only what conservative religious advocates stand against but what they stand for and why they take the positions they do, I next look at their history and the complex ideological structuring that organizes their beliefs in more detail. First, I briefly examine some of the current struggles in which they are engaged. Then, in this and the next chapter, I discuss a number of the key moments in the historical development of fundamentalism and conservative evangelicalism. After that, I engage in a considerably more detailed analysis of the larger ideological assemblage that stands behind the conservative religious attacks on schools.

SECULAR DANGERS

In February 1999, the Committee to Restore American Values, a coalition of conservative leaders that includes Paul Weyrich and Phyllis Schlafly, continued their war over cultural politics. They asked prospective presidential candidates a number of questions to check their conservative and religious credentials. Among the questions were the following:

1. Should the words "In God We Trust" remain on the currency of the United States?
2. Would you support a removal of the words "under God" from the Pledge of Allegiance?
3. Should a constitutional amendment guaranteeing the right to life be enacted?
4. What commitments relative to abortion would you require from appointees to the Supreme Court or lower Federal judiciary appointments?
5. Do you believe gun control reduces crime?
6. Would you place a créche on the White House lawn if ordered to refrain from doing so by the Supreme Court?[28]

Clearly, then, for this group and the organizations they represent, religion, the state, gun control, abortion, and patriotism form a seamless web of religious beliefs and issues that should be uppermost in our minds when we ask someone to lead the nation.

Media reports and headlines in national and local newspapers have highlighted the supposed turmoil within groups such as this, especially the Christian Coalition. The seamless web is supposedly cracking. Problems over finances and leadership are said to be endemic; membership lists are reported to have been inflated. The Coalition's infamous voter guides, ones based on candidates' responses to questions similar to those with which I began this section, were not delivered in the numbers they originally reported. State affiliates of organizations such as this are considerably less strong than before.[29] These reports are being seen as evidence of a loss of power of conservative Christian activists. I believe that the case is much less clear, especially since so much of what the Christian right stands for has become accepted as common-sense and since they have now made such successful inroads into local and regional politics. The Kansas example I used earlier is but the tip of the iceberg.

In *Official Knowledge,* I traced out both how the social democratic accord between capital and labor grew in the years after World War II and how it began to disintegrate under the weight of social protest mobilizations, economic crises, attacks by the corporate sector on labor, and rightist movements.[30] The effects of a new conservative accord are visible all around us in education and the entire social and cultural fabric of this society.

Accords such as this are only temporary. They must be constantly reinforced and rebuilt on the terrain of culture and everyday life if they are not to be seen as outside impositions. For this very reason, "culture wars" are and have been among the most powerful forms of politics. This is the case because "they cut to the heart of how people identify themselves and what they think constitutes acceptable behavior."[31] Education has always found itself caught up in such conflicts. It has been a site of moral crusades throughout its history, some progressive and others decidedly conservative. As I have argued, it is the latter that have attained dominance over the last decades.

While many groups constantly (and often legitimately) raise questions about the content that is taught in schools (e.g., race and gender stereotypes, disability, and homophobia) and the methods used to teach it, the sheer number and range of these protests by religious conservatives exceed those by all other groups.[32] Many members of this particular moral crusade feel as if secular society has in essence declared war on Christians. Hence, for a large number of conservative Christians, "official knowledge" opposes Christianity, lawful authority, the family, the military, and free enterprise while promoting feminism, idolatry, "demon worship," evolution, and secular humanism in general.[33] One conservative protestor who sued his school district defined secular humanism as a "lethal religion," one that denies both moral absolutes and God. "The doctrines of humanism include evolution, self-authority, situation ethics, distorted realism, gun control, sexual permissiveness, anti-Biblical bias, anti-free enterprise, one-world government, and death education."[34] For him, and for a growing segment of the population who feel under cultural and economic threat, any and all of these are evidence of extreme danger to their children's identity and to their own. Some activists go so far as to argue that even such a seemingly benign curricular emphasis in school such as multiculturalism is dangerous. Respect for a wide range of cultures and ideas is suspect, since respecting, say, non-Christian societies and beliefs is often interpreted as an attack on one's foundational belief that an absolute faith in Jesus Christ is the *only* means of salvation.[35]

One of the roots of the "evil" done in schools is John Dewey and his progeny. His emphasis on both personal experience and experimentation is seen as the very embodiment of secular "religion." For these conservative critics, anything that involves moral choice is in fact a religion, whether or not it is grounded in faith in a higher power.[36] Dewey and his followers' faith in experimentation, their rejection of absolutism, their sense of the individual/collective relationship at the core of democracy, and above all the integration of all this in their theories of education have led schools astray.

While many protests against these "secular dangers" begin at a local level, there are national organizations that both sponsor and support them. Among the groups involved in challenging the "biases" in public schools are the American Family Association, based in Mississippi and led by Donald Widmon; Citizens for Excellence in Education, based in California and led by Robert Simons; Concerned Women for America, based in

Washington, DC and led by Beverly LaHaye; the Eagle Forum, based in the Midwest and led by Phyllis Schlafly; Focus on the Family, based in California and led by James Dobson; and the National Legal Foundation, based in Virginia and led by Pat Robertson.[37] There are a number of others, but all of them are deeply committed to turn the nation and our schools back to God.

For these groups and for many conservative evangelicals and fundamentalists, only through a return to inerrantist readings of the Bible can we save ourselves and especially our children from these dangers. The Bible and it alone provides us with the path toward a truly ethical and correct society in all of our institutions. Thus, according to Pat Robertson, the Bible is "a workable guidebook for politics, government, business, families, and all the affairs of mankind." It provides us with universal spiritual laws that are "as valid for our lives as the laws of thermodynamics."[38] As one conservative minister asked his congregation about a vexing social problem, "Does the Bible have anything to say about that? Or are we going to let the government feed us everything they want?"[39]

As I noted earlier, this turn back to the Bible and the entire feeling of endangered Christianity is related to multiple causes. Its connections to antigovernment sensibilities are also complex, but the situation was clearly exacerbated by the decision of the Internal Revenue Service in 1978 to challenge the tax-exempt status of all-white Christian academies. It was also heightened by the profound disappointment among conservative evangelicals that a presidential administration guided by one of their own, Jimmy Carter, did not live up to their expectations. On the aforementioned tax case, on abortion, school prayer, busing, the Equal Rights Amendment to the Constitution, gay rights—on all of these the Carter administration was not "upholding the faith."[40] The results can be seen in the rigorous questioning that presidential candidates now go through that forms the introduction to this section.

This sense of betrayal as a larger theme needs to be taken quite seriously. It is absolutely crucial to understand that for many evangelicals and fundamentalists who see the New Testament as an inerrant history of the early Christian church, one thing is inescapable. To be a Christian is to be *persecuted*.[41] This very theme, so clear in many biblical texts, underpins (though not always at the level of consciousness) much of the emotional economy present within conservative evangelical movements. It has also been one of the central parts of the narrative of this nation (the pilgrims/religious persecution/freedom). A better sense of the history of evangelical movements may help us realize both how this works and why—even given their disagreements with some aspects of the larger alliance—they can be integrated within it.

FROM INSIDERS TO OUTSIDERS

The term *evangelicalism* is derived from the Greek "evangelion," meaning good news. It was a dominant social and intellectual current in American society until the late nineteenth century. As we shall see, over time a number of forces undermined the literal authority of the Bible. Science penetrated the logic of daily lives. The growing pluralism of the United States made it much more difficult for evangelicalism to provide such a diverse people with a common set of values. The increasing separation of public and private spheres of life also helped deprive evangelicalism of its public and political role. This emerging secularization served to remove religious institutions, symbols, and values from the central place they had occupied. In the process, a sea change occurred in the role of evangelicals. There was a steady shift from being what might be called cultural insiders to cultural *outsiders*.[42]

We can date the formal beginnings of the modern evangelical movement as April 7, 1942, when approximately two hundred "moderate fundamentalists" met in St. Louis to launch a religious movement. This group believed that they could both transform conservative Protestantism and radically change the course of religious history in the United States.[43] Thus, the movement started out with grand ambitions. These ambitions have been at least partly met, since more than twenty million Americans identify themselves as part of the evangelical movement.[44] How has this waxing and waning occurred?

The movement actually has quite a long historical tradition. As I noted, well before the well-known battles split the Protestant house into modernist and fundamentalist wings, "conservative Protestantism enjoyed a remarkable public respectability, influence, and relevance."[45] Indeed, it could be said that during the Victorian era in particular, broadly evangelical Protestants were in fact the establishment.[46] This was not just the case in the United States. Throughout the world, American evangelicals "mobilized a missionary enterprise of vast proportions."[47] In the words of Lewis French Stearns in 1890, "Today Christianity is the power which is moulding the destinies of the world. The Christian nations are . . . ascendant. . . . The old promise is being fulfilled; the followers of the true God are inheriting the world."[48]

Overarching all the influence that this set of triumphal perspectives had in the worlds of business, education, culture, and the polity in general was a pervasive belief that the United States was a (the) Christian nation. It was blessed by God; it had a particular destiny to become not only the kingdom of heaven on earth but the place that God would make into a "central spot for the whole earth."[49]

As we shall see shortly, key elements of this position will remain and will resurface with considerable power again later on. However, the dominance of such beliefs began to falter during the end of the nineteenth and the beginning of the twentieth centuries. A more liberal theology, the growth of biblical criticism, and skepticism about the supernatural challenged accepted orthodoxies within the church. The importance of the act of individual conversion was jeopardized in the eyes of a considerable number of evangelicals by the more structural reforms being proposed by the Social Gospel movement. The growth of naturalistic assumptions about reality and the shift within science itself away from the Newtonian paradigm undercut the role of the Bible within the scientific community, a fact that was heightened by the growing influence of Darwinian understandings of evolution. When all this is coupled with rapid industrialization, a radically changing demographics brought about by immigration, and an equally powerful set of religious changes accompanying the increase in Catholic, Jewish, and other populations, the situation made it seem as if conservative Protestantism's hegemony—as the very embodiment of what it meant to be a "civilized and civilizing" nation—was constructed on a foundation of sand. As Christian Smith puts it, "and the rains were pouring down."[50]

For some, the "rains" led to a slow movement away from the old orthodoxy and toward more "modern" and "liberal" positions. For others, much of the orthodox vision was maintained, but perhaps in a somewhat weaker form as they "adjusted to the new reality." But for a significant minority this was a painful process, one that could not and would not be accepted. They chose to fight back against what they deeply believed was an "assault on Christian truth and civilization."[51] From their very beginnings in the first two decades of the twentieth century, the positions of the leaders of this countermovement were clear. They sought to mobilize a conservative coalition whose aim was to combat modernism in churches and schools. Two strategic goals were focused upon: to wrest control of major Protestant denominations from the forces of liberalism and, especially in the South, to make the teaching of Darwinian evolutionism illegal in the public schools. "In time, these fighting conservatives were labeled 'fundamentalist'—a term coined from a booklet series published between 1910 and 1915 called *The Fundamentals*—and their movement, 'fundamentalism.'"[52]

Yet such engagement in the world was actually rather limited. Theological purity was often seen as more important than acting in the outside world. Cooperation with liberal or "inclusive" conservatives was treated with much bitterness by fundamentalists. From the 1920s onward, separatism and a very strong distaste for doctrinal compromise became even stronger. Rejecting the nineteenth-century's postmillennialism—which was seen as being connected to the more liberal Social Gospel movement[53]—the fundamentalists arrived at what was actually a more recent theological position, what has been called "premillennialist dispensationalism." This can be characterized in the following way:

Premillennialism taught that history and society were—in God's plan—inevitably going to grow worse and worse until, just before things hit rock bot-

tom, Christ would return to vindicate his faithful people and establish his
kingdom on earth. This pessimistic view of history suggested that the only
task left for the church was to remain separate from and unblemished by the
world and to "win" as many souls to heaven before the damned ship of history went down. . . . The perspective of many fundamentalists became: let
the worldly intelligentsia, scholars, universities, media, cultural elite, politicians—all who spurned Christian truth and civilization—go to perdition.[54]

This constituted part of what has been described as the "Great Re-
versal": the rejection of the Social Gospel's emphasis on social reform
rather than on saving lost souls through evangelism; the rise of a pessimistic eschatology such as premillennialism; and the turn to social and
political conservatism.[55] Attempting to engage with the world and reform it, hence, was like polishing the brass on a doomed ship. The depth
of the rejection of the reformist commitments behind the Social Gospel
is perhaps nowhere stated more clearly than in the revivalist Billy Sunday's angry message that "We've had enough of this God-less social service nonsense."[56]

I do not want to overstate the fundamentalists' rejection of engagement in the world. Although many such conservative Christians took
the path of resistance to modernity that led to withdrawal, a goodly
number of others took a much more overtly militant and activist stance.
As George Marsden, one of the leading scholars of the evangelical movement, tartly states when discussing this tendency, "A fundamentalist is
an evangelical who is angry about something."[57] These "angry" evangelicals battled against the influence of modernity and liberalism both
in the churches and the schools, again with Darwinism playing a large
role in what they struggled against in the latter. Such militancy had its
attractions and some victories. But ultimately a combination of factors—
with the fear of schism and the humiliation of William Jennings Bryan
at the 1925 Scopes trial being among the most important—led to a loss
of widespread support for fundamentalism.[58]

The fundamentalists, then, ultimately lost ground. But a strong current of militant, inerrantist, antiliberal (and later on, aggressively anti-

communist), and antisecular sentiment was kept alive. It was kept alive in churches and Bible institutes and seminaries. It was given constant transfusions of new blood in the writings and teachings of strongly conservative theologians such as Carl McIntire and others as well. Thus, the movement may have been in cultural "exile," but the flame of politicized resistance still burned—and grew—in the ensuing decades. In fact, as we shall see later on, the flame burned ever more brightly in the 1950s, 1960s, and 1970s with the growth of the New Right. But the roots of this have their genesis in the 1940s.

While fundamentalists sought to protect what they believed was spiritual purity, by the 1940s a number of more "moderate" fundamentalists grew increasingly worried about its tendencies. In their minds, the separatist and judgmental character of fundamentalism had sacrificed one of its most important tasks, "evangelizing American society for Christ." Fundamentalism's tacit (and sometimes overt) anti-intellectualism, its pessimistic premillennial dispensationalism, its disengagement from the real social, political, and economic world—all of this needed to be overcome. For these new heirs to the evangelical legacy—among them Harold Okenga, J. Elwin Wright, Wilbur Smith, Edward Carnell, Carl Henry, Harold Lindsell, Charles Fuller, Gleason Archer, Everett Harrison, Bernard Ramm, and a name that would become even more significant, Billy Graham—such positions had to be replaced by an *engaged orthodoxy.* For them, one could be fully committed to promoting orthodox Protestant beliefs and practices and at the same time be equally vigorous in "bringing Christ to the world."[59]

This vision was institutionalized in the formation of a national movement, the National Association of Evangelicals. It both reached out beyond orthodox fundamentalists by stressing "the need for unity and love among different Protestant traditions for the sake of the Gospel and the world" and provided institutional support for the growing number of evangelical Christians who were convinced that "Jesus Christ was the answer for the world's social, economic, and political problems and wanted to see Christians making a real impact on the world."[60]

This "neoevangelical" movement combined many elements: orthodoxy and tradition, but with a concern for more intellectual respectability than that accorded to the earlier fundamentalists; social and political activism; and spreading the word of the Gospel while avoiding some of the behavioral rigidity of fundamentalism. This gave it more legitimacy and allowed it to spread. It also enabled people who were not as enamored with the anti-intellectual tendencies within previous conservative religious traditions to ground their beliefs in what seemed to be a more "rational" foundation. Neoevangelicalism spawned and in turn was itself spurred by the formation of other religious, educational, and cultural forms. For example, a number of theological seminaries were either founded or transformed into its own image. A considerable number of colleges aligned themselves with the movement. Evangelical missions and ministries saw steady growth—Youth for Christ, Campus Crusade for Christ, Inter-Varsity Christian Fellowship, Teen Challenge, Fellowship of Christian Athletes, the Overseas Missionary Fellowship, the World Evangelical Fellowship, the Evangelical Foreign Missions Fellowship, and the list goes on.

A considerable number of evangelical periodicals were published, accompanied by a growing list of evangelical publishing houses and music production and recording companies. Other aspects of the media and cultural apparatus were not ignored, with organizations such as the National Religious Broadcasters and the Evangelical Press Association being formed. In these ways, a "transdenominational" evangelicalism was both built and defended by networks of "parachurch agencies."[61]

For many of these churches and parachurch agencies, however, a specific kind of engaged orthodoxy came to dominate. Much of this combined particular and exceptionally conservative views on the family, on gender roles within the home and the outside world, on national and international politics, on militant Christianity, and often on race as well. Significant parts of these tendencies can only be explained if we look more deeply at the history of conservative evangelicalism in the South especially.

SOUTHERN CROSS

We are used to hearing evangelicalism's call in a southern voice. While it is a truly national and international phenomenon, much of conservative evangelicalism grew from the soil of specifically southern experiences at first. Oddly enough, far from dominating the South, throughout much of the eighteenth and nineteenth centuries evangelicals were viewed by most white southerners as either odd or subversive.[62] Indeed, many southern whites of all classes believed that evangelicalism would not strengthen, but instead weaken, community ties and eliminate many of the celebrations and social events that gave meaning to life in the region. In particular, evangelicalism's unremitting emphasis on "mankind's sinfulness, hell's torments, and Satan's wiles" had a telling effect. It "estranged men and women from the strong and decent parts of their personalities and plunged them into fathomless darkness."[63] For the majority of southern whites, then, evangelicalism seemed to erase social identity and rupture communal bonds.

Yet, over time, the margin became the center as evangelicalism grew in strength. Partly this increase was a natural outgrowth of cultural elements that were already there—a belief in supernaturalism, in the foretelling power of dreams and portents, in the ability of spirits to take visible form. Thus, at the same time as Thomas Jefferson and other southern leaders helped usher in the "Age of Reason," it was not natural law that dominated the daily lives and beliefs of many southern whites. Rather, they already combined varied forms of supernaturalism with their Christian beliefs. Hence, sensing the "fullness of Satan's sway" was not that large a leap.[64] And evangelicalism enabled the making of that leap. As time passed, while evangelicals still listened to and connected with the region's strong traditions of supernaturalism, they toned down diabolism's (Satan's) terror in their discourse. This too increased their legitimacy across the South by attracting a wider swath of the population.[65]

As in the later periods I have already discussed, economic transformations and crises, immigration, the loss of a firm identity based on one's social location—all of these also had an impact. Yet something else was crucial. Evangelicals drew strength from the feeling that each and every one of them was participating in a cosmic drama. In the struggle between God and Satan, they were on the winning side. As Christine Leith Heyrman recognized in her exceptional history of the growth of evangelicalism in the South, committing oneself to evangelical discipline did begin with a process of self-repentance, in essence of radical self-abasement. Yet it also brought with it a profound sense of individual importance. One's guilt, doubt, and fear—the hidden yet powerful emotions that become even more potent in times of crisis—became of great significance not only to you, but to an entire religious community as well. Individual and community are joined here. As Heyrman says, for many southerners— "those who happened to be black in a society ruled by whites, poor in a society that bowed to wealth, female in a society dominated by males, young in a society that honored age"—being taken seriously was itself *serious*. It made evangelicalism nearly irresistible.[66]

Thus, evangelicalism had multiple roots, often among the least powerful. However, these democratic tendencies often caused a conservative backlash that profoundly changed evangelicalism over time and helped to make it into what it is today.

For example, the emergence of a distinctly African-American Christianity that fused elements of West African traditions with evangelical teachings is part of what must be told here.[67] In fact, evangelicalism in the South had elements that challenged racial superiority, that called for active not passive worship, and were less hierarchical than many other churches. Evangelical gatherings were also at times interracial and provided spaces for bringing in personal experience (and thus allowed for elements and memories of African cultural forms). Because of this, it is clear why many African-Americans saw it positively and transformed it for their own spiritual, cultural, and political purposes.

This led many dominant whites to try to curb the behavior of many of these converts, attempts that in the long run proved less than successful.[68] But it also did not stop some conservative evangelicals who were worried about what would happen in a less racially stratified church and society from seeing African-Americans as the literal embodiment of the devil. The repulsively stereotypical grinning black face became the face of Satan as he came for children to bring them to Hell.[69] Indeed, in their constant search for greater "respectability" in the South, not only did many evangelical churches vigilantly monitor their "black brothers and sisters," but they began erecting barriers against interracial religious intimacy.[70] Dominant whites and slaveholders were increasingly moved to the center. In the words of one well-known evangelical leader, "I am called upon to suffer for Christ's sake, not for slavery."[71] This became the moral calculus for most white southern evangelical leaders. As they themselves moved from margin to center, the margin was again rebuilt—and once again, African-Americans occupied it on the terrain of religion. For the evangelicals, then, reclaiming (white) souls was of the essence and "any concession to the South's ruling race could be justified in the name of that end."[72] This prefigures the often tense relationship authoritarian populist religious activists currently have with people of color today.

The contradictory history of southern evangelicalism—its partially democratic beginnings leading ultimately to a return to dominant forms—can be seen not only in its history of compromise over racial stratification. It is quite visible in the history of its changing vision of the family and gender hierarchies as well. It is ironic that conservative evangelicals—whose embrace of the "traditional family" is one of their identifying marks—were in the early years of their growth in the South in the 1800s among the most powerful forces that challenged traditional family solidarity and values. Those who converted to evangelical faiths had to renounce their previous sinfulness, including many of their family members who continued their "sinful ways." The *church* was one's new family. Criticism of the evangelicals' challenges to the rights of families is what ultimately led them to move toward sanctifying the "natural family." This too was deeply connected historically to issues of race. Evangelicals began their effort to bring their version of family values into accord with white southern mores by retreating from their opposition to slavery.[73] Family values were to be upheld, but not necessarily for slaves.

Gender relations played a major role historically in this valorization of the natural family. Evangelicals showed their resourcefulness by suspending the usual southern belief that nothing good could come out of the North. They enthusiastically embraced a "new" form of patriarchal relations that had originated among middle-class northern evangelicals, "the cult of domesticity." For its proponents, the home is a church. It constitutes an Edenic sanctuary that is tended by wives and mothers. In this Edenic home, religious and moral sensibility were seeds that were incubated in children. A "flowering of rectitude" ennobled husbands and fathers.[74]

Just as it did in the North, the compelling metaphor of home as church evoked powerful positive reactions. However, there were regional differences as to why it struck such a responsive chord. In the North, the growth of commerce and industry fostered the emergence of these new domestic ideals, especially within the middle class. Yankee men increasingly spent their days in offices, factories, and shops, thereby further sanctioning a definition of the public sphere as commercial and male and the private sphere as domestic and female.[75]

In the South, most husbands and fathers were farmers. The household was a workplace for both women and men. However, although homes in the antebellum South did not become only the sphere of women, southern whites found the image of the home as a church more than a little appealing. It restored the moral authority of the "natural family." The evangelical embrace of the natural family, then, was a crucial tactical move. By changing its emphasis from supporting the idea that one's total loyalty must be to God and the church rather than to family and home, to one in which families and homes were created in God's image, tensions were eased and converts could be won. If the home *is* a church, then family claims and religious claims could be made one and the same.[76]

Behind these changes in evangelicalism was something more than the cementing of the bonds of family, household integrity, and order. As I have noted, these transformations over time were dependent on a revivification of gender and racial orders. They were harbingers of things to come. Heyrman summarizes these orders in a striking manner:

> Reinforcing these claims was something sterner—the absolute rule that husbands and fathers exercised over all their dependents—wives, children, and slaves. As a result, during the same years that evangelicals sought to persuade all white southerners that their churches ceded primacy to family solidarity and kinship loyalty, they also tailored their teachings to uphold, even more unequivocally, the authority of male heads of households, particularly over godly women. These ever more rigid teachings on gender roles, along with their changing messages about familial order and the prerogatives of age, transformed the early . . . movements into the evangelical culture that later generations of Americans would identify as epitomizing "family values."[77]

Heyrman is quite insightful here. However, this can be interpreted as giving little agency to those people—women and people of color, for example—who were subjected to such authority. This is not necessarily the case, nor is it her position.

At the same time as evangelicals revivified patriarchal authority, historically the churches themselves provided a space for women to assert themselves as authoritative *in public*.[78] This paradox actually represented in the past and still represents in the present a major achievement on the part of religiously conservative women. In a family structure in which "God has willed" that the man is the head and in which women are to be submissive and/or helpmates, the evangelical churches provided a public arena for women to exercise intelligence, judgment, fortitude, and power. Historically, for women of the South—a region that had long had a culture steeped in misogyny "against which women had become schooled, as their best defense, in habits of submission"—the creation of such a public arena was a liberating force, no matter what its ideological content.[79] As I show in the next chapter, there is no doubt that this continues to this day, as many women in evangelical movements whose official beliefs center around God-given gender roles occupy that public space in creative and powerful ways.[80] In fact, in my mind this is one of the most significant ways in which the contradictions of patriarchal authority are solved within authoritarian populist religious movements. Women are *both* passive and active at the same time.

In this regard, we need to remember that gender relations are exactly that, relations. Thus, spaces for agency created by and for women necessarily imply changes in men's roles as well. And here, once again, evangelicalism wrought contradictory transformations in the past that live with us still today.

For instance, evangelicalism also had an effect on the prevailing definitions of masculinity, especially in the South where white men were asked to forswear their culture's rigidly defined gender roles. Church fellowship seemed to be but a poor replacement for "swaggering male comraderie," but for many men it did provide a different model.[81] While a mistrust of the church for its requirement that men submit to religious authority and God's judgment was widespread, such fears of "unmanly dependence" were assuaged by a vision of male authority in the family. These new forms of masculinity and male authority were also made more legitimate by the development of literature and stories about what might be called "warrior preachers." In these stories and sermons, real men could embrace evangelical faith without sacrificing their masculinity. The stories were extremely popular and often took the form of a confession. Swearing, fighting, gambling, hunting, and more were sins that were recounted in detail. All of them were forsworn on conversion for the mightier challenges and higher glory of becoming God's warrior. The message was clear. It took a tough man to make a tender Christian. For many of the nineteenth-century evangelical clergy and their converts, spreading the gospel was a military campaign requiring nerves of steel, agility, cunning, and courage. One was now a soldier in the army of Jesus.[82]

Thus, just as evangelicalism provided spaces for African-Americans' and white women's agency, it also allowed for a creative solution to the contradictory positions surrounding male authority, a solution still struggled over in such modern forms as the Promise Keepers with their emphasis on strong but godly men. Yet, in the process of creating these spaces, the solutions that were proposed did not—and do not—challenge the fundamental social hierarchies around race, gender, and class that dominated society in both the North and the South. Space was given, but the rules that constituted the social field of power on which it played remained the same. In the final analysis, the world of southern evangelicals converged with the world of southern white male masters. The "muscular Christianity" built in the nineteenth century both solved and re-created problems of power. It changed, but ultimately vindicated, the mastery of white men in the public and private spheres.[83]

There can be no doubt that, in comparison to many religious groups, in a number of ways the early evangelicals were considerably more democratic and egalitarian. Evangelicals were neither an undifferentiated mass, nor were their beliefs static and monolithic. In their early years, evangelical fellowships did promise the prospect of greater fulfillment and freedom to the most subordinated groups within the South—the poor, the female, the young, and the black. However, as the nineteenth century progressed, these very same churches retreated from these earlier promises in order to become more successful. Their energies were invested in upholding the honor and equality of all white men.[84] Present-day evangelicals live in the shadow of the values; theological, social, and educational commitments; and institutions of this legacy, with all its contradictions, strengths, and weaknesses. It is to the current embodiment of this legacy that I now turn.

Chapter 5

God, Morality, and Markets

BRINGING GOD TO THE WORLD

To understand the authoritarian populist religious right, it is crucial to complement the historical excavation of how and why such movements grew. While the historical roots I traced out in Chapter 4 are important, we also have to look at the world through their eyes now. Before I begin, however, it is important to remember that strong religious convictions can go in many directions, including progressive ones. An example of the latter would be such things as base-community movements throughout Latin America and elsewhere.[1] Therefore, we need to realize that such convictions need not inexorably lead to conservative positions. At times, organizations form around considerably more progressive social and political issues. Indeed, some bear a striking resemblance to liberation theology in its taking up of concerns about social justice, poverty, racial segregation, and so on. However, the dominant tendencies of religious activism (at least those that get the most attention in the media), especially in the United States, move in conservative directions for reasons of theology, social position, temperament, and as we just saw, history.

As I demonstrated, after failing to sway the majority of mainline Protestants, fundamentalists largely withdrew. More liberal and "modern" forces flourished until the resurgence of more public forms of conservative evangelicalism in the 1940s and 1950s, stressing an agenda of moral reform and a less internally antagonistic outlook. Though still grounded in the traditional emphasis on private individual salvation, conservative evangelicalism increasingly came to concentrate on public civic issues—but not those that guided the more liberal Social Gospel movement. The emerging conservative bloc recognized that it was crucial to enter the political arena if they were to guarantee the conditions of sustaining the moral order they wished to protect and expand.[2] Indeed, the dispensationalist belief in the cosmic struggle between God and Satan clearly has contributed to the militancy of many conservative Christians.[3] While many religious conservatives have historically objected to a focus on the political sphere, preferring to emphasize individual salvation, for a large portion of Christian right leaders today—such as Jerry Falwell, Pat Robertson, James Dobson, Tim and Beverly LaHaye—activism is utterly essential if we are to restore God's hand as our guide.[4]

This commitment to "bring God to the world" is partly the result of changes in the class composition of evangelicalism. The less overtly political stance of earlier periods was transformed and delegitimated by the growth in upwardly mobile middle-class converts to evangelicalism in the 1970s and 1980s. A new constituency of professional, technical, and business people was formed. These individuals had a much greater interest in politics and social action than did their predecessors,[5] in part because they had come of age in an era of social ferment in which social activism was seen as a legitimate form of expression.

It would be deceptive to assume that because of these changes in class composition and outlook the Christian right is a unitary movement and that it speaks with one voice. Not only is it diverse organizationally, but it is also in constant motion. It is always "in formation," characterized by shifting alliances and tensions caused by changing events and social conditions.[6] However, there *are* central tendencies that push it in particular directions. Within these central tendencies, how do conservative evangelicals understand the world? How do they interpret their own actions? Do they see themselves as many others see them—as people who are attempting to impose their religious beliefs and values on others?

To answer these questions, we need to begin with an empirical question. What are some of the things we know about fundamentalists and conservative evangelicals? I shall direct most of my attention to evangelicals since they are a considerably larger group numerically and are more influential.

The empirical evidence is striking. Of all Christians in the United States, including fundamentalists, evangelicals have the strongest belief in traditional orthodoxy. Ninety-seven percent believe that the Bible is God-inspired and that it is without error. They adhere to a theologically orthodox vision of human nature. Even though we are "created in God's image," human beings are inherently sinful and need God's redemption and restoration. The only way to salvation is through a faith in Jesus Christ. Further, evangelicals—even more than fundamentalists—"are the most likely of all major Christian traditions to affirm a belief in moral absolutes." There is a firm rejection of moral relativism. Not human reason, but God and the Bible, provide the sources of direction for one's life.[7] Human and institutional authority are secondary to these more spiritual groundings.

Overall, though this may not always have been the case, evangelicals report that they are now "no more economically or educationally deprived than others in American society." While they do not seem to believe that they more than others have suffered economically or in terms of status, they consistently voice powerful feelings about America's turn from "the ways of God." They believe that we are witnessing all around us the consequences—social and spiritual—of the nation's and the people's loss of a God-centered life.[8]

Empirically as well, the vast majority of evangelicals state that they *never* have doubts about their faith. In most ways, they seem to be immune to the undermining effects of uncertainty and skepticism—or perhaps the insistent and publicly professed lack of doubt is an armor that guards them from unconscious and dangerous feelings of grave doubt.

Yet it is not just the strength of belief and certainty that separates them from many others. They also exhibit a striking optimism about the probability that a Christian revival will sweep across the United States.[9]

The effects of this strong set of beliefs are not limited to the "private" sphere. For them, such beliefs must also permeate the world of paid work. A "Christian presence" must follow one everywhere, a point to which I return later. Occasionally a cost may be exacted at work for being "moral and honest," but it is still crucial to Christianize the workplace because "God knows more than I do about where my life is going."[10] Perhaps because of this, by and large evangelicals do not question the larger structures of the economy. Corporate behavior is determined not by the norms and structures of the economy, by class or race or gender relations, or by colonial and postcolonial histories. Rather, it is the goodness or badness of individuals who work in these businesses that is determinate.[11] Individual morality and honesty are the answers to economic problems; structural transformation is not a category even used by most conservative evangelicals. "Truth" will rule when moral people act in their businesses, homes, and communities in truthful ways.

It is not only that an unchanging and universal "truth" exists, but evangelicals often see themselves as the ones to whom God had revealed it. Again, empirically, they are much more likely than mainstream Protestants to hold that there are unchanging and absolute moral standards. They are more apt to hold that "Christian morality" should be the law of the land and less apt to believe that other people—even those who are not themselves Christians—should be able to choose their own moral standards. And, more than others, a significant fraction of them tend to believe that public schools must instruct children in distinctly Christian values. It is important to realize, however, that for evangelicals this is not a conscious attempt at dominating others. Rather, it is grounded in a deeply seated belief that the world would be a much better place if everyone followed "God's ways."[12]

This certainty is coupled with a powerful impulse to change American society, not only by example, but by conversion and by action in the political sphere. As Christian Smith puts it, "Talk . . . is cheap. What about actions? . . . Which Christian tradition is actually *doing* the work of trying to influence American society? . . . The evidence suggests that it is the evangelicals who are mostly walking their talk."[13] The acts of "walking their talk" are varied. Compared with all other Christians and with nonreligious Americans, they are most likely by far to vote, to lobby political officials, to work hard to educate themselves about what they take to be important social and political issues, and to defend biblical worldviews in intellectual circles. While, like neoliberals who put their faith in the market and neoconservatives who emphasize character and "proper" values, they may usually be against government programs of assistance, in keeping with their emphasis on personal conduct they are also *most* likely to give money to the poor and the needy. They also are most likely to *personally* evangelize others and, among Christians, to participate in political protests and demonstrations. Further, along with fundamentalists, they donate quite extensive amounts of money to Christian political candidates and organizations.[14]

This belief in moral superiority and following God's way, hence, extends well beyond the sphere of private life. For conservative evangelicals, religion is not a private matter. It is necessary to extend its voice and reach in the public debates over cultural, political, economic, and bodily practices and policies. Although it may be grounded for some evangelicals in a relatively unself-conscious paternalism,[15] it is clearly connected to an extremely strong sense of social mission.

The Christianization of all parts of life can be seen in other ways as well. Not only do evangelicals participate in these political acts of influence, they also engage in more church-related activities than any other part of Christianity. Further, they have exceptionally high rates of engaging in "parachurch" religious activities. For example, their rate of listening to Christian radio is nearly twice as much as even fundamentalists and nearly four times as much as members of more mainstream churches. Their rate of watching specifically Christian television programs exhibits similar tendencies.[16]

POLITICS AND THE CLERGY

Much of this can be understood not only by examining the structure of beliefs of conservative Christians, but also by asking who their ministers are and how these messages are reinforced in other ways. Thus, in many churches, one of the best predictors of political activism is how conservative the clergy are. The more conservative, the more active.[17]

Ministers who are younger and who went to Bible colleges are more apt to be conservative theologically. Ministers from working-class homes and with less-advanced education are also more likely to be conservative. Further, there is an inverse correlation between having a liberal arts background and religious conservatism among ministers. The less background in liberal arts, the less likely one is to hold liberal theological positions.[18] The antipathy between conservative evangelicals toward a secular education, then, may have some of its roots not only in theological and cultural disputes, but in autobiographical ones as well.

Such backgrounds have an effect. Like their church members, conservative clergy insist that social reform comes not from altering social institutions, but from the "changed hearts" of individuals. In the words of a number of orthodox clergy, "Our problems are not drugs, divorce, abortion, greed, etc., but the symptoms of a larger problem, that of alienation from God." Only through mass conversion to faith in Jesus Christ will there be social improvement. Thus, "Jesus is the answer to all problems: social, financial, health, national, international, civil, moral, and educational."[19]

That there are close theological connections between conservative clergy and their church members is important here. A comparison is helpful. Perhaps because of the pervasiveness of conservative discourses in public life, there is a growing gap between liberal clergy and their parishioners. While differences often may exist between conservative clergy and the members of their churches, they are not as wide as those developing between more liberal ministers and their church members. On such things as the death penalty, gay rights, defense spending, school prayer, affirmative action, and similar issues, modernist clergy themselves have noticed growing differences between their parishioners and themselves.[20] This is a crucial fact, since it points to the inroads of a more conservative commonsense even among members of more mainline churches.

The comparison is made more powerful by the fact that recent research also has indicated that members of evangelical churches are more likely to be in the pews on Sunday. They are the most accepting of clerical pronouncements and place a premium on pastoral leadership. Further, they most often take as definitive their minister's "biblical warrant" for political preaching. This stands in stark contrast to more liberal congregations who attend less regularly, are less deferential to pastoral leadership, and may have more disagreement with their ministers in terms of their political views.[21] And while many liberal clergy remain involved in the social gospel, there is a growing trend among conservative clergy to be even more activist than their liberal counterparts in areas such as political and moral pronouncements, endorsing candidates, campaign activities, organizing petition drives, and sponsoring boycotts.[22] Thus, increasingly, political momentum is with the conservatives, sponsored mightily by their clergy.

THE ELECTRONIC CLERGY

While clergy are quite influential in developing and responding to conservative sensibilities at the local level in churches and parachurch organizations, a good deal of the work of bringing God to the world is accomplished through the creative use of media by the Christian right. There has been a tendency to think of this as a recent development. However, the use of the media by Christian broadcasters is not a new phenomenon by any means. It has an exceedingly long history. In fact, in 1921 the first Christian radio broadcast was aired. Even though periods of rise and decline occurred over the next decades, and some tension between fundamentalist and modernizing Christian broadcasters emerged during this period, fundamentalist use of media such as radio was a very real presence on the airwaves by the early 1930s.

As an example, fundamentalist and conservative religious broadcasters accounted for 246 of the 290 weekly quarter-hours of Christian radio programming in Chicago in 1932. In 1939, Charles E. Fuller's "Old Fashioned Revival Hour" had the most extensive prime-time distribution of any radio broadcast in the entire nation. It had airtime on 60 percent of all the licensed stations, with an estimated weekly audience of twenty million.[23] Radio and, later on, television were seen as essential to the New Testament missionary mandate to "go into the world and make disciples."[24]

This "making of disciples" was and is not only national but international as well. Through international networks such as HCJB (Heralding Christ Jesus' Blessings), FEBC (Far East Broadcasting Company), TWR (TransWorld Radio), and other outlets, there is a clear hope that "as many souls as possible" will be drawn to become "followers of Christ." This goal can perhaps best be seen in the joint pledge that HCJB, FEBC, and TWR made in the mid-1980s: "We are committed to provide every man, woman, and child on earth the opportunity to turn on their radio and hear the gospel of Jesus Christ in a language they can understand, so that they can become followers of Christ and responsible members of His church."[25]

A good example, but certainly not the only one, of the use of such media to both communicate and reinforce conservative religious and social worldviews is Pat Robertson's ministry of the air. Robertson, one of the most influential public figures on the conservative religious front and a former candidate for the presidency, is not your "ordinary" televangelist. While there is a sense of rags-to-riches in his personal story, it is also true that his father, Willis A. Robertson, served in Congress for thirty-four years in both the House and the Senate, ultimately serving as chair of the Senate Banking Committee.[26] It is also true that Pat Robertson himself went to Yale Law School and became a minister only after failing the bar examination in New York State.[27]

Robertson's powerful television show, the *700 Club*, began in 1963 with the idea of having seven hundred viewers contribute $10 per month, thereby enabling the television ministry to be self-sustaining.

This has been more than a little successful. As early as 1985, Robertson's annual budget was nearly $230 million. The *700 Club* itself was broadcast on two hundred stations in the United States and syndicated for broadcast in another sixty countries. Money for the broadcasts comes not only from viewers but also from "sympathetic corporations" within the conservative movement.[28] One of Robertson's Christian Broadcasting Network's strokes of genius was to obtain the broadcasting rights to older, "family-friendly," situation comedies such as *I Love Lucy, Gilligan's Island,* and other shows. It reduced its overtly religious programming to 25 percent of its airtime and garnered an increasingly large audience, as well as selling airtime for commercials to a considerable number of major corporations.[29] This made the Christian Broadcasting Network (CBN) something of a media empire (although parts of it have been sold to a secular corporate media giant to provide Robertson and his allies with money for other evangelical work).

Showing family-friendly programs and evangelizing the world have not been the Christian broadcasting movement's only tasks. Politically conservative messages (often radically so) have been promoted side by side with religious and cultural themes. This has extended to "defending the freedom" of truly murderous regimes. For example, Robertson and CBN's stance on international politics not surprisingly has often been supportive of rightist and militaristic social alliances and governments. Thus, Robertson himself was strongly supportive of U.S. intervention in Nicaragua to aid the Contras. He found Roberto D'Aubuisson of El Salvador (widely considered to be the leader of rightist death squads there) to be a "very nice fellow." And he has consistently supported Israel's hardline factions in their repression of Palestinians.[30]

My point is not to decry any use of media to bring one's case before the public. Indeed, the creative use of radio, television, and now the Internet by conservative evangelicals demonstrates how potent a force such media can be, something Rush Limbaugh, Pat Robertson, and other figures on the right have realized for years. Rather, I want us to think about the connections that make this possible. Linda Kintz is quite perceptive when she reminds us that this is not a level playing field. The conservative religious agenda, and its accompanying political and cultural attacks, articulated by Robertson, Ralph Reed, and others is massively overdetermined by its minutely organized electronic and grassroots networks, its media empire, and its ties to conservative and corporate funding and think tanks. Clearly, this way of looking at the world collapses local, national, and international politics into an absolutist Christian agenda based on the words of "our saviour, the central figure of all history, the risen Lord, sovereign over all." It is also the case, as these religious conservatives constantly remind us, that Martin Luther King Jr. and much of the civil rights movement constantly employed biblical language and metaphors to justify their actions and got a good deal of attention in the media. But it is essential to realize that Dr. King did "not have access to an entire political and corporate structure within which to make his language 'literal'."[31]

A CHRISTIAN NATION AND FREE SPEECH

The unquestioning support of imperial and antidemocratic tendencies internationally both in the media and in their other religious work has much to do with how the United States is seen by conservative evangelicals and how this fits directly into a view of the special nature of the chosen group's covenant with God. For the authoritarian populist religious right, the United States is a blessed nation. It has as its mission the spread of liberty and Christianity. In many ways, in the minds of many on the Christian right, this is linked to the purity and innocence of Eden, for America was something of a "new Eden." Robertson and other conservative religious leaders do not deny the realities of racial and class prejudice, of bigotry and injustice. These "moments" happened because our forefathers wandered from keeping "Christ's commission." As with many neoconservatives, our past, then, is not really shameful, no matter what has been done in terms of genocide and slavery. We need only recall the immensity of the positive achievements of America's Christian culture. The achievements of America as a Christian nation constitute a golden age that needs to be relearned and restored. This restorational vision plays an important part in justifying and maintaining the conservative view of America. In Watson's words:

> The assertion that "America is a Christian nation" is a statement of faith about God's special relationship to America. Faith in a national covenant with God, or in the providential role of America, can neither be proved nor disproved. Such assertions are not statements of historical fact, but part of a vision about the meaning of the national experience.[32]

For conservative evangelicals, it is exactly this providential status that is under threat, in much the same way as Eden was ultimately lost. For them, America was *founded* as a Christian nation. Yet it has "turned its back" on this. In fact, its major institutions have become anti-Christian. The result of this is moral degeneration; and the result of this is in turn social degeneration. Public schools, the mass media, political bodies, the courts, feminist and gay and lesbian rights movements, and so on—these have in essence mounted an attack on Christian values. Immorality and an "anything goes" ethic have lead to a rot at the very center of American society. For many evangelicals, it started with the situation I discussed in the previous chapter, when Darwin and evolution took center stage and the Bible was taken out of the schools. This is not seen as only a moral crisis, but a threat to prosperity and freedom as well. America became great because it was based on God's laws and on Christian principles.[33] Turning one's back on these laws and principles can only lead to economic and moral disarray. Any forces inside this society such as these "immoral" movements around feminism and the politics of sexuality and toward "socialism" here in the United States must be overcome. Any external threats—communism, socialism, anti-imperialism, liberation struggles—these too must be fought, with immense military force if necessary.

Thus, there once was a nation that could be an Eden on earth. America was that nation, based on its covenant with God. Its historical role was and is to bring to the world of the unanointed the blessings of freedom. This restorational agenda can be seen in Pat Robertson's statement:

"We want our history back. We want our tradition back. We want our constitution back. And we want God back in the schools of America."[34] For Robertson and others, only religion, especially that into which he has been anointed, can provide a secure basis for morality and for individual self-restraint. It is absolutely necessary for the continued survival of our government in a world dominated by the threat and reality of evil.[35] For those who might be worried about possible negative implications of this vision, Ralph Reed, the former spokesperson for the Christian Coalition and someone whose task until recently was to put a more personable and less-threatening face to its political and moral agenda, continues this kind of argument in a more moderate public tone: "A secular government informed by sacred principles and open to the service of persons of faith not only poses no threat to the Constitution, it is essential to its survival."[36]

External threats are woven together with internal threats to religious freedom. This is deeply connected to the theme of persecution to which I pointed earlier. For many evangelicals, among the most obvious evidence of the threats they believe they face is their perception that the supposed openness of the United States—an openness they see themselves as defending against the infidels and communists—is true for everyone but *them*. Existing cultural and political institutions do not give space or time for "the" Christian perspective. Schools, the media, politics, indeed nearly the entire society, have created the conditions for pushing evangelicals into a second-class position. The church is left out; Christian views are ignored; Christians are discriminated against. In sum, it is not a level playing field where Christians are concerned. What seems like value neutrality is actually the silencing of a committed Christian agenda and should be seen as an infringement of the right to free speech.

For some, this silencing is the result of an active, secular, anti-Christian "religion" that has come to dominate our society. Conspiratorial movements taking leadership from the devil are behind the turn from the Bible.[37] A spiritual battle must be waged throughout every institution in this society to root out the influence of homosexuality, atheism, liberalism, and secularism. For others, their interpretation may be less conspiratorial. But the feeling that Christian rights are being denied—much as the right of religious practice was denied under a number of state bureaucratic socialist regimes—is widespread. Only a lasting campaign of "engaged orthodoxy" can save the world and can restore the American covenant with God.

The issue of silencing is a vexed one for authoritarian populist religious conservatives. One of the claims made by them is that "liberals" have used the issue of censorship to create a situation in which the media focus all their attention on the right, not on what they perceive are the more widespread problems created by "secular humanists." As Phyllis Schlafly puts it in her own usually biting way, "Like the thief who cries 'Stop thief' in order to distract attention from his own crime, many powerful liberals cry 'censorship' in order to hide the fact that *they* are the most ruthless censors of all."[38]

Schlafly, Robertson, and so many others, then, have found the path. Blocking that path is where "real" censorship lies. For them, following "God's way" is the only route to stability, morality, and prosperity nationally and internationally. Other roads inevitably lead to immorality and social disintegration. Powerful secular forces are denying evangelicals their God-given constitutional right to "tell the truth." Yet this very position of certainty creates a tension between their commitment to their religious beliefs and their sense that what makes America special is its legacy of religious, political, and economic freedom. This is an important point since it helps explain why they interpret their actions in particular ways.

A large portion of the evangelical community(ies) is influenced by a resilient voluntarism that mistrusts imposition, that valorizes the individual and her or his personal choice. Because of this, unlike many neoliberals, evangelicals' activism in bringing God to the world is given legitimacy in their minds because it is seen as *transcending self-interest.* Living out one's faith everywhere—in education, in the home, in the paid workplace, in politics—is grounded in "a genuine heartfelt burden for the state of the world, a tremendous sense of personal responsibility to change society."[39] In the words of one strongly committed evangelical woman, "We can't say, 'the world is always going to be a mess and there is nothing I can do about it.' We need to say, 'yes, it's a mess and what part do I play in dealing with that?'"[40] There is, hence, an evangelical *burden* of activism in all spheres of life. Echoing what I said earlier, the world as a whole is seen as an important mission field, from paid jobs to education and child-raising to politics. It is one's personal responsibility both to evangelize the "unsaved" and to bring the wisdom of the gospel to every sphere of life—"not coercively, but to share."[41] The secular commitments of the dominant institutions of this society prevent such "selfless" sharing.

Thus, the separation of public and private is largely rejected by the Christian right. What many people would consider the most private of all matters—one's religious and moral beliefs—are instead viewed as crucial resources for the moral reformation and "healing" of a society as a whole. How could anyone be against such selfless healing? In this way, part of its restorational project is to restore the *public* role and authority of evangelical beliefs, values, and morality in order to help everyone clean up the mess that should be visible to everyone in the nation.

What I discussed above is what might be called the Christian right's "offensive" agenda. Yet a "defensive" agenda exists as well, one that shows the paradox of the evangelical rejection of the separation of public and private. For these same conservatives, the separation of public and private is not wide enough. Thus, in issues of school prayer, abortion, the areas of education and family life, the public intrusion into private life in the form of government policies and regulations has to be resisted.[42] Therefore, there is no simple dichotomy at work here—private is good; public is bad. Bringing the "private" into the public sphere around (their) religious values is good. Bringing "public" values into (their) private sphere is bad. Hence, public can be good, but only when it mirrors evangelical beliefs.

GODLESS SCHOOLS

One part of the public sphere, however, is *consistently* not good, but bad—the public school. It reflects all that is wrong with this godless society.

Education has been a primary arena of struggle because of this. Secularity, liberalism, "statism"—all of these have combined in schools to destroy the central place of religious beliefs. The educational theories advanced by the "public school cartel" have simply been a "vehicle for socialism and anti-religious cleansing."[43] The Christian right's hostility to public education is extended to teachers' organizations such as the National Education Association (NEA). They too are extremely dangerous. They are anti-Christian and radical leftist organizations whose prime thrust is to wean children away from loyalty to "the outdated religious superstitions, loyalty to family, loyalty to the United States, and beliefs in free market economics, and then introduce them to socialism and world citizenship."[44] How can our children be among the "saved," when their daily lives in schools teach them things that are of the "unsaved"?

The sense of difference, of we/they, of saved and unsaved, can lead to withdrawal from public institutions such as public schools and to a greater reliance on home schooling, about which I say more later on in this chapter and in the chapter that follows. However, when connected to the strong sense of mission that many religious conservatives have, it can just as often lead to a reinvigorated commitment to transform public schools. Such active engagement is quite visible in the commitment of some conservative evangelicals to keep their children in such schools, even though they know that some of the viewpoints there will be opposed to what they believe. In their minds, however, the school is a "mini-mission field."[45] Schools will not become more Christian if evangelical Christians and their children are not there.

If the existing public school system cannot be made to support such Christian beliefs, then neoliberal school choice programs such as vouchers—or failing that, charter schools—provide the keys for changing what children will learn and how they will be taught it. As a group that sees itself as being victimized by current laws and by the educational system, many authoritarian populists are convinced that their threatened cultural identity can only be maintained through the use of public money to establish and expand the rights of parents to school their children in any manner they see fit. While some religious conservatives fear that these kinds of programs might actually expand the sphere of state influence into what should be private decisions, for the majority of conservative Christians, voucher plans would enable the cultural survival of their most deeply held beliefs and would ensure that their children adhere to these beliefs. I do not use the term "survival" lightly. In the minds of many of these parents, that is what is at stake, not only in terms of the beliefs and culture that their children are to be taught but in terms of what may happen to the nation and the world given the threat of godlessness and evil.

For leaders such as Pat Robertson (and not just him, of course), educational policies such as vouchers have additional benefits. Free markets are in essence "God's way." Of course, he would say, such competition would create better schools for everyone. But, even if "vouchers would spell the end of public schools in America," he has an answer: "To which we say, so what?"[46] If one believes as Robertson does that the schools in this country are "firmly in the grip of fanatical ideologues whose crackpot theories are fast destroying not only the public school system but an entire generation of our young,"[47] then even though such a response may strike many readers as disturbing, but it is understandable in the face of such fears.

From these comments, it is easy to see why home schooling as well would seem to hold out hope for a safe and Christian future. Home schooling has been written about in a positive manner in the pages of many "mainstream" national publications and on television and radio, but it is truly glorified in publications such as the conservative magazine *Christianity Today*. One of the major benefits cited is that children schooled at home are more free from the pressures of peers than those at public schools. There are elements of good sense in this claim—and as we shall see in Chapter 6, in a number of other claims made by advocates of home schooling—since it is not only the religious right that has serious concerns about the influences of peer culture and the sometimes disturbing realities of life in our schools, especially after such things as the repeated shootings that have occurred in a number of schools.

It is what accompanies these elements of good sense that may make one pause, however. As the president of the Washington state branch of the Moral Majority put it, secular education is a "Godless monstrosity." Hence, "every born-again Christian in America [should] take their children out of public schools." He goes on, condemning the curriculum of public schools and urging the removal of "immoral" materials. "Just as I don't think a black kid should be forced to read Mark Twain because of the word 'nigger,' religious Christians shouldn't be forced to read books offensive to them." He singled out a number of examples of such dangerous books, among them *The Wonderful Wizard of Oz* and *The Diary of Ann Frank.* The first "condoned the practice of witchcraft," the second "promoted the belief that all paths lead to God."[48]

These fears, although perhaps articulated in a manner that might seem rather extreme to many less aggressively ideological evangelicals, may explain one of the reasons that recent research has found that James Dobson's extremely conservative Focus on the Family has emerged as the most popular organization among conservative Christian clergy.[49] In fact, Focus on the Family may now be even more influential in a number of ways than the weakened Christian Coalition. The fact that it brings in annual revenues of more than $100 million provides one indication of its widespread support.[50]

Focus on the Family is not alone by any means of course. Among others, Reverend Don Widmon's American Family Association (what was once called the National Federation for Decency; notice as well the resonance of the word *family*) and its associated AFA Law Center have been active in bringing lawsuits against textbook publishers for their espousal of witchcraft and other "anti-Christian" beliefs. Along with Focus on the Family, the Eagle Forum, Citizens for Excellence in Education, and other groups, they have aggressively challenged textbooks, curricula, and school systems for their purportedly anti-Christian messages and for their own violations of the separation of church and state given these schools' and texts' promotion of secular humanist values.[51]

A good deal of this activism has its roots in the removal of publicly sponsored prayer in schools and in what is perceived to be the federal government's aforementioned attacks on privately run Christian academies that were supposedly only created to guarantee the teaching of proper morality. The removal of school prayer (although it was actually never removed from the daily activities of many schools who simply ignored the ruling) is seen as both a national loss and a cause of what ails the nation. The Supreme Court's decision to "take prayer out of the school" in the 1960s was "a sign of the lifting of God's blessing from our land" and a "major contributing cause of the moral breakup of society."[52] It not only led to social disorder and moral confusion but also brought down God's wrath. The result has been the degradation of Christian America. For Pat Robertson, this assault on Christian America is directed by Satan as part of Satan's plan for a world government that will be formed after the "Christian United States is out of the way."[53] Although not every conservative evangelical takes quite as seriously the "fact" that Satan is behind all of this, once again we can see the ways in which there is a suturing together of America's covenant with God, its special status granted by God, the ever present possibility of evil, the collapse of morality, and the saving grace of commitment to Christianity in all our institutions.

The issue of school prayer, like Darwinism and evolution, hence, cannot be seen in isolation. It is caught up in and related to a much larger assemblage of values, fears, and commitments. Challenges to any one of these is a challenge to all of the authoritarian populists' position. Yet the crisis over school prayer gets even more complicated when coupled with something I mentioned earlier—the establishment of largely all-white Christian academies in the South (and elsewhere in many cases) by conservative parents and churches. The federal government, after years of delay, finally sought to remove the tax exemption these schools had been originally given. In the eyes of the government, this amounted to a public subsidy both of religion and of segregation. In the eyes of the school supporters, this too was clearly a government attack on both parental freedom of choice and religious liberty.

Race, class, and religion were often mixed together here. Faced with the loss of their tax exemption as charitable institutions, many southerners argued that their religious academies (more than ten thousand of which had been founded nationally in the 1960s and 1970s) were not based on race. They were created to avoid secular humanism. Thus, the issue was not race, but religion. Since 60 percent of the students in southern academies came from working-class or lower-middle-class backgrounds, many families that were threatened with a doubling of their tuition bills were less than pleased with this government intervention for economic reasons as well. Reflecting on the situation, Jerry Falwell concluded that because of such intrusions, it is now "easier to open a massage parlor than a Christian school."[54]

This is obviously a complex situation phenomenologically. For the parents and the clergy, race issues (e.g., are my child's chances of mobility and better achievement compromised by attending schools with "low-achieving" minority students?) are coupled with economic worries. And these are in turn connected to religiously based fears about increasingly dominant secular messages and institutions. Antigovernment sentiment is partly understandable here. Once again, the religious right sews all these concerns together and enables racializing logics to be hidden under other themes that seem wholly meritorious—and not racist—to the people who believe that their and their children's lives and values are under severe threat. This makes it *no less* racist in its effects, but functional explanations should not be confused with intentional ones. For the parents and school leaders, their understandings of their behavior was and is that race plays little or no part. Of course, this is how the politics of whiteness usually plays itself out so that race is the absent presence whose overt absence masks its power in our daily lives,[55] a point to which I return in my concluding chapter.

WE ARE NOT DOING ANYTHING DIFFERENT

Race, however, *does* play a large part in the overt arguments of authoritarian populist religious activists. The history of struggles over racism is consistently used to justify their actions.

Groups such as the Christian Coalition do not see themselves as asking for things that are out of the ordinary. Indeed, they see themselves as part of a long tradition of others who have successfully struggled over the politics of recognition. For them, just as African-Americans, Latino/as, Native Americans, Asian-Americans, and others have demanded recognition of their unique cultural identities, evangelicals believe that they ought to receive the same kind of differential recognition.[56]

For example, the Christian Coalition has been quite aggressive in its portrayal of conservative Christians as oppressed. The claiming of "victimhood" is a powerful rhetorical device. It enhances the legitimacy of a group at the same time as it calls out for redress. Thus, its role in building collectivity and providing "moral" justification for collective actions should not be underestimated. This gives meaning to the connections constantly being made between the civil rights movement and conservative Christians. Martin Luther King Jr.'s name, and the entire history of the civil rights movement, is invoked repeatedly by conservative evangelicals as justification for the battles against what are perceived as injustices. For them, this is exactly what conservative Protestants are doing as well. Once again, Pat Robertson provides a telling rhetorical example: "In the 1930s, African-Americans in the South were classified by bigots as 'niggers,' not worthy of respect; today it is evangelical Christians who are considered by the liberal media as 'niggers' and not worthy of respect."[57] And although Ralph Reed has been less blunt than Robertson, he too states: "It is no exaggeration that Christian bashing is the last acceptable form of prejudice in America."[58]

In the minds of such evangelicals, a clear double standard is applied to them differentially. If civil rights leaders such as Martin Luther King Jr. could move from the pulpit to the street and could employ religious and moral criteria and political activity to change unjust laws, why can't the Christian Coalition? Jerry Falwell makes this clear when he argues that the predecessor of the Moral Majority was the early civil rights movement. After all, King took his message "from the pulpit to the streets."[59] Aren't "we" doing exactly what liberals and African-American political activists have done for years? The fact that a much more affluent group, one that has *not* faced centuries of state-sanctioned apartheid and was not subject to murders, lynching, and overt degradation, does not see that there are very few parallels between its own experiences and those of the African-American population is actually what needs to be asked here.

In many ways, the example of King and the civil rights movement is employed for multiple purposes by the Christian right. By claiming, as they often do, that they are following in his footsteps in acting against a society that denies them their "freedom," they seek to take on his mantle. This both justifies their actions *and* it helps shield them from feeling racist because of the effects of the punitive welfare, education, and penal policies they consistently support—policies whose differential effects on the same black people whose leaders they supposedly wish to emulate are simply scandalous.

Ralph Reed also argues that what the Christian Coalition did—for example, in its voter education efforts to convince people to vote for conservative candidates—was no more than what any other movement has done. The only innovation was that each chapter of the Christian Coalition, through its liaisons with local churches, also focused on local elections, including most importantly those for school board.[60] Further, by the very fact that local liaisons are usually not ministers but laypeople, these efforts more likely will be seen as a genuinely populist response. As Reed put it in 1990, "The Christian community got it backwards in the 1980s. We tried to change Washington when we should have been focusing on the states. The real battles of concern to Christians are in the neighborhoods, school boards, city councils, and state legislatures."[61] (The examples of textbook guidelines in Kansas and Alabama with which I began Chapter 4 lend credibility to this position.) Victories at a local level help cement a more conservative "profamily" set of policies into our daily lives—although this has not stopped conservative religious groups from maintaining a very real presence at the national level and in Washington, as evidenced by the example of their candidate screening process I gave earlier.

To the complaint by moderates that the Christian right has taken over the Republican Party, Reed has a direct answer. "The only crime that the Christian Right has committed is the crime of democracy."[62] To paraphrase him, licking envelopes and burning shoe leather are things everyone can do. Critics, however, are quick to point out that what seems to be a simple exercise of democracy is often instead a "stealth" campaign in which conservative religious activists specifically target "pro-family" voters in historically low-turnout elections such as those for school board.[63] Or they run on a platform of fiscal responsibility, hiding the rest of their more aggressive agenda until they have been elected. The use of such tactics is denied, but the Christian Coalition's field director in 1991 did not help their case when he argued that most people do not care about such elections and are not going to vote. Therefore, speaking to the majority of voters made little sense. Nor did it help when in the same year Ralph Reed himself suggested that rather than following Jerry Falwell's approach of large-scale media events and rallies, the Christian Coalition should engage in something like guerrilla warfare: "It's better to move quietly, with stealth, under cover of night."[64] While Reed claimed that he was not speaking literally and that he was quoted out of context, the worries about stealth campaigning have persisted well after Reed left to form a political consulting firm.

Not only do authoritarian populist religious movements see parallels between themselves and civil rights and voter registration movements of the past, paradoxically given their positions on cultural restoration as a return to a golden past, they see parallels between what they do and the struggle over multiculturalism as well. Unlike the claims by disenfranchised Americans whose roots lie in Asia, Latin America, or Africa that their history has never been told, there is an even greater sense of loss among many evangelicals. To them, their history *was* central to the historical narrative of the United States and it now has been purged from its central location. "Campus gurus and thought police have attempted to strip from our society all references to our Christian heritage, to the faith of our fathers, to the artistic and literary achievements of Western Christian civilization."[65]

All this leads to another kind of paradox. What is it that such conservative religious activists want? A restoration of "Christian America"? Simply a recognition of their distinct cultural and religious heritage, values, and beliefs that would enable them to participate more fully in society's public life? The most credible answer is that they want both. "They want their 'place at the table' *and* they want everyone to agree with them. They want a Christian nation *and* religious freedom. As contradictory as it may seem, they want their cake *and* to eat it too."[66] It is this odd combination of an antipluralist set of beliefs (we are the chosen ones, the ones with the truth) and a belief that in the United States everyone's values should be responded to equally (we are an oppressed minority) that makes the case of authoritarian populists such a complex story. Recognition of the complexity should not lead us to ignore the very real dangers associated with its arrogance. But it does mean that we need to listen carefully to the elements of good sense packed into the elements of bad sense in their positions.

THE STRUCTURES OF FEELING OF AUTHORITARIAN POPULISM

How do these contradictory sentiments work at the level of everyday life? The much discussed breakdown of community caused in part by economic demands and crises, by the concomitant creation of possessive individualism, by the mobility of a population, by the blurring of idealized gender roles, and so on has created a situation in which many people feel unmoored, anomic, and isolated. The church has historically provided a central place for building community. It takes on an even more central role for many people today. Conservative visions of homogeneity under God's laws and guidance not only assist in the construction of real social communities through the church; they also help create imagined communities, structures of feeling that connect you with unseen people throughout the nation who are "just like me."[67] As Raymond Williams reminded us, one of the most important underpinnings of social stability and social transformation is the production of "structures of feeling" that are not necessarily conscious, but presage important limits on and possibilities for social action.[68]

Authoritarian populist sentiments act in exactly this way. They do particular kinds of work for people who hold them. As in the past, for many women, for example, such conservatism holds the promise of community, of female agency, and of the security of responsible male behavior.[69] Rather than looking with ironic condescension on the appeal that conservative populism has to so many people, we need to continue the process that I started in earlier sections; we must get inside it. We need to ask why—in the face of conditions that might predict the opposite—large numbers of people have found in such positions answers to the problems they face in their daily lives.

Such conservatism rests on a structure of feeling that might be thought about as a set of concentric circles that are stacked on top of each other and that point upward to heaven: God, property, womb, family, church, free market, global mission, God.[70] In many of the iterations of these circles, the sense-making that lies behind them takes the form of apocalyptic narratives. History is a divinely predetermined totality. Extreme pessimism about the present is accompanied by a strong belief that a crisis is imminent. Yet, even though evil is present, God will eventually triumph over evil. In the words of Elaine Pagels, "The faith that Christ has conquered Satan assures Christians that in their own struggles the stakes are eternal, and victory is certain. Those who participate cannot lose."[71] These narratives hold a central place, for instance, in Pat Robertson's modernized apocalyptic vision and in Ralph Reed's version that has been sanitized for public consumption. For them and for their many followers, Christ is coming; but he can only return if born-again Christians, rather than waiting to be "raptured out of harm's way," prepare the conditions for the Second Coming.[72] Positions such as these create something of an unbridgeable binary—either the absolutism of conservative Christians or the nihilism of a society that is falling apart around us. God versus evil; there is no other choice.

Because the arguments of conservative religious activists are not presented in ways in which perhaps many readers are very comfortable politically or intellectually, we can overlook the very places where politics often matter the most—in our unconscious needs and fears, in our very bodies and emotions, and through faith. Ignoring these areas involves too truncated a definition of rationality. In the words of one of the most astute analysts of how secular processes of interpretation have all too often coded the spheres of feeling and spirituality as "irrational and feminized," it is important to remember that "part of what has happened is that absolutist Christianity has situated meaning in the heart of Christ rather than in the head of Man."[73] Yet this very act of situating meaning in this way has a long rhetorical tradition within religious discourse not only in the United States but in nations throughout the world.

In this narrative of "truth," God sent his son to redeem us. Thus, he gave up his own child for us. This sacrifice, in a time when so many people feel as if they must move earth and stars to keep their families intact economically and emotionally, creates a powerful imaginary connection. All things are linked together, with children often providing a key nexus, a set of connections that links to the restoration and legitimation of an imagined yet sacred past of family, religion, and nation in an almost sensual set of conjoined meanings and relations. It is Christianity, read as a story pregnant not only with past but fully present meanings, that joins one's intimate experiences of family life and its threats, gender relations, economic and emotional security, and so much more into a coherent framework.[74] Given the potent mix of biblical inerrancy (the Bible is correct) and the rich metaphors in which it is written (I can read it in such a way that I can find my own predicaments and ways of dealing with them in it), it is not at all surprising that considerable numbers of people find it powerful.

But how does this power work in largely conservative ways for so many people in the current context? The issue of gender provides a prime example of how such narratives create structures of feeling that can feel so personally freeing and yet paradoxically support dominance.

At its most extreme, the religious right's position on feminism can be seen in Pat Robertson's 1992 statement: "The feminist agenda is not about equal rights for women. It is about a socialist, anti-family political movement that encourages women to leave their husbands, kill their children, practice witchcraft, destroy capitalism, and become lesbians."[75] It is exactly this kind of rhetoric that Ralph Reed tried to refashion so that the Christian right had a more moderate image.

Even with this kind of argument, however, there are contradictory tendencies in conservative evangelicals' positions on gender relations. For example, while evangelicals often cite Ephesians 5:22, which states "Wives, submit to your husbands as to the Lord," at the same time conservative religious groups actively seek out women of faith to take on major roles in mobilizing for "spiritual warfare."[76] "Selfless women," in roles ordained by God, work for the cause, but they must never forget their true calling. This tension is perhaps best exemplified in a quote from Beverly LaHaye, the founder of Concerned Women of America, when she argues that one of the most important things women can do is to help "restore righteousness."

> I believe that God has a particular task for every Christian woman to perform. Some may be called to be "salt and light" in their own church, fulfilling a need there. Others may be called to action in the local community, organizing an anti-abortion rally or protest against pornography being sold at a corner store. . . . Others may fulfill God's purpose by being intercessors or letter writers. . . .
>
> But let me caution those women who are, by nature, "activists." If you are married and have small children, you must know where your primary responsibility lies. . . . Your "call" at this point in your life will be localized and centered within your family. If you travel and lose your own children, you have failed to fulfill God's primary purpose for you at this point—and that is to train your children.[77]

Therefore, for the most conservative of the authoritarian populist leaders such as LaHaye, women cannot serve both God and feminism. Nor, as we shall see, can they accept homosexuality or abortion. Any acceptance of such "immorality" is the result of the acceptance by this society of "Satan's biggest lie"—evolution. "God's truth is that we come from God's hand. . . . By doubting God's truth about creation, we have set ourselves up for a tidal wave that will destroy our very foundations."[78]

Notice what is being said here. It directly connects to my earlier discussion in Chapter 4 of what stands behind the recent events in education in Kansas. It is not that evolution and its teaching is one element to which such conservatives object. In fundamental ways (excuse the double entendre), it is one of the most *central* foundations of their entire world. We are *made* from God's hand. What gives us value is this fact; it is what provides the underpinnings of our belief in scriptural authority. It determines our responsibilities to each other and to nature. Undercutting this does no less than challenge the very foundation of our entire world. "We know that God's truth is only found in God's word. We must defend that truth in our homes, in our schools, and in our country."[79]

How would I know what to do, how would I be guided through a time of chaos, fluidity, and danger, if God does not provide me—as a special creation—with the ethical principles that make me selfless, make me willing to sacrifice—as God's only child did—in my commitment to act as God's willing servant? For authoritarian populists, this selflessness, this feeling of being one who sacrifices, of having turned oneself over to God and his values, enables one to truly believe that she or he is not guilty of political manipulation, hatred, or racism. Selflessness and truth are fused in powerful ways in this couplet, ways that are even more powerful for many conservative women. Let me say more about this since the relations of all this to particular constructions of gender and women's roles are intricate and are integral to the structures of feeling that help establish identities within authoritarian populist religious communities.

The structure of motherhood is exemplary in this regard. Motherhood is a sacred trust. With the centuries of struggle by women both for recognition and redistribution, not only were there transformations in male identities (though not sufficient ones), but this created a crisis in the idealized identities of many traditional women. This crisis has opened a space for absolutist religion. A considerable number of women have turned religious to "satisfy the anguish, the suffering, and the hopes of mothers."[80] Not surprisingly, the (re)construction of religiously based visions of sacred motherhood is

> constructed precisely where much of secular society's contempt and disgust have historically been focused, for mothers are at the same time idealized

and despised. In this religious framework, children become the instruments of a guaranteed, sacred identity for women who have a deep and realistic fear that without such a guarantee, they will inevitably be judged against men and found lacking. Then they and their children will be left at great risk in a society based on masculine competition, whether built by free-market theorists or liberal institutions.[81]

This sense of sacred motherhood is also then employed as a set of intellectual and emotional resources to counter the move toward such things as institutionalized child care. Such arrangements for our children break the bonds of parents—especially mothers—and children and are largely in the interests of "yuppies" or the state's social engineers.[82] As Christian conservative Connie Marshner argues, such "social parenting" is "not in accord with God's plan for raising children." It may be the case that "social parenting has the power to assume a pleasing shape," but—using the words of Shakespeare—Marshner goes on to remind us that "the Devil hath the power to assume a pleasing shape as well."[83]

Sacred motherhood is itself dependent on the sacredness of the nuclear family, God's chosen unit. But the sacredness of motherhood and the sacredness of the family do not stand alone. They are a crucial counterbalance to something else that is divinely inspired and human nature. (Remember, we are created in God's image, so human nature is itself divine.) This additional element is free enterprise. Justification for this can be found, according to Pat Robertson, in the Eighth Commandment: "Thou shalt not steal." This embodies God's recognition of the sanctity of property. God "forbids a citizen to take what belongs to another citizen." The commandment tells us not to take from the rich and give to the poor. The biblical message is indeed clear: "What a man has accumulated [is] his. In God's order there are no schemes of wealth redistribution under which government forces productive citizens to give the fruit of their hard-earned labors to those who are nonproductive."[84]

Thus, for many of these people, corporations are a "natural extension" of God's law. Our moral and religious duty to the rest of the world is to export unregulated "free enterprise" around the globe. In this, as with other couplets that prove significant in conservative religious discourse, corporate and religious discourse are stitched together, each legitimating the other. Here, traditional family and religious values need to be globalized, and in God's plan this can only be accomplished through the advance of multinational capitalism. Corporate capitalism and the export of U.S. culture are now overtly and without apology defined as among the highest expressions of God's will, the missionary expansion of his culture to the rest of the globe.[85] Human nature *is* the market; and unbridled expansion of such a market to all the world's nations (and ultimately to schools as we have seen) is God's will. Identities and their accompanying beliefs and practices that are not disciplined according to market logic are, hence, in essence also ungodly. Many neoliberal ideas, then, can be easily connected to this range of sentiments since they are given a biblical warrant.

In the words of the conservative Catholic "moral economist" Michael Novak, who often finds himself in agreement with the beliefs of rightist Protestant evangelicals, "Personal economic initiative is a fundamental human right and to exercise that right is to fulfill the image of God inherent in every man and women."[86] For Novak, moral responsibility requires the creation of wealth, which is itself the only true guarantor of liberty and democracy. Hence, his advice to "intelligent, ambitious, and morally serious young Christians and Jews" is the following. "They will better save their souls and serve the cause of the Kingdom of God all around the world by restoring the liberty and power of the private sector than by working for the state."[87]

This is closely connected to something I discussed earlier, the politics of whiteness, for there is almost always a racial subtext here. This is evidenced in the fact that for many European-Americans, being middle class is partly defined by not being black. The absence of African-Americans is what makes a neighborhood a "decent place to live."[88] "They" (blacks) tend to be wards of the state. They are neither efficient nor productive, while "we" are. Although all of us are God's children, some of us—especially particular people of color—can only be saved by setting the market loose on them. Here again, religion, markets, antistatism, and racialized and racializing logics are all brought together in ways in which it is God's will that black, red, and brown poor are made into self-reliant citizens "just like us."[89] The fact that government subsidies and tax breaks to the middle class and the wealthy are *far more* extensive than all of the combined programs to support the poor is not part of this self-understanding.

If the Other is raced, she or he is also sexed. Thus, bodily politics provide another key element in this structure of feeling. Homosexuality is a threat to the sacred family, and to the God-given gender roles that constitute it. It can pollute children's minds and their identities as Christians. Schools, themselves, are sites of danger here, because they are clearly promoting a gay agenda. Resources that should be devoted to raising standards, preventing violence, ensuring that teachers are qualified, and so much more in our crisis-ridden schools are being siphoned away to support sex education and an agenda of immorality. This can only be stopped if sex education is devoted to one theme only—abstinence—and if such "private" matters are left to the family. Valorizing the "private"—with all the contradictions this entails—becomes crucial in structuring one's interpretive frame.

However, the sanctity of private life is not extended to gays. They can be "cured," brought back into the fold of sacred gender relations defined by compulsory heterosexual norms and values. Rather than interpreting their actions as forms of bigotry and discrimination, the conservative activists who support such policies see themselves as acting in a wholly meritorious manner. They are acting out of deep love of children and out of a religious conviction that loving the "sinner" means bringing her or him back into a covenant with God, and as truly principled about the fate of the nation.

Like many of the sentiments of the religious right, this logic too is grounded in a strong commitment of "being fair to everyone." The "gay agenda" is seen as an attack on religious rights. Just as important, granting civil rights protections to gays and lesbians grants them the right to use the law to establish that homosexuals are a legitimate minority and deserve the protections accorded to racial minorities, women, and others. It would force schools to teach children that gays and lesbians are "good." In this way, the constitutional rights of parents and children who hold religious beliefs that find homosexuality abhorrent are themselves abrogated by schools.[90] A finely tuned sense of what they see as democratic justice provides an important element in this intellectual/emotional assemblage.

Understanding this sense of justice should not make us lose perspective on the hatefulness that guides much of it. Some of the antigay rhetoric gets quite extreme and can and has been used to justify murderous acts. Consider the following statement made by the antigay activist Paul Cameron on the Christian Broadcasting Network. Supposedly drawing on one of the nation's founders, Cameron said, "Think of Thomas Jefferson, one of our most liberal thinkers in the western world. He said in a considered statement that homosexuals ought to be castrated. He said that homosexual females ought to have a one-inch hole drilled through the cartilage of their nose."[91] Although other conservative evangelicals may take less of a violent position, and even Jerry Falwell has recently met with representatives of gay and lesbian movements to try to lessen the overt hostility, it is clear that for many conservative religious activists the "sin" of homosexuality needs to be punished and eradicated. Indeed, HIV/AIDS, for example, is seen not only as a punishment against gays, but also as a punishment from God against society as a whole because this society has tolerated the "perversion" of homosexuality. "We" (the church and "good" Christians) must fight the social acceptance of homosexuality, "not just in terms of pressing for testing or even quarantining of gays, but in terms of massive action to stop non-monogamous, non-heterosexual activity in its entirety."[92] We shall do this out of love for the homosexual and out of love for this society. How else can they and this society about which we care so much be saved?

A good deal of these structures of feeling center around what is perhaps best named "plain-folks Americanism," an identity with its roots in the populist and libertarian soil of the South and West. It also draws strength from Pentecostal traditions with their own grounding in the work ethic, personal responsibility, and traditional values. Although this plain-folks Americanism was often racist in earlier periods of populism, it also focused on a critique of elites. (Remember, for instance, my point that the now derogatory term *rednecks* had its origins in the fierce pride many farmers and working-class people in the South had in differentiating themselves from those who worked in jobs where their necks would not be reddened by the sun.) In the 1960s and 1970s, these critiques increasingly shifted to people of color, feminists, unions, urban elites, "liberals," and the state.[93] In fact, I do not think it is possible to understand the seductiveness of authoritarian populist messages unless we appreciate the undercurrent of a stern moral critique of elitism that works throughout it. This responds to a deep popular discontent over the directions our culture has taken,[94] a discontent that is itself part of the moral economy that feels righteous when it is expressed by religious conservatives.

From what I have said in this section, it should be clear that the structures of feeling underlying all of this are tense and contradictory, but they do provide meaning and emotional cement that give one a definite place in an uncertain world. They embody certain tendencies. First, there is the horror of mixing, a binary of purity and danger. Second, there is a fear of solitude. Third, there is intense anxiety over the possibility that equality will produce uniformity. These elements lead to an emotional economy in which specific kinds of "circuits of solidarity" are produced and reinforced. The world is to become a perpetual small town in which all know their place and where hierarchies are based on God's plan. But these are not just any circuits of solidarity; they are circuits of *preferential* solidarity. The limited absolutist vision of democracy under God's law turns democracy into an exclusive "patriotic religion."[95] Women, gays and lesbians, people of color, the poor, the dispossessed and oppressed—for them there is to be no recourse through the state. Faith will solve all. Perhaps Michelle LeDoeuff is right when she says that these structures of feeling support "structures of vassalage which are as undemocratic as possible."[96]

HOW CAN HATE SEEM SO NICE?

Structures of vassalage can contain elements that create forms of mis-recognition for those who participate in them, forms that make one feel *powerful* even in the face of the depowering of oneself and especially those whom such discourses position as the Other. For the majority of conservative evangelicals, they themselves are "nice" people, "real Americans" who stand for things that the rest of us have given up on. They are the defenders of all of us. Their power, their willingness to strictly uphold moral principles, stands between us and what is certain to be a future that will be a disaster. Their very "niceness" serves as a major element of their misrecognition. Linda Kintz asks what is perhaps one of the most significant questions in this regard: "How can hate seem so nice?"[97]

While it does not provide a complete explanation, Kelly argues that one of the reasons conservative religions have been growing is actually because of their strictness. The fact that they are so demanding means that they present people with a rich set of meanings. Less-demanding religious groups call forth less sacrifice and less discipline, and therefore are less able to seem relevant to every aspect of one's life.[98] This is true to some extent, but one of the signal accomplishments of modern conservative evangelicalism has been its strategic curbing of some of fundamentalism's rigid absolutism and its separateness from the world. By reducing the level of strictness, and by creating an atmosphere of what can be called "seeker-friendly" churches, evangelicalism enables one to walk the tightrope of religiosity in all parts of life. It helps one deal with the task of not remaining pure from the world, but advancing into it and transforming its very soul.[99]

These actions increase its vitality, its sense of being both traditional *and* modern. Its very lack of one single authoritative creed, guided by one central organizational form, enables conservative evangelicalism to create "a meaningful identity space." In the process, it also provides another kind of space. By its very nature as a transdenominational identity movement, it is characterized by a loose network that is wide open structurally. This enables the development of entrepreneurial and inventive leaders. But it also gives people subject positions, identities, that respond to people's definition of themselves as individuals who have made a personal choice to be reborn.[100] How can I interpret my actions as hateful and authoritarian when I am so strongly committed to personal choice and to seeking the "truth"?

While large numbers of citizens may find such a position to be nothing short of arrogant and aggressive, paradoxically this confirms evangelicalism's correctness for its followers. Christian Smith argues that rather than threatening its growth, evangelicalism is actually made stronger by the tensions and conflicts that its engagement with the public world engenders. It is exactly this engagement that keeps it vital, that gives it its purpose and identity.[101] This is connected to the ways "self" and "others" are produced socially. "Collective identities depend heavily for existence on contrast and negation. Social groups know who they are in large measure by knowing who they are not."[102] Such identities are not necessarily stable. They are constantly being reproduced symbolically and socially by one's daily interactions, interactions that constantly mark the differences between insiders and outsiders, between "we" and "they." In Bourdieu's terms, nearly all cultural symbols and practices act to reproduce distinctions among collective actors. In the case of the growing conservative evangelical movement, these distinctions enable identities to be achieved and reinforced.[103]

> This has been described as something of the "cultural DNA" of evangelicalism. The evangelical tradition's entire history, theology, and self-identity reflects strong cultural boundaries with nonevangelicals; a zealous burden to convert and transform the world outside of oneself; and a keen perception of external threats and crises seen as menacing what it views to be true, good, and valuable.[104]

This means that evangelicalism depends for its very existence on having a "constitutive outside." Its very meaning and identity requires that there be those who are immoral, lazy, burdens on the state, evil, secular humanists, or unsaved. This very binary gives meaning to one's most fundamental sets of interpretive structures. It is one of the reasons that evangelicals have some very real sympathies with neoconservative positions on the importance of character and virtue (but I hasten to add not necessarily with the belief held by many neoconservatives that national and state curricula, standards, and tests are the way forward).

Do not take this as a negative statement about evangelical religion in general. It is not meant to imply that such religious affiliations are built around a false consciousness that somehow wrongly solves the tensions over identity in the modern/postmodern world.[105] There is nothing new in evangelicalism's attempt to do this. Nearly all religious movements have constantly attempted to create communities of meaning, memory, and belonging. This is one of the ways in which they provide a primary basis of making sense of the world. Just as in its early history, evangelicalism's activist rebirth comes about at a time when people are experiencing alienation and rootlessness, isolation, and feelings of insignificance.[106] What would have to be explained would be not the rebirth of activist evangelicalism, but if it had *not* occurred.

However, while much of this is to be expected, conservative evangelicalism has built on, extended, and in part transformed these earlier instances of religious mobilization in distinct ways. It has taken existing themes and creatively transmuted them in such a way that the conservative elements come to the fore. Such creative alterations—ones that are both connected to historical meanings and yet reworked in powerful ways—can be seen in the ways in which conservative evangelicalism resonates and connects with deep-seated American constructions of the embodiment of individualism in our daily lives. As I argued earlier, the forces of conservative restoration and of conservative modernization have been more than a little successful in altering our ideas about democracy and citizenship. They have partly depoliticized them (and then repoliticized them around extremely conservative visions), transforming earlier collective forms into the language of consumption and choice. Evangelicalism is itself both a response to this and a reproduction and extension of it. Just as we saw in my discussion of its earlier history, evangelicalism provides a collectivity, while at the same time making it a result of active individual *choice*. This is clear in the following:

> For . . . modern Americans the ultimate criteria of identity and lifestyle validity is individual choice. It is by choosing a product, a mate, a lifestyle, or an identity that one makes it one's very own, personal, special, meaningful—not "merely" something one inherits or assumes. In the value-epistemology of modern American culture, to believe, to want, or to do something simply because that is what one's parents believe, or what one's friends want, or what somebody else does is considered inferior and unauthentic. . . . That is parochial, acquiescent, and artificial. Rather every such thing must be personalized and substantiated through individual choice. Even if (as is often the case) one chooses what one was already inheriting or assuming, it is only through the observance of individual choice—whether actual or ritualized—that it becomes "real" and personally meaningful.[107]

In a faith-based movement where one of the most important acts is making a "personal decision for Christ," of being "reborn" through an experience of individual conversion, the power of such values can be seen.[108] Making a "choice for Christ" validates individualism (and hence cannot be oppressive to others since it is based on the fundamental value that supposedly guarantees freedom in the United States) and at the same time secures an identity within a larger movement. This is a profoundly creative way of dealing with the contradictions and tensions of authoritarian populist identities today. And it allows what is often based on hate to seem like love.

This is closely tied to another element of the structures of feeling that I described before, antielitism. This is not only a sociological outlook, but also an epistemological one. It reconstructs our understanding of "truth." Truth is simple and clear, unlike the opinions of the "plague of experts" in, say, government, law, the media, and education. This position works off of the populist hostility to experts and to their supposed belief that our problems are too complex for the commonsense solutions held by average citizens.[109] Strategically, this element is more important than many of us might like to admit. Like the critical and deconstructionist tools employed by, say, critical multiculturalists, this view of truth as commonsense supplies a powerful vocabulary for describing and fighting against perceived oppressions. Yet, and this is crucial, while the social and cultural criticism of the former is based on what is often a new and difficult vocabulary taken from critical theory and postmodernism for example,[110] the Christian conservatives speak in familiar terms. They call upon their constituency to employ tools that they *already possess*—a strong Christian faith and commonsense. Whether we like it or not, this gives them a functional and tactical advantage.[111] This connects with the criticisms I made in Chapter 3 of the overly theoretical and rhetorical turn taken by many writers about "critical pedagogy." The tactical advantage that familiarity gives the authoritarian populist right needs to be thought about directly and strategically, not ignored.

TURNING STRAW INTO GOLD

The implications of this "plain speaking" are not small by any stretch of the imagination. This advantage is not sitting unused. The religious right has not been and is not static. It is in constant motion, involved in "reclaiming and reinvigorating lost or dormant themes, traditions, and practices," at the same time as the Christian right often generates new themes and practices. In their interactions with the world and in their modes of interpretation, as I have demonstrated here these groups are often more than a little talented in "using quintessentially modern tools to strengthen and promote their traditional worldviews and ways of life."[112] In one commentator's clever words, evangelical religious movements are more than capable of taking these advantages and "turning the proverbial 'straw into gold.'"[113]

Although this talent should no longer surprise us, given what I have shown in these chapters, it should make us try even harder to understand the creative elements that underpin the structures of feelings and identities of this movement. If we do not, then the institutions in our society may embody a set of values that may not be filled with love—evangelical or any other kind. While Pat Robertson does not speak for all of the many evangelical communities, conservative or otherwise, his statements about the place of religion in public life and in our schools help illuminate the reasons for concern. For him, the current separation of church and state is an "intellectual scandal." For the sake of our children, we must bring God back into the classrooms, homes, and businesses of America. The fact that nonbelievers have the right to citizenship should not be employed to argue that "the ninety-four percent of us who believe in God have any duty whatsoever to dismantle our entire public affirmation of faith in God just to please a tiny minority who don't believe in anything."[114] The tone of this statement gives much cause to worry.

Even with this rhetoric, however, we need to be fair. There are religious impulses that are even more conservative than those I have discussed so far. These range from the Reconstructionist movement to the utterly racist and at times quite violent far-right groups such as neo-Nazis, the followers of Christian Identity, the Order, and others.[115] While in no way do I wish to minimize the dangers of radical paramilitary and racist groups—given the long and murderous history of such action in the United States and given the recent spate of racist killings here—their very presence makes the positions of ultraconservative religious groups seem more "mainstream." That is, their existence gives legitimacy to conservative religious groups that would otherwise be seen as beyond the boundaries of widespread public acceptability. A case in point here is Christian Reconstructionism.

The Reconstructionist movement is relatively small in numbers, but its language and principles have been increasingly influential among charismatic Christians, home schoolers, and the religious right. The core of Reconstructionism centers around "presuppositionalism," the idea that the only way to understand reality is through the lens of the Bible. The Bible, hence, is *the* governing text in education, law, government, and all other areas of public and private life. Family, church, and government are under God's covenant. Under such a covenant, the nuclear family is the basic unit. Wives and children submit to the head, the husband. But he in turn submits to Jesus and to the laws of God as detailed in the Old Testament. All forms of civil government exist only to implement God's laws. Thus, family, church, and government are under God's law, "theonomy."[116] This biblical worldview, then, is not to be applied only to such contentious moral issues as pornography, homosexuality, abortion, or the knowledge that is declared official in schools. Rather, as one noted Reconstructionist theologian argues, as God's chosen people, "the Christian goal for the world is the universal development of Biblical theocratic republics, in which every area of life is redeemed and placed under the Lordship of Jesus Christ and the rule of God's Law."[117]

As one pastor puts it, "We have the word of God. . . . Principle sometimes takes precedent over silly laws."[118] In a similar vein, another leader of Concerned Women for America writes that the "separation of church and state is a bogus phrase. Our country was founded on Biblical principles and we need to turn back to God and his precepts."[119]

While not alone in this belief, central to Reconstructionist calling is the attack on public schools. One of the most vocal of such critics is Gary North, who writes, "Until the vast majority of Christians pull their children out of public schools, there will be no possibility of creating a theocratic republic."[120] For this wing of the movement, the task is not to improve public schools but—ultimately—to shut them down. Urging conservative Christians to pull their children out of school *and* run for their local school boards, the task once elected is to cut off funding for such schools and, finally, "to sink the ship."[121] At the very least, "our" task will be to return to the situation before 1837 when virtually all education in the country was Christian and private. Through Christian schools and home schooling, it is hoped that an entire generation of people will be trained to understand that religious neutrality is, in essence, a fiction. In home school advocate Christopher Klicka's words, "Sending our children to public schools violates nearly every Biblical principle. . . . It is tantamount to sending out our children to be trained by the enemy."[122]

Many religious conservatives have had to distance themselves from any public affiliation with Reconstructionism because it has become too controversial. For example, Pat Robertson has had to defend himself against charges that he wants to establish a theocracy. This is a charge that can be justified by some of his writings, but he has attempted to move away from some of his earlier more aggressive claims about this.[123] Even with such public disavowals, Reconstructionism has helped pull people even further toward the right. The influences that it and similar "biblical worldview" perspectives of this segment of the Christian right have are more widespread than are usually admitted, especially since many conservative evangelicals interact constantly both with figures from this movement and with the symbols to which it gives legitimacy.

For example, televangelist D. James Kennedy's weekly television program airs on over three hundred stations and is broadcast on the Armed Services Network. He hosts a yearly national political conference on "Reclaiming America," which has drawn more than two thousand people, including such conservative luminaries as presidential hopeful Gary Bauer of the Family Research Council, Beverly LaHaye of Concerned Women of America, Bob Dugan of the National Association of Evangelicals, Bob Simonds of Citizens for Excellence in Education, Russ Walton of the Plymouth Rock Foundation, George Grant, the even more ultraconservative Reconstructionist formerly of Coral Ridge Ministries, and others such as former vice-president Dan Quayle. Aside from being a gathering ground for rightist religious figures, the conference is also notable for the participants' recitation of the pledge of allegiance to the "Christian flag." Thus, before Dan Quayle's speech to the assembly, the audience recited "I pledge allegiance to the Christian flag, and to the Saviour, for whose freedom it stands. One Saviour, crucified, risen and coming again, with life and liberty for those who believe."[124] It is probable that not everyone in the audience was fully committed to the principles of Reconstructionism. Yet this pledge shows the reach of its underlying premises.

It is still important to remember, however, that while many evangelicals do want to reassert the power and authority of their morality and beliefs in the public sphere, they have *not* consistently taken the even stronger stance advocated by the more radical Reconstructionist movement. As I documented, as postmillennialists, the Reconstructionists believe that God requires "man" to create the kingdom of God on earth. Rather than the premillennial assumption that time is running out soon, Reconstructionism advocates even more uncompromising and grassroots struggles that leave no room for false ideas of tolerance for other religions.[125] "Time is on our side." Christ is coming and "has willed our victory." Thus, there is no need for compromise and pluralism. While Robertson and other conservative evangelicals may sound this way at times and undoubtedly want to change the world, only dominionists like the Reconstructionists insist that they, and they alone, must run it.[126]

This said, though, it should be absolutely clear that for Robertson, Reed, and so many other authoritarian populist religious leaders and spokespersons religious diversity and pluralism are certainly not things to be fully welcomed. For them, such things are among the ways the forces of secular humanism have engaged in the "de-Christianizing of America."[127] This does not mean that they are necessarily overtly anti-Semitic or anti-Catholic, although that border is sometimes crossed. Their major enemies are those whom they see as antireligion. They have been willing to compromise and to form alliances with conservatives within Judaism and Catholicism (but certainly not with Islam) in the restorational struggle.

In saying that authoritarian populists such as Robertson, Reed, and others are willing to compromise and that they are not quite as radical as, say, Reconstructionists in terms of seeking dominion over every institution so that a "theonomy" is established, I do not want to minimize their constant and often partly successful attempts to reconstruct our commonsense. This actually may make them even more powerful, since their interest is not only in transforming a few laws but in transforming the structures of feeling of an entire culture.

What Robertson and Reed want is a return to a supposed golden era in which it would not occur to anyone to question the propriety of school

Chapter 6

Away with All Teachers: The Cultural Politics of Home Schooling

SITUATING HOME SCHOOLING

Protecting religious identities and transforming both education and the larger world go hand in hand. One of the ways that the differentiation of inside from outside can be accomplished and maintained is through home schooling. If one of the marks of the growing acceptance of ideological changes is their positive presentation in the popular media, then home schooling has clearly found a place in our consciousness. It has been discussed in the national press, on television and radio, and in widely circulated magazines. Its usual presentation is that of a savior, a truly compelling alternative to a public school system that is presented by neoliberals and neoconservatives as a failure. While the presentation of public schools as simply failures is deeply problematic,[1] given the arguments I have developed in the chapters that preceded this, it is the largely unqualified support of home schooling that concerns me here. I am considerably less sanguine.

Data on home schooling are not always accurate and are often difficult to compile. However, a sense of the extent of home schooling can be found in the fact that the National Home Education Research Institute has estimated that as of the 1997–1998 school year, 1.5 million children were being home schooled in the United States. The Institute also has suggested that there has been a growth of 15 percent annually in these numbers since 1990. These data are produced by an organization that is one of the strongest supporters of home schooling, but even given the possible inflation of these figures, this clearly is a considerable number of students,[2] a number that is constantly growing.

Given the range of reforms sponsored under the umbrella of conservative modernization, I cannot deal at length with all the many issues that could be raised about the home schooling movement. Nevertheless, I want to ask a number of critical questions about the dangers associated with it. While it is quite probable that some specific children and families will gain from home schooling, my concerns are larger. As in my previous chapters, these concerns are connected to the more extensive restructuring of this society that I believe is quite dangerous and to the manner in which our very sense of public responsibility is withering in ways that will lead to even further social inequalities. To illuminate these dangers, I shall do a number of things: situate home schooling within the larger movement that provides much of its impetus; suggest its connections with other protectionist impulses; connect it to the history of and concerns about the growth of activist government; and, finally, point to how it may actually hurt many other students who are not home schooled.

At the very outset of this chapter, let me state as clearly as I can that any parents who care so much about the educational experiences of their children that they actively seek to be deeply involved are to be applauded, not chastised or simply dismissed. Let me also say that it is important not to stereotype individuals who reject public schooling[3] as unthinking promoters of ideological forms that are so deeply threatening that they are—automatically—to be seen as beyond the pale of legitimate concerns. Indeed, there are complicated reasons behind the growth of antischool sentiments. As I showed, such beliefs contain elements of "good" sense as well as bad "sense." All too many school systems *are* overly bureaucratic, are apt not to listen carefully to parents' or community concerns, or act in overly defensive ways when questions are asked about what and whose knowledge is considered "official." In some ways, these kinds of criticisms are similar across the political spectrum, with both left and right often making similar claims about the politics of recognition.[4] Indeed, these very kinds of criticisms have led many progressive and activist educators to build more community-based and responsive models of curriculum and teaching in public schools.[5]

This said, however, it is still important to realize that while the intentions of critics such as home schoolers may be meritorious, the effects of their actions may be less so. Although many home schoolers have not made their decision based on religious convictions, a large proportion have.[6] As in the last two chapters, I focus largely on this group, in part because it constitutes some of the most committed parents and in part because ideologically it raises a number of important issues.

As I noted, many home schoolers are guided by what they believe are biblical understandings of the family, gender relationships, legitimate knowledge, the importance of "tradition," the role of government, and the economy.[7] While many home schoolers combine beliefs from three of the tendencies I have identified—neoliberalism, neoconservatism, and authoritarian populism—it is the last one that seems to drive a large portion of the movement. For this reason it is not hard to understand why they are often integrated within the tense alliance that has been built among various segments of "the public" in favor of particular policies in education and the larger social world.

SATAN'S THREAT AND THE FORTRESS HOME

As we saw, for many on the right, one of the key enemies is public education. Secular education is turning our children into "aliens" and, by teaching them to question our ideas, is turning them against us. What are often accurate concerns about public schooling that I noted earlier—

its overly bureaucratic nature, its lack of curriculum coherence, its disconnection from the lives, hopes, and cultures of many of its communities, and more—are here often connected to more deep-seated and intimate worries. These worries echo Elaine Pagels's argument that Christianity has historically defined its most fearful satanic threats not from distant enemies, but in relation to very intimate ones.[8] "The most dangerous characteristic of the satanic enemy is that though he will look just like us, he will nevertheless have changed completely."[9]

Some of the roots of this can be found much earlier in the conservative activist Beverly LaHaye's call for the founding of an organization to counter the rising tide of feminism. In support of Concerned Women of America, she spoke of her concern for family, nation, and religion:

> I sincerely believe that God is calling the Christian women of America to draw together in a spirit of unity and purpose to protect the rights of the family. I believe that it is time for us to set aside our doctrinal differences to work for a spiritually renewed America. Who but a woman is as deeply concerned about her children and her home? Who but a women has the time, the intuition, and the drive to restore our nation? . . . They may call themselves feminists or humanists. The label makes little difference, because many of them are seeking the destruction of morality and human freedom.[10]

It is clear from the preceding quote what is seen as the satanic threat and what is at stake here. These fears about the nation, home, family, children's "innocence," religious values, and traditional views of gender relations are sutured together into a more general fear of the destruction of a moral compass and personal freedom. "Our" world is disintegrating around us. Its causes are not the economically destructive policies of the globalizing economy,[11] not the decisions of an economic elite, and not the ways in which, say, our kind of economy turns *all* things—including cherished traditions (and even our children)—into commodities for sale.[12] Rather, the causes are transferred onto those institutions and people who are themselves being constantly buffeted by the same forces—public sector institutions, schooling, poor people of color, other women who have struggled for centuries to build a society that is more responsive to the hopes and dreams of many people who have been denied participation in the public sphere, and so on.[13]

As I noted at the beginning of this chapter, however, it is important not to stereotype individuals involved in this movement. For example, a number of men and women who are activists in rightist movements believe that some elements of feminism did improve the conditions of women overall. By focusing on equal pay for equal work and opening up jobs and opportunities that had been traditionally denied to women who had to work for pay, women activists had benefited many people. However, as was developed in considerable detail in Chapters 4 and 5, for authoritarian populists, feminism and secular institutions in general still tend to break with God's law. They are much too individualistic and misinterpret the divine relationship between families and God. In so doing, many aspects of civil rights legislation, of the public schools' curricula, and so many other parts of secular society are simply wrong. Thus, for example, if one views the Constitution of the United States literally as divinely inspired, then it is not public institutions but the traditional family—as God's chosen unit—that is the core social unit that must be protected by the Constitution.[14] In a time of seeming cultural disintegration, when traditions are under threat and when the idealized family faces ever more externally produced dangers, protecting our families and our children are key elements in returning to God's grace.[15]

Even without these religious elements, a defensive posture is clear in much of the movement. In many ways, the movement toward home schooling mirrors the growth of privatized consciousness in other areas of society. It is an extension of the "suburbanization" of everyday life that is so evident all around us. In essence, it is the equivalent of gated communities and of the privatization of neighborhoods, recreation, parks, and so many other things. It provides a "security zone" both physically and ideologically. Linda Kintz describes it this way:

> As citizens worried about crime, taxes, poor municipal services, and poor schools abandon cities, the increasing popularity of gated communities, . . .

fortress communities, reflects people's desire to retreat. . . . They want to spend more of their tax dollars on themselves instead of others. Further, they take comfort in the social homogeneity of such communities, knowing that their neighbors act and think much as they do.[16]

This "cocooning" is not just about seeking an escape from the problems of the "city" (a metaphor for danger and heterogeneity). It is a rejection of the entire *idea* of the city. Cultural and intellectual diversity, complexity, ambiguity, uncertainly, and proximity to the Other, all these are to be shunned.[17] In place of the city is the engineered pastoral, the neat and well-planned universe where things (and people) are in their "rightful place" and reality is safe and predictable.

Yet in so many ways such a movement mirrors something else. It is a microcosm of the increasing segmentation of American society in general. As we move to a society segregated by residence, race, economic opportunity, and income, "purity" is increasingly more apt to be found in the fact that upper classes send their children to elite private schools; where neighborliness is determined by property values; where evangelical Christians, ultraorthodox Jews, and others only interact with each other and their children are schooled in private religious schools or schooled at home.[18] A world free of conflict, uncertainty, the voice and culture of the Other—in a word I used before, cocooning—is the ideal.[19]

Home schooling, thus, has many similarities with the Internet. It enables the creation of "virtual communities" that are perfect for those with specialized interests. It gives individuals a new ability to "personalize" information, to choose what they want to know or what they find personally interesting. However, as many commentators are beginning to recognize, unless we are extremely cautious, "customizing our lives" could radically undermine the strength of local communities, many of which are already woefully weak. As Andrew Shapiro puts it,

Shared experience is an indisputably essential ingredient [in the formation of local communities]; without it there can be no chance for mutual understanding, empathy and social cohesion. And this is precisely what personalization threatens to delete. A lack of common information would deprive individuals of a starting point for democratic dialogue.[20]

Even with the evident shortcomings of many public schools, at the very least they provide "a kind of social glue, a common cultural reference point in our polyglot, increasingly multicultural society."[21] Yet, whether called personalizing or cocooning, it is exactly this common reference point that is rejected by many within the home schooling movement's pursuit of "freedom" and "choice."

This particular construction of the meaning of freedom is of considerable moment, since there is a curious contradiction within such conservatism's obsession with freedom. In many ways this emphasis on freedom is, paradoxically, based on a *fear* of freedom.[22] Freedom is valued, but also loathed as a site of danger, of "a world out of control." Many home schoolers reject public schooling out of concern for equal time for their beliefs. They want "equality." Yet they have a specific vision of equality, because coupled with their fear of things out of control is a powerful anxiety that the nation's usual understanding of equality will produce uniformity.[23] But this feared uniformity is not seen as the same as the religious and cultural homogeneity sponsored by the conservative project. It is a very different type of uniformity—one in which the fear that "we are all the same" actually speaks to a loss of religious particularity. Thus, again at the heart of this movement lies another paradox: we want everyone to be like "us" (this is a "Christian nation"; governments must bow before "a higher authority");[24] but we want the right to be different—a difference based on being God's elect group. Uniformity weakens our specialness. This tension between knowing one is a member of God's elect people and thus by definition different, and also being so certain that one is correct that the world needs to be changed to fit one's image, is one of the central paradoxes behind authoritarian populist impulses. For some home schoolers, the paradox is solved by withdrawal of one's children from the public sphere in order to maintain their difference. And for still others, this allows them to prepare themselves and their children with an armor of Christian beliefs that will enable them to go forth into the world later on to bring God's word to those who are not among the elect. Once again, let us declare our particularity, our difference, to better prepare ourselves to bring the unanointed world to our set of uniform beliefs.

ATTACKING THE STATE

At the base of this fear both of the loss of specialness and of becoming uniform in the "wrong way" is a sense that the state is intervening in our daily lives in quite powerful ways, ways that are causing even more losses. It isn't possible to understand the growth of home schooling unless we connect it to the history of the attack on the public sphere in general and on the government (the state) in particular. To better comprehend the antistatist impulses that lie behind a good deal of the home schooling movement, I need to place these impulses in a longer historical and social context. Some history and theory is necessary here.

One of the keys to this feeling of antistatism is the development of what Clarke and Newman have called the "managerial state."[25] This was an active state that combined bureaucratic administration and professionalism. The organization of the state centered around the application of specific rules of coordination. Routinization and predictability are among the hallmarks of such a state. This was to be coupled with a second desirable trait, that of social, political, and personal neutrality, rather than nepotism and favoritism. This bureaucratic routinization and predictability would be balanced by an emphasis on professional discretion. Here, bureaucratically regulated professionals such as teachers and administrators would still have an element of irreducible autonomy based on their training and qualifications. Their skills and judgment were to be trusted, if they acted fairly and impartially. Yet fairness and impartiality were not enough; the professional also personalized the managerial state. Professionals such as teachers made the state "approachable" not only by signifying neutrality but also by acting in nonanonymous ways to foster the "public good" and to "help" individuals and families.[26]

Of course, such bureaucratic and professional norms were there not only to benefit "clients." They acted to protect the state, by providing it with legitimacy. (The state is impartial, fair, and acts in the interests of everyone.) They also served to insulate professional judgments from critical scrutiny. (As holders of expert knowledge, we—teachers, social workers, state employees—are the ones who are to be trusted since we know best.)

Thus, from the end of World War II until approximately the mid-1970s, there was a "settlement," a compromise, in which an activist welfare state was seen as legitimate. It was sustained by a triple legitimacy. There was (largely) bipartisan support for the state to provide and manage a larger part of social life, a fact that often put it above a good deal of party politics. Bureaucratic administration promised to act impartially for the benefit of everyone. And professionals employed by the state, such as teachers and other educators, were there to apply expert knowledge to serve the public.[27] This compromise was widely accepted and provided public schools and other public institutions with a strong measure of support since by and large the vast majority of people continued to believe that schools and other state agencies did in fact act professionally and impartially in the public good.

This compromise came under severe attack as the fiscal crisis deepened and as competition over scarce economic, political, and cultural resources grew more heated in the 1970s and beyond. The political forces of conservative movements used this crisis, often in quite cynical and manipulative—and well-funded—ways. The state was criticized for denying the opportunity for consumers to exercise choice. The welfare state was seen as gouging the citizen (as a taxpayer) to pay for public handouts for those who ignored personal responsibility for their actions. These "scroungers" from the underclass were seen as sexually promiscuous, immoral, and lazy as opposed to the "rest of us" who were hardworking, industrious, and moral. They supposedly are a drain on all of us economically, and state-sponsored support of them leads to the collapse of the family and traditional morality.[28] These arguments may not have been totally accurate, but they were effective.[29]

This blending together of neoliberal and neoconservative attacks led to a particular set of critiques against the state, critiques that connected dramatically with the authoritarian populist mistrust of elites. For many people, the state was no longer the legitimate and neutral upholder of the public good. Instead the welfare state was an active agent of national decline, as well as an economic drain on the country's (and the family's) resources. In the words of Clarke and Newman:

> Bureaucrats were identified as actively hostile to the public—hiding behind the impersonality of regulations and "red tape" to deny choice, building bureaucratic empires at the expense of providing service, and insulated from the "real world" pressures of competition by their monopolistic position. Professionals were arraigned as motivated by self-interest, exercising power over would-be costumers, denying choice through the dubious claim that "professionals know best." Worse still, . . . liberalism . . . was viewed as undermining personal responsibility and family authority and as prone to trendy excesses such as egalitarianism, anti-discrimination policies, moral relativism or child-centeredness.[30]

These moral, political, and economic concerns were easily transferred to public schooling, since for many people the school was and is the public institution closest to them in their daily life. Hence, public schooling and the teaching and curricula found within it became central targets of attack. Curricula and teachers were not impartial, but elitist. School systems were imposing the Other's morality on "us." And "real Americans" who were patriotic, religious, and moral—as opposed to everyone else—were suffering and were the new oppressed.[31] While this position fits into a long history of the paranoid style of American cultural politics and it was often based on quite inaccurate stereotypes, it does point to a profound sense of alienation that many people feel.

Much of this antistatism of course was fueled by the constant attention given in the media and in public pronouncements to "incompetent" teachers who are overpaid and have short working days and long vacations.[32] We should not minimize the effects of the conservative attacks on schools for their supposed inefficiency, wasting of financial resources, and lack of connection to the economy. After years of well-orchestrated attacks, it would be extremely odd if one did not find that the effects on popular consciousness were real. The fact that a number of these criticisms may be *partly* accurate should not be dismissed. There undoubtedly is a small group of teachers who treat teaching as simply a job that gives them many holidays and free time in the summer. Administrative costs and bureaucratic requirements in schools have risen. Parents and local communities do have a justifiable right to worry about whether their daughters and sons will have decent jobs when they leave school, especially in a time when our supposedly booming economy has left millions of people behind and many of the jobs being created are anything but fulfilling and secure.[33] (The fact that the school has very little to do with this is important.)

Yet it is not only worries about teachers that fuel this movement. As I showed, public schools themselves are seen as extremely dangerous places. These schools were institutions that threatened one's very soul. Temptations and godlessness were everywhere within them. God's truths were expunged from the curriculum and God's voice could no longer be heard. Prayers were now illegal and all of the activities that bound one's life to scriptural realities were seen as deviant.

Even with the negative powerful emotions that such senses of loss and disconnection create, an additional element has entered into the emotional economy being created here with a crushing force. For an increasingly large number of parents, public schools are now seen as threatening in an even more powerful way. They are dangerous bodily; that is, they are seen as filled with physical dangers to the very life of one's children. The spate of shootings in schools in the United States has had a major impact on the feelings of insecurity that parents have about their children. Stories of violence-ridden schools, ones that were worrisome but were seen as largely an "urban problem" involving the poor and children of color, were already creating an anti–public school sentiment among many conservative parents. The horrors of seeing students shoot other students, and now not in those supposedly troubled urban schools but in the suburban areas that had grown after people fled the city, exacerbated the situation. If even the schools of affluent suburbia were sites of danger, then the *only* remaining safe haven was the fortress home.[34]

Fears, no matter how powerful they are or whether they are justified or not, are not enough, however. That a person will act on her or his fears is made more or less probable by the availability of resources to support taking action. It is an almost taken for granted point, but important nonetheless, that the growth of home schooling has been stimulated by the wider accessibility to tools that make it easier for parents to engage in it. Among the most important is the Internet.[35] Scores of Web sites are available that give advice, that provide technical and emotional support, that tell the stories of successful home schoolers, and that are more than willing to sell material at a profit. The fact that, like the conservative evangelical movement in general, a larger portion of home schoolers than before seem to have the economic resources to afford computers means that economic capital can be mobilized in antischool strategies in more flexible and dynamic ways than in earlier periods of the home schooling movement.[36]

Since home schooling is often done using the Web, it is useful to see what some of the sites say. The Teaching Home, based in Portland, Oregon, is one of the central resources for conservative Christians who wish to home school.[37] On its Web site, after the following general statement on the question "Why do families home school?" a number of answers are given:

> Many Christian parents are committed to educating their children at home because of their conviction that this is God's will for their family. They are concerned for the spiritual training and character development as well as the social and academic welfare of their children.

Among the advantages listed are:

> Parents can present all academic subjects from a biblical perspective and include spiritual training.

"The fear of the LORD is the beginning of wisdom, and the knowledge of
the Holy One is understanding" (Prov. 9:10 NAS).

Home schooling makes quality time available to train and influence children in all areas in an integrated way.

Each child receives individual attention and has his unique needs met.

Parents can control destructive influences such as various temptations, false
teachings (including secular humanism and occult influences of the
New Age movement), negative peer pressure, and unsafe environments.

Children gain respect for their parents as teachers.

The family experiences unity, closeness, and mutual enjoyment of one another as they spend more time working together.

Children develop confidence and independent thinking away from the peer
pressure to conform and in the security of their own home.

Children have time to explore new interests and to think.

Communication between different age groups is enhanced.

Tutorial-style education helps each child achieve his full educational potential.

Flexible scheduling can accommodate parents' work and vacation times and
allow time for many activities.

This list is broader than might be allowed in some of the stereotypes of
what home schooling advocates—particularly religiously conservative
ones—are like. There is a focus on wanting their children to explore, to
achieve their full academic potential, to have "his" needs met. Yet, in this
diverse list of advantages, certain themes come to the fore, themes that resonate deeply with those I described in the prior two chapters. At the top is
biblical authority, with knowledge and understanding connected with "fear
of the LORD." "Real" knowledge is grounded in what the Holy One has
ordained. The role of the parent is largely one of "training," of influencing
one's children in all areas so that they are safe from the outside influences
of a secular society. God/home/family is pure; the rest of the world—
secular humanism, peers, popular culture—are forms of pollution, temptations, dangers. That the male pronoun is used throughout is indicative
of God's wish for the man of the house to be God's chosen leader.[38]

Yet saying these things must not be used as an excuse to deny the elements of concern that parents such as these express. They are *deeply* worried about the lives and futures of their children, children for whom they are fully willing to sacrifice an immense amount. They do want there to be a caring environment for their children, one in which all family members respect and care for each other. There are powerful positive moments in these statements. In a time when many groups of varying religious and political sentiments express the concern that children are ignored in this society, that they are simply seen as present and future consumers by people who only care whether a profit is made off of them, that our major institutions are less responsive than they should be, and that there are elements of popular culture that are negative as well as positive—all these sentiments are central to the concerns of home schoolers as well.

Given what I have just said, we do need to recognize that there are elements of good sense in the critique of the state made by both the left and the right, such as the home schoolers I have discussed above. The government has assumed all too often that the only true holders of expertise in education, social welfare, and so on are those in positions of formal authority. This has led to a situation of overbureaucratization. It has also led to the state being partly "colonized" by a particular fraction of the new middle class that seeks to ensure its own mobility and its own positions by employing the state for its own purposes.[39] Some schools have become sites of danger given the levels of alienation and meaninglessness in this society—and the dominance of violence as an "imaginary solution" in the "popular" media. However, there is a world of difference between, say, acknowledging that the state has some historical tendencies to become overly bureaucratic and to not listen carefully enough to the expressed needs of the people it is supposed to serve and a blanket rejection of public control and public institutions such as schools. This has not only led to cocooning, but it threatens the gains made by large groups of disadvantaged people for whom the possible destruction of public schooling is nothing short of a disaster. The final section of my analysis turns to a discussion of this.

PUBLIC AND PRIVATE

We need to think *relationally* when we ask who will be the major beneficiaries of the attack on the state and the movement toward home schooling. What if gains that are made by one group of people come at the expense of other, even more culturally and economically oppressed groups? As we shall see, this is not an inconsequential worry in this instance.

A helpful distinction here is that between a politics of redistribution and a politics of recognition. In the first (redistribution), the concern is for socioeconomic injustice. Here, the political-economic system of a society creates conditions that lead to exploitation (having the fruits of your labor appropriated for the benefit of others), and/or economic marginalization (having one's paid work confined to poorly paid and undesirable jobs or having no real access to the routes to serious and better paying jobs), and/or deprivation (being constantly denied the material that would lead to an adequate standard of living). All these socioeconomic injustices lead to arguments about whether this is a just or fair society and whether identifiable groups of people actually have equality of resources.[40]

The second dynamic (recognition) is often related to redistribution in the real world, but it has its own specific history and differential power relations as well. It is related to the politics of culture and symbols. In this case, injustice is rooted in a society's social patterns of representation and interpretation. Examples of this include cultural domination (being constantly subjected to patterns of interpretation or cultural representation that are alien to one's own or even hostile to it), nonrecognition (basically being rendered invisible in the dominant cultural forms in the society), and disrespect (having oneself routinely stereotyped or maligned in public representations in the media, schools, government policies, or in everyday conduct).[41] These kinds of issues surrounding the politics of recognition are central to the identities and sense of injustice of many home schoolers. Indeed, they provide the organizing framework for their critique of public schooling and their demand that they be allowed to teach their children outside of such state control.

Although both forms of injustice are important, it is absolutely crucial that we recognize that an adequate response to one must not lead to the exacerbation of the other. That is, responding to the claims of injustice in recognition by one group (say religious conservatives) must not make the conditions that lead to exploitation, economic marginalization, and deprivation more likely to occur for other groups. Nor must it lead to the denial of recognition to those who are even more oppressed. Unfortunately, this may be the case for some of the latent effects of home schooling.

Because of this, it is vitally important not to separate the possible effects of home schooling from what we are beginning to know about the possible consequences of neoliberal policies in general in education. As I argued earlier and as Whitty, Power, and Halpin have shown in their review of the international research on voucher and choice plans, one of the latent effects of such policies has been the reproduction of traditional hierarchies of class and race. That is, the programs clearly have differential benefits in which those who already possess economic and cultural capital reap significantly more benefits than those who do not. This is patterned in very much the same ways as the stratification of economic, political, and cultural power produces inequalities in nearly every socioeconomic sphere.[42] One of the hidden consequences that is emerging from the expanding conservative critique of public institutions, including schools, is a growing antitax movement in which those who have chosen to place their children in privatized, marketized, and home schools do not want to pay taxes to support the schooling of the Other.[43]

The wider results of this are becoming clear—a declining tax base for schooling, social services, health care, housing, and anything "public" for those populations (usually in the most economically depressed urban and rural areas) who suffer the most from the economic dislocations and inequalities that so deeply characterize this nation. Thus, a politics of recognition—I want to guarantee "choice" for my children based on my identity and special needs—has begun to have extremely negative effects on the politics of redistribution. It is absolutely crucial that we recognize this. If it is the case that the emergence of educational markets has consistently benefited the most-advantaged parents and students and has consistently disadvantaged both economically poor parents and students and parents and students of color,[44] then we need to critically examine the latent effects of the growth of home schooling in the same light. Will it be the case that social justice loses in this equation just as it did and does in many of the other highly publicized programs of "choice"?

We now have emerging evidence to this effect, evidence that points to the fact that social justice often does lose with the expansion of home schooling in some states. A case in point is the way in which the ongoing debate over the use of public money for religious purposes in education is often subverted through manipulation of loopholes that are only available to particular groups. Religiously motivated home schoolers are currently engaged in exploiting public funding not only in ways that are hidden, but also in ways that raise serious questions about the drain on economic resources during a time of severe budget crises in all too many school districts.

Let me say more about this, since it provides an important instance of my argument that gains in recognition for some groups (say, home schoolers) can have decidedly negative effects in other spheres such as the politics of redistribution and in claims to recognition by other groups. In California, for example, charter schools have been used as a mechanism to gain public money for home schoolers. Charter school legislation in California has been employed in very "interesting" ways to accomplish this. In one recent study, for example, 50 percent of charter schools were serving home schoolers. "Independent study" charter schools (a creative pseudonym for computer-linked home schooling) have been used by both school districts and parents to gain money that otherwise might not have been available. While this does demonstrate the ability of school districts to strategically use charter school legislation to get money that might have been lost when parents withdraw their children to home school them, it also signifies something else. In this and other cases, the money given to parents for enrolling in such independent study charter schools was used by the parents to purchase religious material produced and sold by Bob Jones University, one of the most conservative religious schools in the entire nation.[45]

Thus, public money not legally available for overtly sectarian material is used to purchase religious curricula under the auspices of charter school legislation. Yet unlike all curricula used in public schools that *must* be publicly accountable in terms of its content and costs, the material purchased for home schooling has no public accountability whatsoever. While this does give greater choice to home schoolers and does enable them to act on a politics of recognition, it not only takes money away from other students who do not have the economic resources to afford computers in the home, but it denies them a say in what the community's children will learn about themselves and their cultures, histories, values, and so on. Given that a number of textbooks used in fundamentalist religious schools expressly state such things as Islam is a false religion and embody similar claims that many citizens would find deeply offensive,[46] serious questions can be raised about whether it is appropriate for public money to be used to teach such content without any public accountability.

Thus, two things are going on here. Money is being drained from already hard-pressed school districts to support home schooling. Just as important, curricular materials that support the identities of religiously motivated groups are being paid for by the public *without* any accountability, even though these materials may act in such a way as to deny the claims for recognition of one of the fastest-growing religions in the nation, Islam. This raises more general and quite serious issues about how the claims for recognition by religious conservatives can be financially supported when they may at times actually support discriminatory teaching. Here, one form of recognition politics interferes with another group's justifiable claims to recognition and legitimacy, and especially a group (Islam) that has suffered immensely from both stereotyping and discrimination in the United States and elsewhere.

I don't wish to be totally negative here. After all, this is a complicated issue in which there may be justifiable worries among home schoolers that their culture and values are not being listened to. But it must be vative cultural and political movements into the arms of such alliances by their defensiveness and lack of responsiveness and by their silencing of democratic discussion and criticism. Of course, sometimes these criticisms are unjustified or are politically motivated by undemocratic agendas. However, this must not serve as an excuse for a failure to open the doors of our schools to the intense public debate that makes public education a living and vital part of our democracy.[47]

We have models for doing exactly that, as my points about the democratic schools movement in earlier chapters demonstrate.[48] While I do not want to be overly romantic here, I argue in more detail in my concluding chapter that there *are* models of curricula and teaching that are related to community sentiment, that are committed to social justice and fairness, and that are based in schools where both teachers and students want to be. If schools do not do this, all too many parents may be pushed in the direction of antischool sentiment. This would be a tragedy both for the public school system and for our already withered sense of community that is increasingly under threat. Even though state-supported schools have often served as arenas through which powerful social divisions are partly reproduced, at least in the United States such schools have also served as powerful sites for the mobilization of collective action and for the preservation of the very possibility of democratic struggle.[49] As one of the few remaining institutions that *is* still public, struggles over it are crucial. This is obviously a tightrope we need to negotiate. How do we uphold the vision of a truly public institution at the same time as we rigorously criticize its functioning? In the United States, this is one of the tasks that the critical educators involved in *Democratic Schools* and the National Coalition of Education Activists have set for themselves.[50] They have recognized that schools have both contradictory impulses and pressures upon them, especially in a time of conservative modernization. It is not romantic to actively work on and through those contradictions so that the collective memory of earlier and partly successful struggles is not lost. Nor is it romantic to engage in what I have called elsewhere "nonreformist reforms," reforms whose aim is to expand the space of counterhegemonic action in public institutions.[51] Yet, to do this, it is necessary to defend the public nature of such public spaces.

Raymond Williams may have expressed it best when—positioning himself as an optimist without any illusions—he reminded us of the importance of the *mutual* determination of the meanings and values that should guide our social life. In expressing his commitment toward "the long revolution," his words are worth remembering. "We must speak for hope, as long as it doesn't mean suppressing the nature of the danger."[52] There are identifiable dangers to identifiable groups of people in public schooling as we know it. But the privatizing alternatives may be much worse. This tension between realism and hope forms the context for my concluding chapter.

Chapter 7

Righting Wrongs and Interrupting the Right

CULTURE COUNTS

My task in this book has not simply been to castigate the right, although there is a bit of fun in doing so. Rather, in each chapter I have also sought to illuminate the elements of good sense, not only bad sense, that are found within the various factions of the rightist alliance. I have several reasons for doing so. First, people who find certain elements of conservative modernization relevant to their lives are not puppets. They are not dupes who have little understanding of the "real" relations of this society. This smacks of earlier reductive analyses that were based in ideas of "false consciousness." My position is very different. I maintain that the reason that some of the arguments coming from the various factions of this new hegemonic bloc are listened to is because they *are* connected to aspects of the realities that people experience. The tense alliance of neoliberals, neoconservatives, authoritarian populist religious activists, and the professional and managerial new middle class only works because there has been a very creative articulation of themes that resonate deeply with the experiences, fears, hopes, and dreams of people as they go about their daily lives. The right has often been more than a little manipulative in its articulation of these themes. It has integrated them within racist nativist discourses, within economically dominant forms of understanding, and within a problematic sense of "tradition." But this integration could only occur if they were organized around people's understanding of their real material and cultural lives.

The second reason I have stressed the tension between good and bad sense—aside from my profound respect for Antonio Gramsci's writings about this—has to do with my belief that we have witnessed a major educational accomplishment over the past three decades in many countries. All too often, we assume that educational and cultural struggles are epiphenomenal. The real battles occur in the paid workplace—the "economy." Not only is this a strikingly reductive sense of what the economy is (its focus on paid, not unpaid, work; its neglect of the fact that, say, cultural institutions such as schools are also places where paid work goes on, etc.),[1] it also ignores what the right has actually done. Conservative modernization has radically reshaped the commonsense of society. It has worked in every sphere—the economic, the political, and the cultural—to alter the basic categories we use to evaluate our institutions and our public and private lives. It has established new identities. It has recognized that to win in the state, you must win in civil society. The accomplishment of such a vast educational project has many implications. It shows how important cultural struggles are. And, oddly enough, it gives reason for hope. It forces us to ask a significant question. *If the right can do this, why can't we?*

I do not mean this as a rhetorical question. As I have argued throughout this book, the right has shown how powerful the struggle over meaning and identity can be. While we should not want to emulate rightist groups' often cynical and manipulative processes, the fact that they have had such success in pulling people under their ideological umbrella has much to teach us. Granted there are real differences in money and power between the forces of conservative modernization and those whose lives are being tragically altered by the policies and practices coming from the alliance. But the right wasn't as powerful thirty years ago as it is now. It collectively organized. It created a decentered unity, one where each element sacrificed some of its particular agenda to push forward on those areas that bound them together. Can't we do the same?

I believe that we can, but only if we face up to the realities and dynamics of power in unromantic ways. As I argued in Chapter 3, the romantic possibilitarian rhetoric of some of the writers on critical pedagogy is not sufficiently based on a tactical or strategic analysis of the current situation nor is it sufficiently grounded in its understanding of the reconstructions of discourse and movements that are occurring in all too many places. Here I follow Cameron McCarthy, who wisely reminds us, "We must think possibility within constraint; that is the condition of our time."[2]

As I have been at pains to show in this book, cultural struggles are not epiphenomenal. They *count,* and they count in institutions throughout society. For dominant groups to exercise leadership, large numbers of people must be convinced that the maps of reality circulated by those with the most economic, political, and cultural power are indeed wiser than other alternatives. Dominant groups do this by attaching these maps to the elements of good sense that people have and by changing the very meaning of the key concepts and their accompanying structures of feeling that provide the centers of gravity for our hopes, fears, and dreams about this society. The right has been much more successful in doing this than the left, in part because it has been able to craft—through hard and lengthy economic, political, and cultural efforts—a tense but still successful alliance that has shifted the major debates over education and economic and social policy onto its own terrain.

Evidence of this is all around us in the terms we use, in the arguments in which we engage, indeed even in many of the cultural resources we employ to imagine alternative futures. For example, as I am completing the writing of this book, one of the top-selling books on the *New York Times* fiction list is Tim LaHaye (yes, the same Tim LaHaye) and Jerry Jenkins's *The Indwelling,* the seventh of a series of books about "true believers" who confront the "Antichrist."[3] The imagined future is a time of "rapture" where the good are taken up to heaven and the bad are condemned to eternal damnation. The identity of each of these groups is predictable, given what I described in the previous three chapters. In a number of ways, then, the authoritarian populist "outside" has indeed moved to become the inside. It has creatively learned how to use the codes of popular adventure and science fiction novels to build an imaginative space of possibility, and a "muscular" yet sensitive Christianity, that gives meaning to people's daily lives and hopes.[4]

Just as these spaces create imagined futures, so too do they help create identities. Neoliberalism creates policies and practices that embody the enterprising and constantly strategizing entrepreneur out of the possessive individualism it establishes as the ideal citizen. Neoconservatism creates imagined pasts as the framework for imagined and stable futures, futures in which identities are based on people knowing the knowledge and values that neoconservatives themselves have decided "have stood the test of time." Authoritarian populist religious conservatives also have an imagined past where a society, based on God's knowledge and values, has pregiven identities that enable women and men to rearticulate the neoliberal ideology of "choice" and to act in what are seen as godly ways toward bringing society to God. And managerialism establishes new identities for the professional and managerial middle class, identities that give new meaning to their lives and enable them to recapture their feelings of worthiness and efficacy. Out of all these multiple spaces and identities, and the conflicts, tensions, and compromises that their interactions generate, policies evolve. These policies are almost never purely from only one of the elements within this bloc. Rather, they often embody a rich mix that somehow must accommodate as many themes as possible from within the multiple forces of conservative modernization—without alienating those groups believed to be significant who are not yet integrated under the hegemonic umbrella of the right but who the right would like to bring under its leadership in the future.

This is a truly difficult task, and it is filled with contradictory impulses. Yet, even with this movement's contradictions and tensions, it has moved the balance of forces significantly to the right. Educational policies have been part of that move. In fact, education not only has been drawn along by the pressure of these rightist waves, it has actually played a major role in building these waves. The conservative alliance has paid attention to education—both formal and informal—and it has paid off for them. As I showed in Chapter 3, even in my critical deconstruction of the effects of neoliberal, neoconservative, and managerial policies and practices in a number of countries, it is *their* policies that have provided the outlines of the debates in which we engage.

CONTRADICTORY REFORMS

Throughout this book, I have demonstrated that policies often have strikingly unforeseen consequences. Reforms that are instituted with good intentions may have hidden effects that are more than a little problematic. I have shown that the effects of some of the favorite reforms of neoliberals and neoconservatives, for instance—voucher plans, national or statewide curricula, and national or statewide testing can serve as examples—quite often reproduce or even worsen inequalities. Thus, we should be very cautious about accepting what may seem to be meritorious intentions at face value. Intentions are too often contradicted by how reforms may function in practice. This is true not only for large-scale transformations of educational policies and governance, but also about moves to change the ways curriculum and teaching go on in schools.

The framework I have employed to understand these tendencies is grounded in what in cultural theory is called the act of repositioning. It in essence says that the best way to understand what any set of institutions, policies, and practices does is to see it from the standpoint of those who have the least power.[5] That is, every institution, policy, and practice—and especially those that now dominate education and the larger society—establish relations of power in which some voices are heard and some are not. While it is not preordained that those voices that will be heard most clearly are also those who have the most economic, cultural, and social capital, it is most likely that this will be the case. After all, we do not exist on a level playing field. Many economic, social, and educational policies when actually put in place tend to benefit those who already have advantages.

These points may seem overly rhetorical and too abstract, but unfortunately there is no small amount of truth in them. For example, in a time when all too much of the discourse around educational reform is focused on vouchers and choice plans on the one hand and on proposals for national or state curricula, standards, and testing on the other, as I have shown throughout this volume a good deal of international evidence now indicates that such policies may actually reproduce or even worsen class, gender, and race inequalities. Thus, existing structures of economic and cultural power often lead to a situation in which what may have started out in some educators' or legislators' minds as an attempt to make things better, in the end is all too usually transformed into another set of mechanisms for social stratification.

Although much of this situation is due to the ways in which race, gender, class, and "ability" act as structural realities in this society, some of it is related to the hesitancy of policymakers to take seriously enough the complicated ways in which education is itself a political act. These very politics and the structurally generated inequalities that stand behind them provide much of the substance underpinning the organizational principles of this volume.

Near the end of the introductory section of a recent volume on the politics of educational policies and practices, *Learning as a Political Act,* the editors state that as progressives they are committed to an "intellectual solidarity that seeks to lay bare the ideas and histories of groups that have been silenced in mainstream educational arenas."[6] There are several key concepts in this quote—intellectual solidarity, laying bare, silencing. Each speaks to a complicated history, and each phrase again says something about the position from which this book has been written. These too are what I called "key words" in Chapter 1. They come from a very different tradition than that provided by the linguistic mapping of markets. They also speak to a different politics of official knowledge.

Over the past decade, it has become increasingly clear that the school curriculum has become a battleground. Stimulated in large part by neoliberal complaints about "economically useless" knowledge, neoconservative laments about the supposed loss of discipline and lack of "real knowledge," and by religious authoritarian populists' relentless attacks on schools for their supposed loss of God-given "traditional" values, discussions of what should be taught in schools and how it should be taught are now as contentious as at any time in our history.

Evidence of this is not hard to find. In his repeated call for a return to a curriculum of "facts," E. D. Hirsch Jr. argues that schools have been taken over by progressive educators from Rousseau to Dewey,[7] a claim that has almost no empirical warrant at all and largely demonstrates how disconnected Hirsch is from the daily life of schools. Most schooling in the United States is already fact-driven. In addition, school districts throughout the country are constantly looking over their shoulders, worried that their reading, social studies, or mathematics programs will be challenged by the forces of the authoritarian religious right—although as I demonstrate in *Cultural Politics and Education,* sometimes school systems themselves create the conditions for the growth of rightist anti-school movements in their own communities by being less than democratic in their involvement of the community.[8] Other evidence of such contentiousness is visible in the fact that the contents of the mathematics curriculum was even recently debated in the editorial pages of the *New York Times,* where spokespersons for constructivist and traditional curricula went head to head. Many more instances might be cited. But clearly the debate over "What knowledge is of most worth" has taken on more than a few political overtones.[9]

Much of the debate over this goes on with little empirical substance. For example, the argument that we must "return" to teaching, say, mathematics in "traditional" ways is obviously partly an ideological one. (We need to restore discipline; students have too much freedom; "bad" knowledge has pushed "good" knowledge to the sidelines.) Yet it is also based on a claim that such a return will lead to higher achievement and ultimately to a more competitive economy. Here, neoliberal and neoconservative emphases are joined with authoritarian populist mistrust of child-centeredness. This is where Jo Boaler's recent richly detailed qualitative and quantitative comparison of mathematics curricula and teaching enters.[10]

Boaler engages in a fine-grained analysis of two secondary schools with decidedly different emphases. While her book is based on data from England, as in my analysis of the international literature in Chapter 3 its implications are again profound for debates over curriculum and teaching in the United States and elsewhere as well. Both schools are largely working class, with some minority and middle-class populations as well. Both sets of students had attended our equivalent of middle schools that were dominated by more traditional academic methods. And both had similar achievement profiles. One school overtly focused on preparing its students for national tests. Its program was almost totally teacher directed, organized around textbooks that were geared to the national tests, ability grouped, and run in such a way that speed and accuracy of computations and the learning of procedural rules for dealing with mathematical problems were highly valued—all those things that traditionalists here say are currently missing in mathematics instruction. Furthermore, the boundary between mathematics and both the real world and other subjects was strong.[11] The other school did not group by ability. It was decidedly more "progressive" both in its attitude toward students (there was a more relaxed communication style between teachers and students; student input was sought on the curriculum) and in its mathematics program. In this second school, the instruction was project-based, with a minimum of textbook-based teaching and a maximum of cooperative work among the students. The boundary between mathematics and "real-world" problems was weak.

The first school was quiet, on-task, well organized–the very embodiment of the dream of nearly all elements of conservative modernization. The second was more noisy, students were not always fully on-task, and had very flexible time schedules. Both schools had dedicated and hardworking teachers. Yet the differences in the results were striking, both in terms of overall achievement and in terms of the differential effects of each orientation on the students themselves.

The more traditional school, with its driving concern for "covering material" that would be on the test, stressed textbook knowledge and moved relatively rapidly from topic to topic. The more student centered approach of the second school sacrificed some coverage, but it also enabled students to more fully understand the material. By and large, students in the first school actually did less well on the standardized tests than the second, especially but not only on those parts of the tests that needed them to actually think mathematically, in large part because they could not generalize to new contexts as well as did those students who had used their mathematics in more varied (though more time-consuming) projects. Further—and of great importance for equity—young women in the second school did consistently better in a more cooperative atmosphere that stressed understanding and use rather than coverage. The same held true for social class. Working-class students were consistently disadvantaged in the more pressured and text- and test-based agenda of traditional mathematics instruction.

This is a complex situation and Boaler is talking about general tendencies here. But her overall conclusions are clear and are supported by a very nice combination of data. In sum, the claim that a return to (actually, given the fact that most mathematics instruction is still chalk and talk and textbook based, it would be much more honest to say the *continuation of*) the traditional mathematics programs that the critics are demanding neither increases students' mathematical competence nor their ability to use their mathematical knowledge in productive ways. While it may keep classrooms quiet and students under control, it may also systematically disadvantage young women—including, as Boaler shows, the brightest young women—and economically disadvantaged students.[12] Finally, it may have one other effect, a strengthening of students' dislike of mathematics and their feelings that it is simply irrelevant for their future. If this is true for mathematics, it is worth considering the hidden negative effects of the more general policies being proposed by neoconservative reformers who wish to return to what they have constructed, rather romantically, as "the tradition" in all subjects.

If Boaler's conclusions are even partly generalizable, as I think they may very well be, the hidden effects of certain reform movements may not be what we had in mind. Tighter control over the curriculum, the tail of the test wagging the dog of the teacher and the curriculum, more pressure, more reductive accountability plans—all this may lead to less equitable results, not more. Boredom, alienation, and increased inequalities are not the ideal results of schooling. Once again, looking outside of our usual all-too-limited and parochial boundaries can be more than a little beneficial. The careful research underpinning Boaler's volume needs to be taken seriously by anyone who assumes that in our unequal society there is a direct relationship between policy intentions and policy results. There isn't.

One of the most important tasks of critical education, therefore, is an empirical one. Just as Boaler did, we need to make research public not only on the negative effects of the policies of conservative modernization, but just as importantly on the positive effects of more socially and educationally critical alternatives. A good example of this is the SAGE program in Wisconsin, where significantly reducing class size within schools that historically have served a larger portion of dispossessed people has had much more robust results than, say, marketization and voucher plans.[13] This is one form of interrupting dominant discourses and policies, and much more of it needs to be done. However, in doing this we cannot simply rely on the dominant forms of what counts as evidence. In Linda Tuhiwai Smith's words, we need "decolonizing methodologies."[14] I return to the issue of making such things as alternative policies and practices public later on in this concluding chapter.

"RACING" TOWARD EDUCATIONAL REFORM

How else can these retrogressive movements be interrupted? Let me first speak relatively generally about facing the realities of differential power head on and what this means. The commitment to face such reality rests once again on what I argued at the outset of this chapter—the act of repositioning, of seeing the world through the eyes of the most oppressed of our fellow citizens.

In a number of other books, I have brought together data demonstrating the nature of the structured inequalities that characterize this society. I shall not rehearse them here. Suffice it to say that in spite of our overly individualized discourses to describe the society in which we live, class, race, and gender structures and dynamics are powerfully significant.[15] These structures and dynamics are not simply abstractions, but they inflect even the most mundane aspects of our daily lives. While too many people have either ignored or given up on the power of class analysis, a neglect I have fought consistently for years,[16] perhaps some of my more general points can best be grasped by focusing on race. In their exceptional analysis of the way the discourses of race have operated in the United States, Omi and Winant argue that race is not an "add-on," but is truly constitutive of many of our most taken for granted daily experiences, a point I have reiterated in my discussions of the elements of conservative modernization throughout this book:

> In the U.S., race is present in every institution, every relationship, every individual. This is the case not only for the way society is organized—spatially, culturally, in terms of stratification, etc.—but also for our perceptions and understandings of personal experience. Thus as we watch the videotape of Rodney King being beaten, compare real estate prices in different neighborhoods, size up a potential client, neighbor, or teacher, stand in line at the unemployment office, or carry out a thousand other normal tasks, we are compelled to think racially, to use racial categories and meaning systems in which we have been socialized. Despite exhortations both sincere and hypocritical, it is not possible or even desirable to be "color-blind."[17]

Not only is it not possible to be color-blind, as they go on to say "opposing race requires that we notice race, not ignore it." Only by noticing race can we challenge it, "with its ever-more-absurd reduction of human experience to an essence attributed to all without regard for historical or social context." By placing race squarely in front of us, "we can challenge the state, the institutions of civil society, and ourselves as individuals to combat the legacy of inequality and injustice inherited from the past" and continually reproduced in the present.[18]

Although Omi and Winant were analyzing racial dynamics in the United States, I would hope that by now it is equally clear that their claims extend well beyond these geographical borders to include the UK and many other nations. It would not be possible to understand the history, current status, and multiple effects of educational policy in a large array of nations without placing race as a core element of one's analysis.

Placing race at the center is less easy than one might expect, for one must do this with due recognition of its complexity. Race is not a stable category. What it means, how it is used, by whom, how it is mobilized in public discourse, and its role in educational and more general social policy—all this is contingent and historical. Indeed, it would be misleading to talk of race as an "it." "It" is not a thing, a reified object that can be measured as if it were a simple biological entity. Race is a *construction,* a set of fully social *relationships.* This unfortunately does not stop people from talking about race in simplistic ways that ignore the realities of differential power and histories.[19] Yet complexity needs to be recognized here as well. Racial dynamics have their own histories and are relatively autonomous. But they also participate in, form and are formed by, other relatively autonomous dynamics involving, say, class, colonial and postcolonial realities, and so on—all of which are implicated in and related to the social construction of race. Further, racial dynamics can operate in subtle and powerful ways even when they are not overtly on the minds of the actors involved.

We can make a distinction between intentional and functional explanations here. Intentional explanations are those self-conscious aims that guide our policies and practices. Functional explanations, on the other hand, are concerned with the latent effects of policies and practices.[20] In my mind, the latter are more powerful than the former.

In essence, this rightly turns what is called the genetic fallacy in logic on its head, so to speak. Let me be specific here. We are apt to think of the genetic fallacy in particular ways. We tend to castigate authors who assume that the import and meaning of any position is totally determined by its original grounding. Thus, for example, it is clear that E. L. Thorndike—one of the founders of educational psychology—was a confirmed eugenicist and was deeply committed to the project of "race betterment" and had a vision of education that was inherently undemocratic. Yet one is on shaky ground if one concluded that every aspect of his work is totally "polluted" by his (repugnant) social beliefs. Thorndike's research program may have been epistemologically and empirically problematic, but a different kind of evidence and a more complex analysis is required to debunk all of it than to simply claim (correctly) that he was often racist, sexist, and elitist.[21] Indeed, it is not difficult to find progressive educators drawing on Thorndike's work for support of what were then seen to be radical positions.

When we are talking about racism and reform in current policies, we need to turn the genetic fallacy around. The overt motivations of the sponsors of New Labour's policies in the UK or of the proposals for education such as the establishment of voucher programs or national and state testing in the United States may not have been about race or may have assumed that such proposals would "level the playing field" for everyone. Their intentions may have been self-consciously "meritorious." (I very much mean this play on words.) Yet, as I have shown repeatedly throughout this book, conscious originating motives do not guarantee at all how arguments and policies will be employed, what their multiple and determinate functions and effects will be, whose interests they will ultimately serve, and what identifiable patterns of differential benefits will emerge, given existing and unequal relations of economic, cultural, and social capital and given unequal strategies of converting one form of capital to another in our societies. Indeed, race gets a good deal of its power through its very hiddenness. Nowhere is this more true than in the discourse of markets and standards.

For example, while some commentators may be correct that "the competitive schools market in the UK as envisioned by neo-liberals was created without reference to implications for ethnic minorities,"[22] this may be true only at the level of conscious intentions. While race talk may be overtly absent in the discourse of markets—except as a form of legitimation talk[23]—it remains an absent presence that I believe is fully implicated in the goals and concerns surrounding support for the marketization of education. The sense of economic and educational decline, the belief that private is good and public is bad, and so on is coupled with an often unarticulated sense of loss, a feeling that things are out of control, an anomic feeling that is connected to a sense of loss of one's "rightful place" in the world (an "empire" now in decline), and a fear of the culture and body of the Other. The "private" is the sphere of smooth-running and efficient organizations, of autonomy and individual choice. The "public" is out of control, messy, heterogenous. "We" must protect "our" individual choice from those who are the controllers or the "polluters" (whose cultures and very bodies are either exoticized or dangerous). Thus, I believe that there are very close connections between support for neoliberal visions of markets and free individuals; the concerns of neoconservatives with their clear worries about standards, "excellence," and decline; the worries of authoritarian populists that lead to home schooling; and the emphasis on certainty, testing, and control that plays such a large part in new middle-class managerialism.

In this regard, I believe that it is also the case that under current conditions national and state standards and curricula all too often actually represent a step backward in antiracist education (although we should never romanticize the situation before; not all that much antiracist education was actually going on I fear). This is clear in Linda McNeil's important research I mentioned earlier on the destructive effects of the move toward standardized and state-mandated curricula and testing—especially among schools with high concentrations of African-American and Latino/a students that had made major gains in building curricula and teaching that were responsive to and respectful of local cultures, values, and knowledge and that also had led to increased achievement and school attendance.[24] Isn't it odd that just as gains were being made in decentering dominant narratives, dominance returns in the form of national and state curricula (and national and state testing) that specify—often in distressing detail—what "we" are all like? Of course, as I stated, in many nations the attempts at building national curricula and/or national standards were and are forced to compromise, to go beyond the mere mentioning of the culture and histories of the Other. (Certainly, this was and is the case in the United States.) And it is in such compromises that we see hegemonic discourse at its most creative best.

I hope you will forgive me if I repeat myself here, but I can think of no better indication of what I am describing. Take again the example I mentioned in an earlier chapter, the new national history standards in the United States and the attempt in textbooks to respond to the standards' creation of a multicultural narrative that binds "us" all together, to create that elusive "we." As I noted, such a discourse, while having a number of progressive-sounding elements, demonstrates how hegemonic narratives creatively erase historic memory and the specificities of difference and oppression. While all too many textbooks in our schools construct the history of the United States as the story of "immigrants," such a story totally misconstrues the different conditions that existed. As I stated, some "immigrants" came in *chains,* were enslaved, and faced centuries of repression and state-mandated apartheid. Others were subjected to death and forced enclosure as official policies. And there is a world of difference here between the creation of (an artificial) "we" and the destruction of historical experience and memory.

This destruction and how it is accomplished is again related to how race functions as an absent (at least for some people) presence in our societies. This can be made clearer by directing our attention to the invisibility of whiteness. Indeed, I want to suggest that those who are deeply committed to interrupting the forces of conservative modernization and are equally committed to antiracist curricula and teaching need to place much more of their focus on white identity.

It may be unfortunate, but it is still true that many whites believe that there is a social cost not to being a person of color but to being *white.* For them, whites are the "new losers" in a playing field that they believe has been leveled now that the United States is a supposedly basically egalitarian, color-blind society. Since "times are tough for everybody," policies to assist "underrepresented groups"—such as affirmative action—are unfairly supporting "nonwhites." Thus, whites can now claim the status of victims, in much the same way as conservative evangelicals claimed to be oppressed, even though for some of them there is a loss of collective memory of how in the early years of the movement in the South a conscious choice was made to become less integrated in order to become part of a dominant racial order.[25] These feelings are of considerable importance in the politics of education in the United States as well as in many other nations. As it is being shaped by the conservative restoration, whiteness as an explicit cultural product is taking on a life of its own. In the arguments of the conservative discourses now so powerfully circulating, the barriers to social equality and equal opportunity have been removed. Whites, hence, have no privilege. Much of this is untrue, of course. Although undercut by other dynamics of power, there is still considerable advantage to "being white" in this society. However, it is not the truth or falsity of these claims that are at issue here. Rather, it is the production of retrogressive white identities.

The implications of all this are profound politically and culturally. For, given the right's rather cynical use of racial anxieties, given the economic fears and realities many citizens experience, and given the historic power of race on the U.S. psyche and on the formation of identities in so many other nations, many members of these societies may develop forms of solidarity based on their "whiteness." To say the least, this is not inconsequential in terms of struggles over meaning, identity, and the characteristics and control of our major institutions.

How do we interrupt these ideological formations? How do we develop antiracist pedagogic practices that recognize white identities and yet do not lead to retrogressive formations? These are complex ideological and pedagogical questions. Yet these issues cannot be dealt with unless we focus directly on the differential power relations that have created and been created by the educational terrain on which we operate. And this requires an insistent focus on the role of the state, on state policies, on the shift to the right in government policies and by political parties in so many nations, and on the reconstruction of common-sense in which the right has successfully engaged.

If we were to be true to the historical record, whiteness is certainly not something we have just discovered. The politics of whiteness has been enormously, and often terrifyingly, effective in the formation of coalitions that unite people across cultural differences, across class and gender relations, and against their best interests.[26] It would not be possible to write the history of "our" economic, political, legal, health, educational, indeed all of our institutions, without centering the politics of whiteness either consciously or unconsciously as a core dynamic. Of course, I am saying little that is new here. As critical race theorists and postcolonial writers have documented, racial forms and identities have been and are constitutive building blocks of the structures of our daily lives, imagined and real communities, and cultural processes and products.[27]

Let us look at this situation a bit more closely. Race as a category is usually applied to "nonwhite" peoples. White people are usually not seen and named. They are centered as the human norm. "Others" are raced; "we" are just people.[28] Richard Dyer speaks to this in his telling book, *White*.

> There is no more powerful position than that of being "just" human. The claim to power is the claim to speak for the commonality of humanity. Raced people can't do that—they can only speak for their race. But non-raced people can, for they do not represent the interests of a race. The point of seeing the racing of whites is to dislodge them/us from the position of power, with all of the inequities, oppression, privileges, and sufferings in its train, dislodging them/us by undercutting the authority with which they/we speak and act in and on the world.[29]

"Our" very language speaks to the invisibility of power relations in our ordinary talk about whiteness. "We" speak of a sheet of white paper as "blank." A room painted all white is seen as perhaps "needing a bit of color." Other examples could be multiplied. But the idea of whiteness as neutrality, as a there that is not there, is ideally suited for designating that social group that is to be taken as the "human ordinary."[30]

In the face of this, in the face of something that might best be called an absent presence, a crucial political, cultural, and ultimately pedagogic project then is *making whiteness strange*.[31] Thus, part of our task in terms of pedagogy and political awareness and mobilization is to tell ourselves and teach our students that identities are historically conferred. We need to recognize that "subjects are produced through multiple identifications." We should see our project as not reifying identity, but both understanding its production as an ongoing process of differentiation, *and* most importantly as subject to redefinition, resistance, and change.[32]

There are dangers in doing this, of course. Having whites focus on whiteness can have contradictory effects, ones we need to be well aware of. It can enable one to acknowledge differential power and the raced nature of everyone—and this is all to the good. Yet it can also serve other purposes than challenging the authority of, say, the white West. As I argue in *Cultural Politics and Education*, it can just as easily run the risk of lapsing into the possessive individualism that is so powerful in this society. That is, such a process can serve the chilling function of simply saying "But enough about you, let me tell you about me." Unless we are very careful and reflexive, it can still wind up privileging the white, middle-class woman's or man's need for self-display. This is a seemingly endless need among many people. Scholars within the critical educational community will not always be immune to these tensions. Thus, we must be on our guard to ensure that a focus on whiteness doesn't become one more excuse to recenter dominant voices and to ignore the voices and testimony of those groups of people whose dreams, hopes, lives, and their very bodies are shattered by current relations of exploitation and domination.

Further, focusing on whiteness and the complex roles it plays in current "reforms" can simply generate white guilt, hostility, or feelings of powerlessness. It can actually prevent the creation of those "decentered unities" that speak across differences and that can lead to broad coalitions that challenge dominant cultural, political, and economic relations. Thus, doing this requires an immense sensitivity, a clear sense of multiple power dynamics in any situation, and a nuanced and (at times risky) pedagogy.[33]

Issues of whiteness may seem overly theoretical to some readers or one more "trendy" topic that has found its way to the surface of the critical educational agenda. This would be a grave mistake. What counts as "official knowledge" consistently bears the imprint of tensions, struggles, and compromises in which race plays a substantial role.[34] Further, as Steven Selden has so clearly shown in his recent history of the close connections between eugenics and educational policy and practice, almost every current dominant practice in education—standards, testing, systematized models of curriculum planning, gifted education, and so much more—has its roots in such concerns as "race betterment," fear of the Other, and so on.[35] And these concerns were themselves grounded in the gaze of whiteness as the unacknowledged norm. Thus, issues of whiteness lie at the very core of educational policy and practice. We ignore them at our risk.

Of course, this is partly an issue of the politics of "identity," and increasing attention has been paid over the past decade to questions of identity in education and cultural studies. However, one of the major failures of research on identity is its failure to adequately address the hegemonic politics of the right. As I have been at pains to show here and elsewhere, the conservative restoration has been more than a little successful in creating active subject positions that incorporate varied groups under the umbrella of a new hegemonic alliance. It has been able to engage in a politics inside and outside of education in which a fear of the racialized Other is connected to fears of nation, culture, control, and decline—and to intensely personal fears about the future of one's children in an economy in crisis. All of these are knit together in tense but creative and complex ways. Given this, those of us who are committed to antiracist educational policies and practices and who are engaged in bearing witness to the actual functioning of existing and newly proposed educational "reforms" would be wise to direct our attention not only to the racial effects of markets and standards, but just as much to the creative ways neoliberal and neoconservative (and in the United States and a number of other nations, authoritarian populist religious conservative) movements work to convince so many people (including many of the leaders of the Labour Party in the UK and in the Democratic Party in the United States) that these policies are merely neutral technologies. They're not.

MAKING CHALLENGES PUBLIC

My arguments in the previous section of this concluding chapter have been at a relatively general level because I did not want us to lose sight of the larger picture. Let me now get more specific and tactical, since I am convinced that it is important to interrupt rightist claims immediately, within the media, in academic and professional publications, and in daily life.

One crucial example of such interruption is found in the Educational Policy Project formed under the auspices of the Center for Education Research, Analysis, and Innovation. This involves the ongoing construction of an organized group of people who are committed to responding very rapidly to material published by the right. This group includes a number of well-known educators and activists who are deeply concerned that the right has successfully used the media to foster its own ideological agenda, just as it has devoted a considerable amount of resources to getting its message to the public. For example, a number of conservative foundations have full-time staff members whose responsibility it is, for example, to fax synopses of reports to national media, to newspapers, and to widely read journals of opinion and to keep conservative positions in the public eye. Progressives have been much less successful in comparison, in part because they have not devoted themselves to the task as rigorously or because they have not learned to work at many levels, from the academic to the popular, simultaneously. In recognition of this, a group of socially and educational critical educators met first in Milwaukee and has been continuously meeting to generate an organized response to conservative reports, articles, research, and media presentations.

A full-time staff member was hired by the Center to focus on conservative material, to identify what needs to be responded to, and to help edit responses written by individual members of the group. A Web site has been developed that publishes these responses and/or original publications of more progressive research and arguments. The project also focuses on writing "op-ed" pieces, letters to the editor, and other similar material and on making all of this available to the media. This requires establishing contacts with journals, newspapers, radio, and television, and so on. This is exactly what the right did. We can and must do similar things. It requires hard work, but the Educational Policy Project is the beginning of what we hope will be a larger effort involving many more people. The reader can see the kinds of things that have been done by going to the following Web site for the Educational Policy Project of the Center for Education Research, Analysis, and Innovation: www.uwm.edu/Dept/CERAI/project.html.

To give a sense of the kinds of pieces that are being produced and widely circulated, I am including my response to Gary Rosen's arguments for vouchers that he published in the neoconservative journal *Commentary.*[36]

Are Vouchers Really Democratic?
A Response to "Are School Vouchers Un-American?"
By Gary Rosen

By Michael W. Apple
February 2000

Over the past decade, conservative groups in particular have been pressing for public funding for private and religious schools. At the forefront of this movement have been voucher plans. Voucher proponents argue that only by forcing schools onto a competitive market will there be any improvement. Writing in the neo-conservative journal *Commentary,* Gary Rosen attempts to synthesize the arguments for vouchers and against public schools and teachers.[1]

Voucher proposals do not stand alone. They are connected to other widespread attacks on public institutions and public employees. This more extensive agenda—often not available for scrutiny—shows itself when one looks carefully at Rosen's position.

Rosen seeks to rebut arguments that vouchers for religious schools violate the US constitutional principle of church-state separation, and arguments that they would have a corrosive effect on common public education and therefore would undermine national identity and unity. Such arguments by public school partisans, Rosen asserts, are self-serving; private schools, he claims, do a better job of civic education and are more racially integrated than public schools. Private school vouchers, he concludes, can reverse a trend in which growing numbers of minority inner city teenagers emerge unprepared from today's urban public schools—by providing some of those students an alternative, while goading public schools to improve for the rest. "What could be more democratic— or more American—than this?"[2]

While he is very selective in those arguments against vouchers to which he chooses to respond, Rosen presents them as simply a tool to improve the lives of inner city students. While that may be the aim of some voucher advocates, it ignores the realities of the larger voucher movement, which has a much more ambitious agenda. In Wisconsin, Polly Williams, a Democratic, African American legislator, allied with the Republican governor a decade ago to craft a voucher plan limited to poor children in inner city schools in Milwaukee. She assumed that its aim, as Rosen states, was to give African American and poor parents the right to exit public schools. Yet once the State Supreme Court, in a close vote, ruled the program was constitutional, conservative proponents of the program began calling for its expansion to include all parents—a clear, direct attack on public schools while providing public money to support even affluent parents who wished to pull their children out of public education. Ms. Williams, though still a supporter of vouchers targeted only to low-income families, attacked her erstwhile allies, accusing them of not having the interests of her constituents at the heart of their policies.[3]

The issue is not simply one of competing social beliefs, though. It is also about what research actually says. Voucher proponents are extremely selective in their use of data to support their cause, and Rosen in his essay is no exception. Rosen points to Paul E. Peterson's data on the "success" of vouchers and then quotes from the recent long term study of these programs by John Witte to further bolster the argument. Yet, Rosen does not report Witte's own conclusion that vouchers are not necessarily effective in raising achievement and that the research does not clearly support vouchers at all.[4] At best, the available research is still quite unclear. It cannot be used to give a ringing endorsement to vouchers.

Witte's cautions are not alone here, though. Internationally, a number of studies have powerfully demonstrated the effects of policies to privatize schools and turn education into a market-driven institution. Study after study has shown that, except for a very limited group of students, placing schools on a market merely reinforces existing hierarchies, further stratifying education.[5] Poor and working class children are even more marginalized. While a small number of children of color do get the right to exit, the vast majority of these same children either gain no benefits whatsoever, or they and their schools are left in even worse condition than before.

The data also indicate worrisome effects on teachers and administrators. While Rosen, without supporting data, claims that vouchers do not cause added hardship for schools, an extensive body of international research on placing schools in a competitive market can lead to exactly the opposite conclusion. Much more time is spent on maintaining the image of a "good" school, with much less time spent by teachers and administrators on curricular substance. Since it is comparative test scores that determine whether a school is "good" or "bad," children who do perform well on such reductive tests are seen as welcome. Those who do not are often discouraged or are marginalized. Once again, the vast majority of children harmed by such reforms are exactly those whom Rosen and others state they are supporting. These conditions exist not because teachers do not already work extremely hard or are uncaring. Rather, markets in schools seem to worsen, rather than improve, work load, pressure, and access to resources.

The issue of teachers is significant. Rosen's essay not only fails to report much of the countervailing data, but it is clearly an attack on teachers and on teachers unions. Words and phrases such as teachers' "mock concern" and "disingenuous" behavior point to a powerful antipathy to public employees. This is unfortunate, since any institution that acts in dismissive and undemocratic ways to the employees who work every day in it cannot be considered democratic.

Much of the literature in support of vouchers assumes that the root cause of the supposed decline in education is directly related to unprepared teachers and overly bureaucratic schools. There undoubtedly are some ill-prepared teachers and there are schools districts that are overly bureaucratic. To place the blame only on teachers and schools, however, ignores the larger structural realities that have nearly destroyed public services in our inner cities. It is simply not possible to understand what has happened in education unless we honestly link schooling to the growth of poverty. One of the most consistent research findings over the past decades has been that income inequality and other social and economic factors—not type of school—have the most power in determining success in schools.[6] This is not to ignore the role of schooling in enhancing mobility, but it does ask us to be very honest. It was not schools that caused the massive decline of respectful jobs with decent pay in our inner cities, thereby creating a crisis in faith about the future among generations of parents and children. It was not schools that caused capital flight as factories fled to non-unionized, lower paid parts of the world. And it was not schools that led to the willful neglect of the families, health care, and decent housing in these inner cities. To blame teachers for this is to live in a world divorced from reality.

Yet, even given the unfortunate relationship between schooling and an unequal economy, there are things that can be done and that have been proven to work. Effective schooling does not necessarily mean turning our schools over to a market. There are other, and even more proven, choices. The democratic schools movement growing throughout the country shows how educators and local communities can jointly build responsive and effective education that makes a real difference in the lives of children, teachers, and communities. Schools such as Central Park East in New York, Fratney Street School in Milwaukee, and the Rindge School of Technical Arts in the Boston area all provide telling examples of public schools that treat their teachers, students, and local communities with the respect they deserve.[7] Programs in Tennessee and Wisconsin to reduce class size have shown a much more robust set of results than any of those reported for voucher plans.[8]

Most of the debates about vouchers have been conducted around one issue, whether or not they raise scores on standardized tests. There are other crucial issues that must not be ignored, however. Voucher plans, like all market-driven and privatized models, are part of a larger and quite aggressive ideological movement to change how we think about our society and our participation in it. They assume without question that public is by definition bad and private is by definition good. Instead of collectively building and rebuilding our institutions, voucher plans are part of the larger effort by conservatives to change the very meaning of citizenship. Citizenship is now to be defined as simply consumer choice. The unattached individual makes choices about her or his life, without caring what its effects are on the rest of society.[9] The reduction of democracy to selfish individualism may in fact be Un-American. I doubt that this is what we as a society want.

NOTES

1. Gary Rosen, "Are School Vouchers Un-American?" *Commentary,* Vol. 109, No. 2, February 2000, pp. 26–31.

2. Ibid.

3. It is important to understand as well that many of the same foundations that are pouring money into the campaign for voucher plans are those which provided financial and logistical support for such volumes as Richard Herrnstein and Charles Murray, *The Bell Curve* (New York: Free Press, 1994). Widely discredited in the scientific literature, the volume claimed that African Americans were on the whole less intelligent than European Americans. While this does not discredit all of the arguments in favor of vouchers, it should make us extremely cautious about how voucher plans fit into the larger sets of social commitments that guide many of their proponents.

4. John Witte, *The Market Approach to Education: An Analysis of America's First Voucher Program* (Princeton, N.J.: Princeton University Press, 2000).

5. See the following:

Geoff Whitty, Sally Power, and David Halpin, *Devolution and Choice in Education* (Philadelphia: Open University Press, 1998).

Hugh Lauder and David Hughes, *Trading in Futures: Why Markets in Education Don't Work* (Philadelphia: Open University Press, 1999).

David Gillborn and Deborah Youdell, *Rationing Education: Policy, Practice, Reform, and Equity* (Philadelphia: Open University Press, 2000).

Sharon Gewirtz, Stephen Ball, and Richard Bowe, *Markets, Choice, and Equity in Education* (Philadelphia: Open University Press, 1995)

6. Grace Kao, Marta Tienda, and Barbara Schneider, "Race and Ethnic Variation in Academic Performance," *Research in Sociology of Education and Socialization* 11:263–297. 1996.

7. Michael W. Apple and James A. Beane, eds. *Democratic Schools* (Washington, DC: Association for Supervision and Curriculum Development, 1995).

8. The entire issue of *Educational Evaluation and Policy Analysis* 21, 2 (Summer 1999) is devoted to evaluating various programs that lower class size.

9. Michael W. Apple, *Cultural Politics and Education* (New York: Teachers College Press, 1996).

This is just one example of one strategy for bringing what we know to parts of the public in more popular forms. Many other examples are posted on the Web site and published as reports, responses in journals, letters to the editor, and op-ed pieces. While this project is relatively new, it shows considerable promise. In combination with the use of talk radio, call-in shows, and similar media strategies in *multiple* languages,[37] these kinds of activities are part of a larger strategy to bring both more public attention to what the dangers are in the "solutions" proposed by the right and to what the workable alternatives to them might be. Integrating the educational interventions within a larger focus on the media is absolutely crucial.[38]

LEARNING FROM OTHER NATIONS

During one of the times I was working in Brazil with Paulo Freire, I remember him repeatedly saying to me that education must begin in critical dialogue. These last two words were crucial to him. Education both must hold our dominant institutions in education and the larger society up to rigorous questioning and at the same time this questioning must deeply involve those who benefit least from the ways these institutions now function. Both conditions were necessary, since the first without the second was simply insufficient to the task of democratizing education.

Of course, many committed educators already know that the transformation of educational policies and practices—or the defense of democratic gains in our schools and local communities—is inherently political. Indeed, this is constantly registered in the fact that rightist movements have made teaching and curricula the targets of concerted attacks for years. One of the claims of these rightist forces is that schools are "out of touch" with parents and communities. While there are elements of insight in such criticisms, we need to find ways of connecting our educational efforts to local communities, especially those members of these communities with less power, that are more truly democratic than those envisioned by the right.

I talked earlier on, in Chapter 1, about the efficacy of turning to the experiences of other nations to learn about what the effects of neoliberal and neoconservative policies and practices actually are. Yet we can learn many more things from other nations' struggles. For example, currently in Porto Alegre, Brazil, the policies of participatory budgeting are helping to build support for more progressive and democratic policies there in the face of the growing power of neoliberal movements at a national level. The Workers Party ("PT" as it is known there) has been able to increase its majority even among people who had previously voted in favor of parties with much more conservative educational and social programs *because* it has been committed to enabling even the poorest of its citizens to participate in deliberations over the policies themselves and over where and how money should be spent. By paying attention to more substantive forms of collective participation and, just as important, by devoting resources to encourage such participation, Porto Alegre has demonstrated that it is possible to have a thicker democracy, even in times of both economic crisis and ideological attacks from neoliberal parties and from the conservative press. Programs such as the "Citizen School" and the sharing of real power with those who live in "favelas" (slums) provide ample evidence that thick democracy offers realistic alternatives to the eviscerated version of thin democracy found under neoliberalism.[39] Just as important is the pedagogic function of these programs. They develop the collective capacities among people to enable them to continue to engage in the democratic administration and control of their lives.[40] This is time-consuming, but time spent in such things now has proven to pay off dramatically later on.

A similar story can be told about another part of Brazil. In Belem, a "Youth Participatory Budget" process was instituted. It provided resources and space for the participation of many thousands of youth in the deliberations over what programs for youth needed to be developed, how money should be spent, and over creating a set of political forums that could be used by youth to make public their needs and desires. This is very different from most of the ways youth are dealt with in all too many countries, where youth are seen as a "problem" not as a resource.[41] A similar instance is found in New Zealand, where under the original leadership of the International Research Institute on Maori and Indigenous Education, multi-racial groups of youth are formed in communities to publicly discuss the ways in which youth see their realities and advance proposals for dealing with these realities.[42] In this way, alliances that begin to cut across race, class, and age are being built. There are models, then, of real participation that we can learn from and that challenge the eviscerated vision of democracy advanced by neoliberals by putting in place more substantive and active models of actually "living our freedoms." The issue is not the existence of such models; it is ensuring that they are made widely visible.

THINKING HERETICALLY

To build counterhegemonic alliances, we may have to think more creatively than before—and, in fact, may have to engage in some nearly heretical rethinking. Let me give an example. I would like us to engage in a thought-experiment. I believe that the right has been able to take certain elements that many people hold dear and connect them with other issues in ways that might not often occur "naturally" if these issues were less politicized. Thus, for instance, one of the reasons populist religious groups are pulled into an alliance with the right is because such groups believe that the state is totally against the values that give meaning to their lives. They are sutured into an alliance in which other elements of rightist discourse are then able to slowly connect with their own. Thus, they believe that the state is antireligious. Others also say that the state seeks to impose its will on white working-class parents by giving "special treatment" to people of color and ignoring poor white people. These two elements do *not* necessarily have to combine. But they slowly begin to be seen as homologous.

Is it possible that by taking, say, religion out of the mix that some parts of the religious community that currently find collective identities on the right would be less susceptible to such a call if more religious content was found in school? If religious studies had a more central place within the curriculum, is it less likely that people who find in religion the ultimate answers to why they are here would be less mistrustful of the state, less apt to be attracted to a position that public is bad and private is good? I am uncertain that this would be the case. But I strongly believe that we need to entertain this possibility.

Do not misunderstand me. I am decidedly not taking the position that we should use vouchers to fund private religious schools, nor am I saying that the authoritarian populist religious right should be pandered to. Rather, I am taking a position similar to that espoused by Warren Nord that I noted in Chapter 1. Our failure to provide a clear place for the study of religion in the curriculum makes us "illiberal." Yet I do not want to end with Nord's position. Rather, I see it as a starting point. In earlier books and here, I have argued that at times people "become right" because of the lack of responsiveness of public institutions to meanings and concerns that are central to their lives. Teaching more *about,* not for, religion doesn't just make us more "liberal" in Nord's words. It may also help interrupt the formation of antipublic identities. This has important implications for it can point to strategic moves that can be made to counter the integration of large numbers of people under the umbrella of conservative modernization.

As I have demonstrated elsewhere, people often become right at a local level, not through plots by rightist groups but because of local issues and sentiments. Making schools more responsive to religious sentiments may seem like a simple step, but it can have echoes that are profound since it may undercut one of the major reasons some populist groups who are also religious find their way under the umbrella of rightist attacks on schools and on the public sphere.

I am not a romantic about this. I do think that it could be dangerous and could be exploited by the religious right. After all, some of them do have little interest in "teaching about" and may hold positions on Christianity and other religions that both construct and leave little room for the Other. Yet the centrality of religious sentiments need not get pushed toward neoliberalism. It need not be connected to a belief that public schools and teachers are so totally against religious people that marketization and privatization are the only answers. Thus, I'd like us to think seriously—and very cautiously—about the possible ways members of some of the groups currently found under the umbrella of the conservative alliance might actually be pried loose from it and might work off the elements of good sense they possess. In saying this, I am guided by a serious question. In what ways can religious commitments be mobilized for socially progressive ends? Our (often justifiable) worries about religious influences in the public sphere may have the latent effect of preventing such a mobilization by alienating many people who have deep religious commitments and who might otherwise be involved in such struggles. If many evangelicals do commit themselves to helping the poor, for example, in what ways can these sentiments be disarticulated from seeing capitalism as "God's economy" and from only helping the "deserving poor" and rearticulated toward greater social and economic transformation. It would seem well worth studying the recent histories of religious involvement in, say, the anti-WTO struggles to understand this better. At the very least, we cannot act as if religious beliefs about social and educational justice are outside the pale of progressive action, as too many critical educators do. A combination of caution, openness, and creativity is required here.

Yet another example is to take advantage of the shared elements of good sense among groups who usually have very different agendas in order to work against specific policies and programs that are being instituted by other elements within the new hegemonic alliance. That is, there *are* real tensions within conservative modernization that provide important spaces for joint action.

This possibility is already being recognized. Because of this, for example, some truly odd political couplings are emerging today. Both the populist right and the populist left are occasionally joining forces to make strategic alliances against some neoliberal incursions into the school. For instance, Ralph Nader's group Commercial Alert and Phyllis Schlafly's organization the Eagle Forum are building an alliance against Channel One. Both are deeply committed to fight the selling of children in schools as a captive audience for commercials. They are not alone. The Southern Baptist Convention has passed a resolution opposing Channel One. Groups such as Donald Wildmon's American Family Association, and even more important, James Dobson's powerful organization Focus on the Family, have been working with Nader's groups to remove Channel One from schools and to keep it out of schools where it is not already established. This tactical alliance has also joined together to support antigambling initiatives in a number of states and to oppose one of the fastest-growing commercial technology initiatives in education—ZapMe! Corp. ZapMe! provides free computers to schools at the cost of collecting demographic data on students, which it then uses to target advertising specifically at these children.[43]

The tactical agreement is often based on different ideological positions. While the progressive positions are strongly anticorporate, the conservative positions are grounded in a distaste for the subversion of traditional values, "the exploiting of children for profit," and a growing rightist populist tension over the decisions that corporations make that do not consider the "real folks" in America. This latter sentiment is what the rightist populist and nativist Pat Buchanan has worked off of for years. In the words of Ron Reno, a researcher at Focus on the Family, we need to fight "a handful of individuals exploiting the populace of America to make a buck."

This teaming up on specific causes is approached more than a little cautiously on both sides, as you would imagine. As Ralph Nader says, "You have to be very careful because you can start tempering your positions. You can be too solicitous. You have to enter and leave on your own terms. You tell them, 'Here's what we're doing, if you want to join us fine. If not, fine.'" Phyllis Schlafly portrays her own reasons this way. "[Nader and I] agree that the public schools should not be used for commercial purposes. A captive audience of students should not be sold for profit. I agree with that. I don't recall his objection to the content of the news, which is what stirs up a lot of conservatives."[44]

Schlafly's comments show the differences as well as similarities in the right-left division here. While for many people across the divide, there is a strong distaste for selling our children as commodities, divisions reappear in other areas. For one group, the problem is a "handful of individuals" who lack proper moral values. For the other, the structural forces driving our economy create pressures to buy and sell children as a captive audience. For conservatives, the content of the news on Channel One is too "liberal"; it deals with issues such as drugs, sexuality, and similar topics. Yet, as I have shown in my own analysis of what counts as news in the major media and in Channel One, even though there is some cautious treatment of controversial issues, the content and coding of what counts as news is more than a little conservative and predominantly reinforces dominant interpretations.[45]

These differences should not detract from my basic point. Tactical alliances are still possible, especially where populist impulses and anticorporate sentiments overlap. These must be approached extremely carefully, however, since the grounding of much of the populism of the right is also in a racist nativism, a very dangerous tendency that has had murderous consequences. A recognition, though, of the anticorporate tendencies that do exist here is significant, since it also points to cracks in the alliance supporting some aspects of conservative modernization in general and to similar fissures within the ranks of authoritarian populism itself. For example, the fact that Ralph Reed was hired as a consultant to burnish Channel One's image has also created a number of tensions within the authoritarian populist ranks.[46]

Another area that is ripe for such coalitions is that of national and state curricula and testing. Neither the populist right nor the populist left believe that such policies leave room for the cultures, histories, or visions of legitimate knowledge that they are so deeply committed to. Although the specific content of such knowledge is decidedly dissimilar for each of these groups, the fact that there is agreement both on a generally antielitist position and on the fact that the very processes involved are antidemocratic provides room for tactical alliances not only against these processes but as a block against even further incursions of managerialism into schools. In addition, given the ideological segregation that currently exists in this society, working (carefully) with such groups has the advantage of reducing stereotypes that they may hold (and perhaps that we might also hold?). It increases the possibility that the populist right will see that progressives may in fact be able to provide solutions to serious issues that are so distressing in populist movements of multiple orientations. This benefit should not be minimized.

My position here, hence, embodies a dual strategy. We can and must build tactical alliances where this is possible and where there is mutual benefit—and where such an alliance does not jeopardize the core of progressive beliefs and values. At the same time, we need to continue to build on more progressive alliances between our core constituencies around issues such as class, race, gender, sexuality, ability, globalization and economic exploitation, and the environment. That such a dual strategy can be used to organize both within already existing alliances and to work across differences is made clear in the anti-WTO mobilizations in Seattle, in Washington, and in a number of other cities throughout the world.

Once the issue of tactical alliances is raised, however, it is nearly impossible to ignore charter schools. For a number of people on both the left and the right, charter schools have been seen as a compromise that can satisfy some of the demands of each group. Here, though, I would urge even more caution. Much of the discussion of these schools has been more than a little romantic. It has accepted the rhetoric of "debureaucratization," experimentation, and diversity as the reality. Yet, as Amy Stuart Wells and her colleagues have demonstrated, charter schools can and do often serve less meritorious ends. As I showed in Chapter 6, they can be manipulated to provide public funding for ideologically and educationally problematic programs, with little public accountability. Beneath the statistics of racial equality they supposedly produce, they can exacerbate white flight and can be captured by groups who actually have little interest in the culture and futures of those whom they assume are the Other. They are used as the "constitutive outside" in attacks on public schooling for the majority of children in schools throughout the United States, by deflecting attention to what must be done there. Thus, they often can and do act to deflect attention from our lack of commitment to provide sufficient resources and support for schools in urban and rural areas. And in a number of ways they threaten to become an opening wedge for voucher plans.[47]

Having said this, however, I do not believe that charter schools will go away. Indeed, during the many periods of time when I have lectured and engaged in educational and political work in countries in, say, Latin America and Asia, it has become ever more clear to me that there is considerable interest in the charter school movement. This is especially the case in those nations that have a history of strong states and strong central control over the curriculum, teaching, and evaluation and where the state has been inflexible, highly bureaucratic, and unresponsive. Given this situation, it is absolutely crucial that the terrain of charter schools *not* be occupied by the forces within the conservative alliance. If charter schools become, as they threaten to, primarily a site where their function is to deflect attention from schools where the vast majority of students go, if they are allowed to be used as vouchers "in cognito," if they serve to legitimate concerted attacks on teachers and other educators, then the effects will not be limited to the United States. This will be a worldwide tragedy. For these very reasons, it is crucial that some of our empirical, educational, and political energy goes into guaranteeing that charter schools are a much more progressively inclined set of possibilities than they are today. We need to work so that the elements of good sense in the movement are not lost by it being integrated under the umbrella of conservative modernization.[48]

MAKING CRITICAL EDUCATIONAL PRACTICES PRACTICAL

You will notice that I said "some" of our energy in the previous paragraph. Once again we need to be extremely cautious that by focusing our energies on "alternatives" such as charter schools we are not tacitly enhancing the very real possibility that progressives will spend so much of their attention on them that action in the vast majority of schools will take a back seat. While all of the tactical and strategic foci I have mentioned are important, I believe that one area in particular should be at the center of our concerns as educators—providing real answers to real practical problems in education. By showing successful struggles to build a critical and democratic education in real schools and real communities with real teachers and students today, attention is refocused on action not only in charter schools but on local elementary, middle, and secondary schools in communities much like those in which most of us spend our lives. Thus, publicizing such "stories" makes critical education seem actually "doable," not merely a utopian vision dreamed up by "critical theorists" in education. For this very reason, as I have stressed repeatedly throughout this book, political/educational interventions such as the popular and widely translated book *Democratic Schools* and the increasingly influential journal *Rethinking Schools* become even more important.[49] As I showed in Chapter 3, this is crucial if we are indeed to interrupt the right. Since the right does have an advantage of speaking in "common-sense" and in "plain-folks Americanism"—and peoples' common-sense *does* have elements of good and bad sense within itself—we can also use these progressively inclined elements to show that it is not only the right that has answers to what are real and important issues of educational practice.

For example, the specific vocational and academic programs in which curricula and teaching are linked to paid work and to the economy in socially progressive ways in the Rindge School of Technical Arts in the Boston area powerfully demonstrate that those students and parents who are (justifiably) deeply concerned about their economic futures do *not* have to turn to neoliberal policies to find practical answers to their questions.[50] I can think of little that is more important than this. The forces of conservative modernization have colonized the space of practice and of providing answers to the question of "What do I do on Monday?" in part not because the right has all the answers, but because the left has too often evacuated that space.

Here again, we have much to learn from the right. While we do not need progressive imitators of, say, E. D. Hirsch, we do need to be much more active in actually attempting to provide answers to teachers, community members, and an increasingly skeptical public that questions such as *what* will I teach, *how* will I teach it, *how* will I evaluate its success—in essence, all those practical questions that people have a right to ask and to which they are entitled to get sensible answers—are taken very seriously. In the absence of this, we are left standing on the sidelines while the right reconstructs not only common-sense but the schools that help produce it.

This is where the work engaged in by several critically inclined practicing educators has proven to be so important. Debbie Meier and her colleagues at Central Park East School in New York and at Mission Hill School in Boston; Bob Peterson, Rita Tenorio, and their colleagues at Fratney Street School in Milwaukee; the staff at Rindge School; and many other educators in similar schools throughout the country provide critical models of answering the day-to-day questions that I have noted. They also directly respond to the arguments that are made by neoliberals, neoconservatives, and authoritarian populists. They do this not only by defending the very idea of a truly public school (although they are very good at marshaling such a defense),[51] but also by demonstrating workable alternatives that are based both on high expectations for their diverse students and on a deep-seated respect for the cultures, histories, and experiences of these students and their parents and local communities.[52] Only in this way can the neoliberal, neoconservative, and managerial factions of the new alliance be undercut at the level of the school.

HOPE AS A RESOURCE

Much more could be said about interrupting the right and about building workable alternatives, but there is a limit to what can be done in any one book. I have written this book to contribute to an ongoing set of crucial debates about the means and ends of our educational institutions and about their connections to larger institutions and power relations. Keeping such debates alive and vibrant is one of the best ways of challenging "the curriculum of the dead." To stimulate such discussion, I want to continue a practice that I began in *Official Knowledge* by again giving my postal and e-mail address for people to raise questions about or affirm my arguments here, or to send your own stories about successful interruptions of the conservative tendencies now so powerful in education. I can be reached at the University of Wisconsin, Department of Curriculum and Instruction, 225 North Mills Street, Madison, WI 53706, USA or at the following email address: apple@education.wisc.edu. Building and defending a truly democratic and critical education is a collective project. We have much to learn from each other.

Let me end with something that I always want to keep in the forefront of my own consciousness when times are difficult. Sustained political and cultural transformations are impossible "without the hope of a better society that we can, in principle and in outline, imagine."[53] One of my hopes is that this volume will contribute to the larger movement that is struggling to loosen the grip of the narrow concepts of "reality" and "democracy" that have been circulated by neoliberals and neoconservatives in education and so much else over the past decades. As I showed in Chapter 1, there historically have been alternatives to the limited and increasingly hypocritical conception of democracy that, unfortunately, even social democratic parties (under the label of the "third way") in many nations have come to accept. In the words of Panitch and Leys, we need "to insist on a far fuller and richer democracy than anything now available. It is time to reject the prevailing disparagement of anything collective as 'unrealistic' and to insist on the moral and practical rightness, as well as the necessity, of egalitarian social and economic arrangements." As they go on to say, this requires "the development of popular democratic capacities and the structures that nurture rather than stifle or trivialize them."[54] The movements I have analyzed in *Educating the "Right" Way* may be "wrong," not "right." They may in fact "stifle or trivialize" a vision of democracy that is based on the common good. But they certainly don't have trivial effects, not only on my former student Joseph but on millions of people all over the world. Our children, our teachers, and our communities deserve something better.

Endnotes

Chapter 1

1. For a discussion of this and of the problems of using this dichotomy between phonics and whole language, see Gerald Coles, *Reading Lessons* (New York: Hill & Wang, 1998).

2. I have demonstrated these connections in a number of places. See, for example, Michael W. Apple, *Ideology and Curriculum,* 2d ed. (New York: Routledge, 1990); Michael W. Apple, *Education and Power,* 2d ed. (New York: Routledge, 1995); Michael W. Apple, *Teachers and Texts* (New York: Routledge, 1988); and Michael W. Apple, *Official Knowledge,* 2d ed. (New York: Routledge, 2000). See also James Loewen, *Lies My Teacher Told Me* (New York: The New Press, 1995).

3. See Stephen Ball, *Education Reform: A Critical and Post-Structural Approach* (Buckingham, England: Open University Press, 1994).

4. An articulate and thoughtful analysis of these relations is Jean Anyon's *Ghetto Schooling: A Political Economy of Urban Educational Reform* (New York: Teachers College Press, 1997). See also Grace Kao, Marta Tienda, and Barbara Schneider, "Race and Ethnic Variation in Academic Performance," in *Research in Sociology of Education and Socialization, Volume 11,* ed. Aaron Pallas (Greenwich, CT: JAI Press, 1996), 263–97.

5. This is described in considerably more detail in Michael W. Apple, *Cultural Politics and Education* (New York: Teachers College Press, 1996), 68–90.

6. Edward Wyatt, "Investors See Room for Profit in the Demand for Education," *The New York Times,* 4 November 1999, p. A-1.

7. Ibid.

8. Ibid.

9. Richard Rorty, *Achieving Our Country: Leftist Thought in Twentieth Century America* (Cambridge: Harvard University Press, 1998), 14.

10. See, for example, Michael W. Apple and James A. Beane, eds., *Democratic Schools* (Alexandria, VA: Association for Supervision and Curriculum Development, 1995) and Michael W. Apple and James A. Beane, eds., *Democratic Schools: Lessons from the Chalk Face* (Buckingham, England: Open University Press, 1999).

11. Noam Chomsky, *Profits Over People: Neoliberalism and the Global Order* (New York: Seven Stories Press, 1999), 145.

12. See, for example, Raymond Williams, *Keywords: A Vocabulary of Culture and Society* (New York: Oxford University Press, 1983).

13. Eric Hobsbawm, *The Age of Extremes: A History of the World, 1914–1991* (New York: Pantheon, 1994), 3.

14. Eric Foner, *The Story of American Freedom* (New York: W. W. Norton, 1998), 4.

15. Ibid.

16. Ibid., 4.

17. Ibid., 7–8.

18. Ibid., 8.

19. Ibid., 9. See also Nancy Fraser and Linda Gordon, "A Genealogy of Dependency," *Signs* 19 (winter 1994): 309–36.

20. Foner, *Story of American Freedom*, 10.

21. Ibid., xx. Foner's book is absolutely essential for anyone interested in the continuing struggle over what freedom means and how it has been embodied in our daily life.

22. Ibid., 264.

23. Ibid., 269.

24. Ibid., 308–9.

25. William Bennett, Chester E. Finn Jr., and John T. E. Cribb Jr., *The Educated Child* (New York: The Free Press, 1999) and William Bennett, *Our Children and Our Country* (New York: Simon & Schuster, 1988).

26. Foner, *Story of American Freedom*, 310–11.

27. Ibid., 317–18.

28. Charles W. Mills argues insightfully that nearly all of our economic, political, and cultural/educational institutions in the past and today are undergirded by what he calls "the racial contract" that marginalizes people of color. See Charles W. Mills, *The Racial Contract* (Ithaca, NY: Cornell University Press, 1997).

29. Robert McChesney, "Introduction" to Noam Chomsky, *Profit Over People: Neoliberalism and the Global Order* (New York: Seven Stories Press, 1999), 7.

30. Ibid., 8.

31. Apple, Cultural Politics and Education.

32. McChesney, "Introduction," 11.

33. Chomsky, *Profit Over People,* 39.

34. Adam Smith, *The Wealth of Nations* (Oxford: Clarendon Press, 1976), 709–10.

35. Stuart Hall, "The Problem of Ideology: Marxism Without Guarantees," in *Stuart Hall: Critical Dialogues in Cultural Studies,* ed. David Morley and Kuan-Hsing Chen (New York: Routledge, 1996), 40.

36. Ibid., 37.

37. Apple, *Cultural Politics and Education;* see especially pp. 68–90.

38. Jorge Larrain, "Stuart Hall and the Marxist Concept of Ideology," in *Stuart Hall: Critical Dialogues in Cultural Studies,* ed. David Morley and Kuan-Hsing Chen (New York: Routledge, 1996), 68.

39. Foner, *Story of American Freedom,* 119.

40. Ibid., 121.

41. Ibid., 134.

42. Ibid., 26.

43. Ibid., 26–27.

44. Warren A. Nord, *Religion and American Education: Rethinking a National Dilemma* (Chapel Hill: University of North Carolina Press, 1995), 8.

45. Ibid.

46. Ibid., 32.

47. Karl Marx and Friedrich Engels, *Manifesto of the Communist Party,* in *Marx and Engels: Basic Writings on Politics and Philosophy,* ed. Lewis S. Feuer

(New York: Anchor Books, 1959), 10. For a more personal account of what this meant to Marx, see Francis Wheen, *Karl Marx: A Life* (New York: W. W. Norton, 1999).

48. The writings on this issue are vast and filled with a good deal of empirical and theoretical debate. For a brief overview, see, for example, James A. Beckford, *Religion and Advanced Industrial Society* (New York: Routledge, 1989).

49. Nord, *Religion and American Education,* 50.

50. Ibid., 51.

51. Ibid., 65.

52. Ibid., 65.

53. Ibid., 67.

54. Beckford, *Religion and Advanced Industrial Society,* 25.

55. Ibid., 18.

56. Ibid., 6–7.

57. Ibid., 89–105.

58. Michel Foucault, "The Subject and Power," in *Michel Foucault: Beyond Structuralism and Hermeneutics,* ed. Herbert Dreyfus and Paul Rabinow (Chicago: University of Chicago Press, 1982), 215.

59. Beckford, *Religion and Industrial Society,* 132–33.

60. Ibid., 142. See also Stuart Hall and Lawrence Grossberg, "On Postmodernism and Articulation: An Interview with Stuart Hall," in *Stuart Hall: Critical Dialogues in Cultural Studies,* ed. David Morley and Kuan-Hsing Chen (New York: Routledge, 1996), 142.

61. John Clarke and Janet Newman, *The Managerial State* (Thousand Oaks, CA: Sage, 1997), 27–28.

62. Ibid., 93.

63. See the analysis of managerial discourse in James Paul Gee, Glynda Hull, and Colin Lankshear, *The New Work Order: Behind the Language of the New Capitalism* (Boulder: Westview Press, 1996).

64. Clarke and Newman, *The Managerial State,* 76. Clarke and Newman argue that corporate missions have moved from the bare pursuit of efficiency to the pursuit of "excellence" and the achievement of continuous improvement. In their words, there has been an "epidemic of quality." There is of course nothing necessarily wrong with pursuing quality, but much of this represents the

colonization of professional discourse by corporate models whose ultimate concern is not quality, but profit.

65. Ibid., 30.

66. Jennifer Daryl Slack, "The Theory and Method of Articulation in Cultural Studies," in *Stuart Hall: Critical Dialogues in Cultural Studies,* ed. David Morley and Kuan-Hsing Chen (New York: Routledge, 1996), 113.

67. Ibid.

Chapter 2

1. Madeleine Arnot, "Schooling for Social Justice," unpublished paper, University of Cambridge, Department of Education, 1990.

2. William Greider, *One World, Ready or Not* (New York: Simon & Schuster, 1997).

3. See Michael W. Apple, *Cultural Politics and Education* (New York: Teachers College Press, 1996) and Michael W. Apple, *Official Knowledge,* 2d ed. (New York: Routledge, 2000).

4. I am drawing upon Roger Dale, "The Thatcherite Project in Education," *Critical Social Policy* 9 (winter 1989/1990): 4–19. Because of the size and complexity of the United States, I cannot focus on all the policy issues and initiatives now being debated or implemented. For further descriptions, see the chapters on policy research in William Pink and George Noblit, eds., *Continuity and Contradiction: The Futures of the Sociology of Education* (Cresskill, NJ: Hampton Press, 1995).

5. Apple, *Cultural Politics and Education* and Ted Honderich, *Conservatism* (Boulder: Westview Press, 1990).

6. Given the current emphasis on this by neoliberals, it may be the case that while Bowles and Gintis's book on the relationship between education and capitalism, *Schooling in Capitalist America,* was reductive, economistic, and essentializing when it first appeared in 1976, oddly it may be more accurate today. See Samuel Bowles and Herbert Gintis, *Schooling in Capitalist America* (New York: Basic Books, 1976). For criticism of their position, see Michael W. Apple, *Teachers and Texts* (New York: Routledge, 1988); Michael W. Apple, *Education and Power,* 2d ed. (New York: Routledge, 1995); and Mike Cole, ed., *Bowles and Gintis Revisited* (New York: Falmer Press, 1988).

7. See Michael W. Apple, *Ideology and Curriculum,* 2d ed. (New York: Routledge, 1990).

8. Stephen Ball, *Education Reform* (Philadelphia: Open University Press, 1994) and Apple, *Cultural Politics and Education.*

9. Apple, *Teachers and Texts,* 31–78 and Sandra Acker, "Gender and Teachers' Work," in *Review of Research in Education, Volume 21,* ed. Michael W. Apple (Washington, DC: American Educational Research Association, 1995), 99–162. A number of the larger gender implications of neoliberalism in education and the economy can be seen in Jacky Brine, *Under-Educating Woman; Globalizing Inequality* (Philadelphia: Open University Press, 1992) and Madeleine Arnot, Miriam David, and Gaby Weiner, *Closing the Gender Gap: Postwar Education and Social Change* (Cambridge, England: Polity Press, 1999).

10. John Chubb and Terry Moe, *Politics, Markets, and America's Schools* (Washington, DC: The Brookings Institution, 1990). See also, Ernest House, *Schools for Sale* (New York: Teachers College Press, 1998).

11. See Amy Stuart Wells, *Time to Choose* (New York: Hill & Wang, 1993); Jeffrey Henig, *Rethinking School Choice* (Princeton, NJ: Princeton University Press, 1994); Kevin Smith and Kenneth Meier, eds., *The Case Against School Choice* (Armonk, NY: M. E. Sharpe, 1995); Bruce Fuller, Elizabeth Burr, Luis Huerta, Susan Puryear, and Edward Wexler, *School Choice: Abundant Hopes, Scarce Evidence of Results* (Berkeley and Stanford: Policy Analysis for California Education, University of California at Berkeley and Stanford University, 1999); and John F. Witte, *The Market Approach to Education* (Princeton, NJ: Princeton University Press, 2000).

12. Geoff Whitty, "Creating Quasi-Markets in Education," in *Review of Research in Education, Volume 22,* ed. Michael W. Apple (Washington, DC: American Educational Research Association, 1997), 17. See also Chubb and Moe, *Politics, Markets, and America's Schools* and Gary Rosen, "Are Schools Vouchers Un-American?" *Commentary* 109 (February 2000): 26–31.

13. Quoted in Whitty, "Creating Quasi-Markets in Education," 17.

14. See, for example, Geoff Whitty, Sally Power, and David Halpin, *Devolution and Choice in Education* (Philadelphia: Open University Press, 1998) and Hugh Lauder and David Hughes, *Trading in Futures: Why Markets in Education Don't Work* (Philadelphia: Open University Press, 1999).

15. See Apple, *Cultural Politics and Education,* especially Chapter 4, for a description of the ways in which many current social and educational policies often widen racial gaps.

16. Whitty, "Creating Quasi-Markets in Education," 58.

17. Henig, *Rethinking School Choice,* 22.

18. See Whitty, "Creating Quasi-Markets in Education," Lauder and Hughes, *Trading in Futures,* and Apple, *Cultural Politics and Education.*

19. Many times, however, these initiatives are actually "unfunded mandates." That is, requirements such as these are made mandatory, but no additional funding is provided to accomplish them. The intensification of teachers' labor at all levels of the education system that results from this situation is very visible. On the history of education for employment, see Herbert Kliebard, *Schooled to Work: Vocationalism and the American Curriculum, 1876–1946* (New York: Teachers College Press, 1999). For clear and thoughtful analyses of other effects on higher education, see Geoffrey White, ed., *Campus, Inc.* (Amherst, NY: Prometheus Books, 2000) and Sheila Slaughter and Larry L. Leslie, *Academic Capitalism* (Baltimore, MD: Johns Hopkins University Press, 1997).

20. I have engaged in a much more detailed analysis of Channel One in Apple, *Official Knowledge,* 89–112. See also Alex Molnar, *Giving Kids the Business* (Boulder: Westview Press, 1996). A good example as well is provided by financially troubled ZapMe!, which gives free computer equipment in return for demographic information on children in schools. Of course, there is a history of resistance to things such as Channel One. UNPLUG, a student-led group, has been in the forefront of contesting the commercialization of schools. Further, as I discuss in my final chapter, both conservative and progressive groups have joined forces to act against Channel One.

21. Apple, *Cultural Politics and Education,* 68–90 and Greider, *One World, Ready or Not.*

22. Ibid. See also, Christopher Cook, "Temps Demand a New Deal," *The Nation,* 27 March 2000, pp.13–19.

23. Nancy Fraser, *Unruly Practices* (Minneapolis: University of Minnesota Press, 1989), 168.

24. Ibid., 172. See also the discussion of how gains in one sphere of social life can be "transported" into another sphere in Samuel Bowles and Her-

bert Gintis, *Democracy and Capitalism* (New York: Basic Books, 1986) and Apple, *Teachers and Texts*. On the history of such positions in health care, see Sandra Opdycke, *No One Was Turned Away* (New York: Oxford University Press, 1999).

25. Fraser, *Unruly Practices,* 172.

26. Roger Dale, *The State and Education Policy* (Philadelphia: Open University Press, 1989).

27. For further discussion of residual and emergent ideological forms, see Raymond Williams, *Marxism and Literature* (New York: Oxford University Press, 1977).

28. See Allen Hunter, *Children in the Service of Conservatism* (Madison: University of Wisconsin, Institute for Legal Studies, 1988) and Apple, *Cultural Politics and Education.*

29. See, for example, E. D. Hirsch Jr., *The Schools We Need and Why We Don't Have Them* (New York: Doubleday, 1996). For an insightful critique of Hirsch's position, see Kristen L. Buras, "Questioning Core Assumptions: A Critical Reading of E. D. Hirsch's *The Schools We Need and Why We Don't Have Them,*" *Harvard Educational Review* 69 (spring 1999): 67–93. See also Susan Ohanian, *One Size Fits Few: The Folly of Educational Standards* (Portsmouth, NH: Heinemann, 1999).

30. William Bennett, *The Book of Virtues* (New York: Simon & Schuster, 1994).

31. William Bennett, *Our Children and Our Country* (New York: Simon & Schuster, 1988), 8–10.

32. See Amy Stuart Wells, *Beyond the Rhetoric of Charter School Reform* (Los Angeles: University of California at Los Angeles, Graduate School of Education and Information Studies, 1999).

33. Mary Douglas, *Purity and Danger* (London: Routledge, 1966).

34. See, for example, Cameron McCarthy and Warren Crichlow, eds., *Race, Identity, and Representation in Education* (New York: Routledge, 1994).

35. This is treated in greater depth in Apple, *Ideology and Curriculum.*

36. Lawrence Levine, *The Opening of the American Mind* (Boston: Beacon Press, 1996), 20.

37. Ibid.

38. Ibid., 15. See also Apple, *Ideology and Curriculum* and Herbert Kliebard, *The Struggle for the American Curriculum,* 2d ed. (New York: Routledge, 1995).

39. Levine, *The Opening of the American Mind,* 15.

40. Catherine Cornbleth and Dexter Waugh, *The Great Speckled Bird* (New York: St. Martin's Press, 1995).

41. For a counternarrative on the history of the United States, see Howard Zinn, *A People's History of the United States* (New York: HarperCollins, 1999). See also Howard Zinn, *The Howard Zinn Reader* (New York: Seven Stories Press, 1997) and Howard Zinn, *The Future of History* (Monroe, ME: Common Courage Press, 1999).

42. This is often done through a process of "mentioning" where texts and curricula include material on the contributions of women and "minority" groups but never allow the reader to see the world through the eyes of oppressed groups. Or as is the case in the discourse of "we are all immigrants," compromises are made so that the myth of historical similarity is constructed at the same time as economic divides among groups grow worse and worse. See Apple, *Official Knowledge,* 42–60.

43. Diane Ravitch, *National Standards in American Education* (Washington, DC: The Brookings Institution, 1995).

44. In the face of concerted criticism, the NCTM recently has officially voted to return to more of an emphasis on traditional mathematical concerns and methods of teaching. See Anemona Hartocollis, "Math Teachers Back Return of Education to Basic Skills," *The New York Times,* 15 April 2000, p. A16.

45. This is discussed in more detail in Michael W. Apple, *Power, Meaning, and Identity* (New York: Peter Lang, 1999) and Apple, *Cultural Politics and Education.* See also Ohanian, *One Size Fits Few.*

46. This distinction is developed in more depth in Dale, *The State and Education Policy.*

47. For a detailed critical discussion of the effects of this on curricula, teaching, and evaluation, see Linda McNeil, *Contradictions of School Reform* (New York: Routledge, 2000).

48. See Apple, *Education and Power;* Apple, *Teachers and Texts;* and Acker, "Gender and Teachers' Work." Clear gender and class antagonisms are at work

here, ones that have a long history. Analyses of the ways in which race intersects with these dynamics and helps construct the history and labor process of teaching has been somewhat less developed. However, the ongoing work of Michelle Foster and Michael Fultz is quite helpful in this regard.

49. Richard Herrnstein and Charles Murray, *The Bell Curve* (New York: Free Press, 1994).

50. See Michael Omi and Howard Winant, *Racial Formation in the United States,* 2d ed. (New York: Routledge, 1994) and Steven Selden, *Inheriting Shame* (New York: Teachers College Press, 1999). Selden's book in particular demonstrates how very prevalent constructions of race were in a wide range of educational policies and practices, including many programs and individuals whose participation in, say, the popular eugenics movement is little known.

51. Ibid. See also Richard Dyer, *White* (New York: Routledge, 1997) and Cornel West, *Race Matters* (New York: Vintage Books, 1994).

52. Rebecca Klatch, *Women of the New Right* (Philadelphia: Temple University Press, 1987). For criticism of some of these positions, and especially those espoused by Herrnstein and Murray, see Joe Kincheloe, Shirley Steinberg, and Aaron D. Gresson, eds., *Measured Lies* (New York: St. Martin's Press, 1996).

53. For further discussion of this, see Apple, *Cultural Politics and Education,* 11–13.

54. Hunter, *Children in the Service of Conservatism,* 15.

55. Quoted in Ibid., 57.

56. Ibid.

57. The power of the text and its contradictory impulses have been detailed in Apple, *Teachers and Texts* and Apple, *Official Knowledge.* For more discussion of the ways in which struggles over the textbook help mobilize conservative activists, see Apple, *Cultural Politics and Education,* 42–67.

58. Delfattore, *What Johnny Shouldn't Read,* 123.

59. Ibid., 139.

60. The history and influence of the state's role in defining official knowledge and in textbooks is developed in much more depth in Apple, *Teachers and Texts* and Apple, *Official Knowledge.* See also Cornbleth and Waugh, *The Great Speckled Bird.*

61. See Delfattore, *What Johnny Shouldn't Read;* Ralph Reed, *After the Revolution* (Dallas: Word Publishing, 1996); and Fritz Detwiler, *Standing on the Premises of God* (New York: New York University Press, 1999).

62. Anita Oliver and I provide an analysis of a concrete instance of this in Apple, *Cultural Politics and Education,* 42–67.

63. Although he limits himself to a discussion of the nation as an "imagined community," I am extending Benedict Anderson's metaphor to include religious communities as well since many of the attributes are the same. See Benedict Anderson, *Imagined Communities* (New York: Verso, 1991).

64. Fraser, *Unruly Practices,* 172–73.

65. Basil Bernstein makes an important distinction between those fractions of the new middle class who work for the state and those who work in the private sector. They may have different ideological and educational commitments. See Basil Bernstein, *The Structuring of Pedagogic Discourse* (New York: Routledge, 1990). For more on the ways "intermediate" classes and class fractions operate and interpret their worlds, see Erik Olin Wright, ed., *The Debate on Classes* (New York: Verso, 1998); Erik Olin Wright, *Classes* (New York: Verso, 1985); Erik Olin Wright, *Class Counts* (New York: Cambridge University Press, 1997); and Pierre Bourdieu, *Distinction* (Cambridge: Harvard University Press, 1984).

66. See Bourdieu, *Distinction;* Pierre Bourdieu, *Homo Economicus* (Stanford: Stanford University Press, 1988); and Pierre Bourdieu, *The State Nobility* (Stanford: Stanford University Press, 1996).

67. A combination of the work of Bernstein, Wright, and Bourdieu would be useful in understanding this class. A satirical, but still interesting, analysis of a segment of this class can be found in the work of the conservative commentator David Brooks. See David Brooks, *Bobos in Paradise* (New York: Simon & Schuster, 2000).

68. See Apple, *Cultural Politics and Education,* 22–41.

69. See especially Michael W. Apple and James A. Beane, eds., *Democratic Schools* (Alexandria, VA: Association for Supervision and Curriculum Development, 1995); Michael W. Apple and James A. Beane, eds., *Democratic Schools: Lessons from the Chalk Face* (Buckingham, England: Open University Press, 1999); and Gregory Smith, *Public Schools That Work* (New York: Rout-

ledge, 1993). Also of considerable interest here is the work on detracking and educational reform by Jeannie Oakes. See Jeannie Oakes, Karen H. Quartz, Steve Ryan, and Martin Lipton, *Becoming Good American Schools* (San Francisco: Jossey-Bass, 2000).

70. See Jacques Steinberg, "Blue Books Closed, Students Boycott Standardized Tests," *The New York Times,* 13 April 2000, pp. A1, A22. It remains to be seen whether this will grow. It is also unclear whether children of the poor and culturally and economically disenfranchised will participate widely in this. After all, affluent children *do* have options and can compensate for not having tests scores. This may not be the case for the children of those this society calls the "Other."

71. See, for example, the journal *Rethinking Schools.* It is one of the very best indicators of progressive struggles, policies, and practices in education. Information can be gotten from Rethinking Schools, 1001 E. Keefe Avenue, Milwaukee, WI 53212, USA or via its Web site at <www.rethinkingschools.org>.

Chapter 3

1. Geoff Whitty, "Sociology and the Problem of Radical Educational Change," in *Educability, Schools, and Ideology,* ed. Michael Flude and John Ahier (London: Halstead Press 1974), 112–37.

2. Pierre Bourdieu, *Distinction* (Cambridge: Harvard University Press, 1984).

3. Herbert Kliebard, *The Struggle for the American Curriculum,* 2d ed. (New York: Routledge, 1995).

4. John Rury and Jeffrey Mirel, "The Political Economy of Urban Education," in *Review of Research in Education, Volume 22,* ed. Michael W. Apple (Washington, DC: American Educational Research Association, 1997), 49–110; Kenneth Teitelbaum, *Schooling for Good Rebels* (New York: Teachers College Press, 1996); and Steven Selden, *Inheriting Shame* (New York: Teachers College Press, 1999).

5. Michael W. Apple, *Official Knowledge,* 2d ed. (New York: Routledge, 2000) and Michael W. Apple, *Cultural Politics and Education* (New York: Teachers College Press, 1996).

6. Richard Herrnstein and Charles Murray, *The Bell Curve* (New York: Free Press, 1994). See also Joe Kincheloe, Shirley Steinberg, and Aaron D. Gresson, eds., *Measured Lies* (New York: St. Martin's Press, 1997).

7. Apple, *Cultural Politics and Education,* 22–41.

8. Stuart Ranson, "Theorizing Educational Policy," *Journal of Education Policy* 10 (July 1995): 427.

9. David Gillborn, "Race, Nation, and Education," unpublished paper, Institute of Education, University of London, 1997, p. 2.

10. Gary McCulloch, "Privatising the Past," *British Journal of Educational Studies* 45 (March 1997): 80.

11. See E. D. Hirsch Jr., *The Schools We Need and Why We Don't Have Them* (New York: Doubleday, 1996).

12. Quoted in McCulloch, "Privatising the Past," 78.

13. Ibid.

14. Ibid.

15. John Chubb and Terry Moe, *Politics, Markets, and American Schools* (Washington, DC: The Brookings Institution, 1990) and Geoff Whitty, "Creating Quasi-Markets in Education," in *Review of Research in Education, Volume 22,* ed. Michael W. Apple (Washington, DC: American Educational Research Association, 1997), 3–47.

16. David Gillborn, "Racism and Reform," *British Educational Research Journal* 23 (June 1997): 357.

17. Michael W. Apple, *Power, Meaning, and Identity* (New York: Peter Lang, 1999) and Michael W. Apple, *Teachers and Texts* (New York: Routledge, 1988). Of course, there has been a considerable amount of literature on the question of "clarity" in critical educational writings, with contributions on both sides made by Burbules, Giroux, Lather, Gitlin, myself, and a number of others. My own position on this is that such a debate is essential and that while there is a danger in sacrificing theoretical elegance and the richness and subtlety of language in our attempts to be clear, there is still a good deal of arrogance and truly sloppy and merely rhetorical writing within the multiple communities of critical educational work. Obviously, there is a need to respond to complexity, but there is also a need not to marginalize sympathetic readers.

18. Gillborn, "Racism and Reform," 353.

19. Ibid.

20. Herrnstein and Murray, *The Bell Curve* and Hirsch, *The Schools We Need and Why We Don't Have Them.*

21. Roger Dale quoted in Ian Menter, Yolande Muschamp, Peter Nicholls, Jenny Ozga, with Andrew Pollard, *Work and Identity in the Primary School* (Philadelphia: Open University Press, 1997), 27.

22. Menter et al., *Work and Identity in the Primary School,* 27.

23. See Whitty, "Creating Quasi-Markets in Education." See also Geoff Whitty, Tony Edwards, and Sharon Gewirtz, *Specialization and Choice in Urban Education* (London: Routledge, 1993) and Apple, *Cultural Politics and Education.* The integration of markets, standards, and performance indicators is clearly expressed in David Stearns and James Harvey, *A Legacy of Learning: Your Stake in Standards and New Kinds of Public Schools* (Washington, DC: The Brookings Institution, 2000). This book is an intriguing example of "plain talk" and manages to strike a series of populist notes while at the same time placing the needs of the economy and efficiency at the very center of its proposals for "democracy."

24. Chubb and Moe, *Politics, Markets, and American Schools.*

25. Sally Power, David Halpin, and John Fitz, "Underpinning Choice and Diversity," in *Educational Reform and Its Consequences,* ed. Sally Tomlinson (London: IPPR/Rivers Oram Press, 1994), 27.

26. Whether there have been significant changes in this regard given the victory by "New Labour" over the Conservatives in the last election is open to question. Certain aspects of neoliberal and neoconservative policies have already been accepted by Labour, such as the acceptance of stringent cost controls on spending put in place by the previous Conservative government and an aggressive focus on "raising standards" in association with strict performance indicators. See, for example, David Gillborn and Debbie Youdell, *Rationing Education* (Philadelphia: Open University Press, 2000).

27. See Power, Halpin, and Fitz, "Underpinning Choice and Diversity" and Gillborn and Youdell, *Rationing Education.*

28. Stephen Ball, Richard Bowe, and Sharon Gewirtz, "Market Forces and Parental Choice," in *Educational Reform and Its Consequences,* ed. Sally Tomlinson (London: IPPR/Rivers Oram Press, 1994), 39.

29. Ibid., 17–19.

30. Mark Olssen, "In Defense of the Welfare State and of Publicly Provided Education," *Journal of Education Policy* 11 (May 1996): 340.

31. Ball, Bowe, and Gewirtz, "Market Forces and Parental Choice," 19.

32. See the discussion of the racial state in Michael Omi and Howard Winant, *Racial Formation in the United States* (New York: Routledge, 1994) and the analyses of race and representation in Cameron McCarthy and Warren Crichlow, eds., *Race, Identity, and Representation in Education* (New York: Routledge, 1994) and Cameron McCarthy, *The Uses of Culture* (New York: Routledge, 1998).

33. Bourdieu, *Distinction.*

34. Ball, Bowe, and Gewirtz, "Market Forces and Parental Choice," 20–22.

35. Michelle Fine and Lois Weis, *The Unknown City* (Boston: Beacon Press, 1998) and Mitchell Duneier, *Sidewalk* (New York: Farrar, Straus & Giroux, 1999).

36. Pierre Bourdieu, *The State Nobility* (Stanford: Stanford University Press, 1996) and David Swartz, *Culture and Power* (Chicago: University of Chicago Press, 1997).

37. Apple, *Teachers and Texts* and Apple, *Official Knowledge,* 113–36.

38. Whitty, Power, and Halpin, *Devolution and Choice in Education,* 12–13.

39. Ibid., 36.

40. Olssen, "In Defense of the Welfare State and Publicly Provided Education."

41. Whitty, Power, and Halpin, *Devolution and Choice in Education,* 37–38. See also the discussion of managerialism and the state in John Clarke and Janet Newman, *The Managerial State* (Thousand Oaks, CA: Sage, 1997).

42. This is discussed in greater detail in Michael W. Apple, *Education and Power,* 2d ed. (New York: Routledge, 1995).

43. See Omi and Winant, *Racial Formation in the United States;* Debbie Epstein and Richard Johnson, *Schooling Sexualities* (Philadelphia: Open University Press, 1998); and Sue Middleton, *Disciplining Sexualities* (New York: Teachers College Press, 1998).

44. Whitty, Power, and Halpin, *Devolution and Choice in Education,* 60–62.

45. Among the best work here is Nancy Fraser, *Unruly Practices* (Minneapolis: University of Minnesota Press, 1989) and Nancy Fraser, *Justice Interruptis* (New York: Routledge, 1997).

46. Whitty, Power, and Halpin, *Devolution and Choice in Education,* 63.

47. Ibid., 67–68. See also Gillborn and Youdell, *Rationing Education.*

48. Youdell and Gillborn's *Rationing Education* demonstrates this clearly. What is also important here is that this has consistently happened even in the face of overt attempts to use such policies to alter existing inequalities. See also Whitty, Power, and Halpin, *Devolution and Choice in Education,* 119–20.

49. Whitty, Power, and Halpin, *Devolution and Choice in Education,* 80.

50. Ibid. See also Gillborn and Youdell, *Rationing Education* and Sharon Gewirtz, Stephen Ball, and Richard Bowe, *Markets, Choice, and Equity in Education* (Philadelphia: Open University Press, 1995). We need to be very cautious of employing these data to legitimate the "model minority" stereotype of Asian students. See Stacey Lee, *Unraveling the Model-Minority Stereotype* (New York: Teachers College Press, 1996).

51. Hugh Lauder and David Hughes, *Trading in Futures* (Philadelphia: Open University Press, 1999), 2.

52. Ibid., 29. See also Phil Brown, "Cultural Capital and Social Exclusion," in *Education: Culture, Economy, and Society,* ed. A. H. Halsey, Hugh Lauder, Phil Brown, and Amy Stuart Wells (New York: Oxford University Press, 1997), 736–49.

53. Lauder and Hughes, *Trading in Futures,* 101.

54. Ibid., 132.

55. Petter Aasen, "What Happened to Social Democratic Progressivism in Scandinavia?: Restructuring Education in Sweden and Norway," unpublished paper, Department of Education, Norwegian University of Science and Technology, Trondheim, Norway, 1998.

56. On the issue of a racial contract that underpins nearly all social arrangements in our kind of society, see Charles W. Mills, *The Racial Contract* (Ithaca: Cornell University Press, 1997). I am drawing as well on Benedict An-

derson's position that nations are themselves based on "imagined communities." See Benedict Anderson, *Imagined Communities* (New York: Verso, 1991).

57. See, for example, the analysis of the gender dynamics surrounding neoliberal policies in Madeleine Arnot, Miriam David, and Gaby Weiner, *Closing the Gender Gap* (Cambridge: Polity Press, 1999). The ways in which neoconservative policies act on and through the politics of sexuality and the body as well are nicely described in Epstein and Johnson, *Schooling Sexualities.*

58. Whitty, Power, and Halpin, *Devolution and Choice in Education,* 98. See also Amy Stuart Wells, *Beyond the Rhetoric of Charter School Reform* (Los Angeles: University of California at Los Angeles, Graduate School of Education and Information Studies, 1999).

59. Whitty, Power, and Halpin, *Devolution and Choice in Education,* 112–13.

60. Ibid., 14.

61. Ibid., 42.

62. Jeffrey R. Henig, *Rethinking School Choice: Limits of a Market Metaphor* (Princeton, NJ: Princeton University Press, 1994), 222. See also some of the comments in Michael Engel, *The Struggle to Control Public Education* (Philadelphia: Temple University Press, 2000).

63. See especially the discussion of the role of the state in this in Bourdieu, *The State Nobility.*

64. Loic Wacquant, "Foreword" to Bourdieu, *The State Nobility,* xiii.

65. Bourdieu, *The State Nobility,* 273.

66. Ball, Bowe, and Gewirtz, "Market Forces and Parental Choice," 24.

67. Menter et al., *Work and Identity,* 8.

68. Ibid., 57. The work of Susan Robertson on the global effects of these transformations, especially on teachers, is exceptional. See, for example, Susan Robertson, *A Class Act: Changing Teachers' Work, the State, and Globalization* (New York : Falmer Press, 2000).

69. Ibid., 9.

70. Ibid., 24.

71. Ibid.

72. Apple, *Cultural Politics and Education,* 22–41.

73. Ball, Bowe, and Gewirtz, "Market Forces and Parental Choice," 23.

74. Power, Halpin, and Fitz, "Underpinning Choice and Diversity," 38.

75. Ranson, "Theorizing Educational Policy," 436.

76. Ibid. See also Misook Kim Cho and Michael W. Apple, "Schooling, Work, and Subjectivity," *British Journal of Sociology of Education* 19 (summer 1998): 269–90.

77. Ranson, "Theorizing Educational Policy," 437.

78. Richard Hatcher and Barry Troyna quoted in Ibid., 438.

79. Ranson, "Theorizing Educational Policy," 438.

80. Philip O'Hear, "An Alternative National Curriculum," in *Educational Reform and Its Consequences,* ed. Sally Tomlinson (London: IPPR/Rivers Oram Press, 1994), 66.

81. Ibid., 55–57.

82. Ibid., 68.

83. Ibid., 65–66.

84. Catherine Gipps and Patricia Murphy, *A Fair Test?* (Philadelphia: Open University Press, 1994), 204.

85. See Basil Bernstein, *The Structuring of Pedagogic Discourse* (New York: Routledge, 1990), Basil Bernstein, *Pedagogy, Symbolic Control, and Identity* (Bristol, PA: Taylor & Francis, 1996), and Apple, *Official Knowledge,* 61–88.

86. John Evans and Dawn Penney, "The Politics of Pedagogy," *Journal of Education Policy* 10 (January 1995): 27–44. See also Ting-Hong Wong and Michael W. Apple, "Rethinking the Education/State Formation Connection," unpublished paper.

87. Ibid., 41–42.

88. See, for example, Robert Linn, "Assessment and Accountability," *Educational Researcher* 29 (March 2000): 4–16; Jeannie Oakes, "Can Tracking Research Inform Practice?" *Educational Researcher* 21 (March 1992): 12–21: Jeannie Oakes, Amy Stuart Wells, Makeba Jones, and Amanda Datnow, "Detracking: The Social Construction of Ability, Cultural Politics, and Resistance to Reform," *Teachers College Record* 98 (spring 1997): 482–510; and Amy Stuart Wells, Alejandra Lopez, Janelle Scott, and Jennifer Holme, "Charter Schools as Postmodern Paradox: Rethinking Social Stratification in an Age of Deregulated School Choice," *Harvard Educational Review* 69 (summer 1999): 172–204.

89. See, for example, Michael W. Apple and James A. Beane, eds., *Democratic Schools* (Alexandria, VA: Association for Supervision and Curriculum Development, 1995).

90. Gillborn and Youdell, *Rationing Education.*

91. See, for example, Stephen Jay Gould, *The Mismeasure of Man* (New York: W. W. Norton, 1981) and Steven Selden, *Inheriting Shame* (New York: Teachers College Press, 1999).

92. Gillborn and Youdell, *Rationing Education,* 194.

93. Ibid., 195.

94. Linda McNeil, *Contradictions of School Reform* (New York: Routledge, 2000).

95. See Glen Y. Wilson, "Effects on Funding Equity of the Arizona Tax Credit Law," paper presented at the annual meeting of the American Educational Research Association, New Orleans, April 2000 and Michele S. Moses, "The Arizona Tax Credit and Hidden Considerations of Justice," paper presented at the annual meeting of the American Educational Research Association, New Orleans, April 2000. See also Mary Lee Smith, Walter Heinecke, and Audrey Noble, "Assessment Policy and Political Spectacle," *Teachers College Record* 101 (winter 1999): 157–91.

96. Terri Seddon, "Markets and the English," *British Journal of Sociology of Education* 18 (June 1997): 165–66.

97. Alan Luke, "Series Editor's Introduction" to Jay Lemke, *Textual Politics* (Bristol, PA: Taylor & Francis, 1995), vi–vii.

98. *Rethinking Schools* is one of the best examples of the ways critical academics, elementary/middle/high school teachers, students, and community activists can work together in nonelitist ways. Information can be gotten from *Rethinking Schools,* 1001 E. Keefe Avenue, Milwaukee, WI 53212, USA. For faxes, the number is 414–964–7220. The Web site is <www.rethinkingschools.org>. For an articulate discussion of Freire's work and of the complexities of putting it into practice in schools, see Maria Pilar O'Cadiz, Pia Lindquist Wong, and Carlos Alberto Torres, *Education and Democracy: Paulo Freire, Social Movements, and Educational Reform in Sao Paulo* (Boulder: Westview Press, 1998). Freire's work, however, has too often been appropriated in rhetorical and/or depoliticized ways in the United States. See my discussion of this

in Michael W. Apple, *Power, Meaning, and Identity* (New York: Routledge, 1999).

99. Apple and Beane, eds., *Democratic Schools.*

100. Translations of this volume have been or are due to be published in Japan, Argentina, Brazil, Spain, Portugal, and elsewhere. A Commonwealth edition for the UK, Australia, New Zealand, and other nations has also recently appeared. See Michael W. Apple and James A. Beane, eds., *Democratic Schools: Lessons from the Chalk Face* (Buckingham, England: Open University Press, 1999). Thus, it is clear that providing critical answers to the pressing issues of "What do I do on Monday?" is seen as crucial in a number of nations.

101. Apple, *Teachers and Texts* and Apple, *Power, Meaning, and Identity.*

102. Dennis Carlson and Michael W. Apple, "Critical Educational Theory in Unsettling Times," in *Power/Knowledge/Pedagogy,* ed. Dennis Carlson and Michael W. Apple (Boulder: Westview Press, 1998), 1–38.

103. Henry Giroux, *Border Crossings* (Routledge, 1992), 219.

104. One of the clearest discussion of the ethical and political dilemmas of doing critical theoretical and empirical work with due recognition of the importance of connecting this work to the lived culture of social actors in their everyday lives can be found in Fine and Weis, *The Unknown City,* 264–88. See also Carlson and Apple, *Power/Knowledge/Pedagogy* and Linda Tuhiwai Smith, *Decolonizing Methodologies* (New York: Zed Books, 1999).

Chapter 4

1. Joan Delfattore, *What Johnny Shouldn't Read* (New Haven: Yale University Press, 1992), 93.

2. Pam Belluck, "Board for Kansas Deletes Evolution From the Curriculum," *The New York Times,* 12 August 1999, pp. A1, A13. The Board allowed the teaching of microevolution—genetic adaptation and natural selection *within* a species. Macroevolution—the origin of species—was purged.

3. Belluck, "Board for Kansas Deletes Evolution From Curriculum," p. A13.

4. Ibid.

5. Ibid.

6. For further discussion of the political economy of publishing, see Michael W. Apple, *Teachers and Texts* (New York: Routledge, 1988) and Michael W. Apple, *Official Knowledge,* 2d ed. (New York: Routledge, 2000).

7. Delfattore, *What Johnny Shouldn't Read,* 120.

8. Ronald L. Numbers, *Darwinism Comes to America* (Cambridge: Harvard University Press, 1998), 8–10.

9. Ibid., 10.

10. Ibid., 9.

11. Ibid., 9–11. See also Ronald L. Numbers and John Stenhouse, "Antievolutionism in the Antipodes: From Protesting Evolution to Promoting Creationism in New Zealand," *British Journal for the History of Science,* in press, and Ronald L. Numbers, "Creationists and Their Critics in Australia," unpublished paper, Department of the History of Medicine, University of Wisconsin, Madison.

12. See Ronald L. Numbers, *The Creationists* (New York: Knopf, 1992) for more on the historical roots of such positions.

13. Numbers, *Darwinism Comes to America,* 109.

14. Ibid., 2.

15. Ibid.

16. Ibid., 3.

17. Ibid., 4.

18. Ibid., 5–6.

19. In *Cultural Politics and Education,* for instance, I show how the battle over textbooks doesn't just reflect, but helps form, rightist movements at a local level. See Michael W. Apple, *Cultural Politics and Education* (New York: Teachers College Press, 1996), 42–67.

20. Numbers, *Darwinism Comes to America,* 6.

21. Ibid., 55–56.

22. See Edward Larson, *Trial and Error: The American Controversy over Creation and Evolution* (New York: Oxford University Press, 1989).

23. For a perceptive and detailed analysis of the Scopes trial, see Edward Larson, *Summer of the Gods: The Scopes Trial and America's Continuing Debate over Science and Religion* (New York: Basic Books, 1997). Additional material can be found in Numbers, *Darwinism Comes to America.*

24. Numbers, *Darwinism Comes to America,* 74.

25. I discuss this at greater length in Apple, *Official Knowledge.*

26. Numbers, *Darwinism Comes to America,* 91.

27. Justin Watson, *The Christian Coalition: Dreams of Restoration, Demands for Recognition* (New York: St. Martin's Press, 1997), 27.

28. Richard Berke, "Conservatives Look For Believers Amid G.O.P. Presidential Field," *The New York Times,* 4 February 1999, p. A19.

29. Laurie Goodstein, "Coalition's Woes May Hinder Goals of Christian Right," *The New York Times,* 2 August 1999, p. A1.

30. Apple, *Official Knowledge,* especially Chapter 2.

31. Kenneth J. Heineman, *God is a Conservative: Religion, Politics, and Morality in Contemporary America* (New York: New York University Press, 1998), 265.

32. Delfattore, *What Johnny Shouldn't Read,* 4.

33. Ibid., 14.

34. Ibid., 21.

35. Ibid., 32.

36. Ibid., 82.

37. Ibid., 6.

38. Pat Robertson, *The Secret Kingdom* (Nashville: Thomas Nelson Publishers, 1982), 44.

39. James L. Guth, John C. Green, Corwin E. Smidt, Lyman A. Kellstedt, and Margaret Poloma, *The Bully Pulpit: The Politics of Protestant Clergy* (Lawrence, KS: The University of Kansas Press, 1997), 2.

40. Watson, *The Christian Coalition,* 20.

41. Ibid., 3.

42. Ibid., 12–13.

43. Christian Smith, *American Evangelicalism: Embattled and Thriving* (Chicago: University of Chicago Press, 1998), 1.

44. Ibid., 2.

45. Ibid.

46. Ibid.

47. Ibid., 3.

48. Ibid.

49. Ibid., 5.

50. Ibid., 7.

51. Ibid., 6.

52. Ibid.

53. Ibid., 8.

54. Ibid.

55. Watson, *The Christian Coalition,* 17. Fundamentalists found evidence for Christ's imminent return to establish a thousand-year period of holiness in Revelations 20.

56. Ibid., 17.

57. George Marsden, *Understanding Fundamentalism and Evangelicalism* (Grand Rapids, MI: Eerdmans, 1991), 1.

58. Ibid., 14. However, the initial sense among fundamentalists was that Bryan and the anti-Darwinian cause had totally vanquished their opponents. See, for example, Numbers, *Darwinism Comes to America.*

59. Christian Smith, *American Evangelicalism,* 10.

60. Ibid., 10–11.

61. Ibid., 12–13.

62. Christine Leigh Heyrman, *Southern Cross: The Beginnings of the Bible Belt* (New York: Knopf, 1997), 6.

63. Ibid., 33.

64. Ibid., 61.

65. Ibid., 73.

66. Ibid., 41.

67. Ibid., 6. See also Cornel West, *Prophesy Deliverance!* (Philadelphia: Westminster Press, 1982) for a discussion of the socially and religiously progressive tendencies within the African-American churches historically and currently.

68. Heyrman, *Southern Cross,* 46–53.

69. Ibid., 56.

70. Ibid., 68–69.

71. Ibid., 76.

72. Ibid.

73. Ibid., 155.

74. Ibid., 158.

75. Useful documents on the "cult of domesticity" can be found in Nancy Cott, ed., *Roots of Bitterness: Documents of the Social History of Women* (New York: E. P. Dutton, 1972). Of course, these positions were both class and race specific and were not accepted passively. They were mediated, contested constantly, and actively used for other purposes by women in quite complex and contradictory ways. See Carroll Smith-Rosenberg, *Disorderly Conduct: Visions of Gender in Victorian America* (New York: Oxford University Press, 1985) and Alice Kessler-Harris, *Out to Work: A History of Wage-Earning Women in the United States* New York: Oxford University Press, 1982).

76. Heyrman, *Southern Cross,* 159–60. This too was class and race specific. See Catherine Clinton, *The Plantation Mistress: Woman's World in the Old South* (New York: Pantheon Books, 1982).

77. Heyrman, *Southern Cross,* 160.

78. Ibid., 166.

79. Ibid., 173. This did create tensions among men over male authority, however. See Ibid., 189.

80. See, for example, Rebecca Klatch, *Women of the New Right* (Philadelphia: Temple University Press, 1987).

81. Heyrman, *Southern Cross,* 214.

82. Ibid., 214, 232–39.

83. Ibid., 248–52.

84. Ibid., 254–55.

Chapter 5

1. See, for example, Johannes Van Vught, *Democratic Organizations for Social Change: Latin American Christian Base Communities and Literacy Campaigns* (New York: Bergin & Garvey, 1991).

2. James L. Guth, John C. Green, Corwin E. Smidt, Lyman A. Kellstedt, and Margaret Poloma, *The Bully Pulpit* (Lawrence, KS: University Press of Kansas, 1997), 13–14. This public agenda of moral reform was, of course, not new. A focus on gambling, drinking, prostitution, and education has consistently characterized conservative religious activists historically, as well as activists in more progressive causes.

3. Ibid., 46.

4. Ibid., 63–65.

5. Ibid., 20.

6. Justin Watson, *The Christian Coalition* (New York: St. Martin's Press, 1997), 6.

7. Christian Smith, *American Evangelicalism* (Chicago: University of Chicago Press, 1998), 23–24. Smith also found that there were no generational differences among evangelicals. Younger evangelicals were equally orthodox. See p. 26.

8. Ibid., 84.

9. Ibid., 31.

10. Ibid.

11. Ibid., 206–10.

12. Ibid., 127–29.

13. Ibid., 39. Stress in original.

14. Ibid., 39–43. The relative *lack* of activism among "liberal" Christians is striking in comparison. See p. 43.

15. Ibid., 132–33.

16. Ibid., 34–35.

17. Guth et al., *The Bully Pulpit*, 137.

18. Ibid., 54–55. The connection between evangelical ministries and youth is not new. See, for example, Christine Leigh Heyrman, *Southern Cross* (New York: Knopf, 1997), 77–116.

19. Guth et al., *The Bully Pulpit*, 59.

20. Ibid., 112. This can and does go both ways, of course. There have been moves toward more liberal social beliefs within some churches as well. See Ibid., 121.

21. Ibid., 143–44.

22. Ibid., 183.

23. Sara Diamond, *Spiritual Warfare: The Politics of the Christian Right* (Boston: South End Press, 1989), 3.

24. Ibid., 4.

25. Ibid., 10.

26. Ibid., 12.

27. For more on Robertson's biography, see Watson, *The Christian Coalition.*

28. Ibid., 13.

29. Ibid., 20.

30. Ibid., 17–18.

31. Linda Kintz, *Between Jesus and the Market: The Emotions That Matter in Right-Wing America* (Durham, NC: Duke University Press, 1997), 106.

32. Watson, *The Christian Coalition,* 91. Of course, many neoconservative commentators would part with the authoritarian populists' position that this is a "Christian nation." For neoconservative Jewish commentators, it is the history of openness, cultural pluralism, and "making it" economically that sets the United States aside as *the* special nation. See, for example, Norman Podheretz, *My Love Affair with America: The Cautionary Tale of a Cheerful Conservative* (New York: Free Press, 2000).

33. Smith, *American Evangelicalism,* 136–40.

34. Pat Robertson, "Law Must Embrace Morality," *Christian America,* April 1995, p. 17.

35. Watson, *The Christian Coalition,* 107.

36. Ralph Reed, *Politically Incorrect* (Dallas: Word Publishing, 1994), 79.

37. Smith, *American Evangelicalism,* 140–43.

38. Phyllis Schlafly, "Fact and Fiction About Censorship" (Washington, DC: National Defense Committee, National Society, Daughters of the American Revolution, 1984), 1. See also Eugene F. Provenzo Jr., *Religious Fundamentalism and American Education* (Albany: State University of New York Press, 1990).

39. Smith, *American Evangelicalism,* 44.

40. Ibid.

41. Ibid., 50.

42. Heyrman, *Southern Cross,* 21.

43. Pat Robertson, *The Turning Tide* (Dallas: Word Publishing, 1993), 227–28.

44. Pat Robertson, *The New Millennium* (Dallas: Word Publishing, 1990), 174–75.

45. Smith, *American Evangelicalism,* 136.

46. Robertson, *The Turning Tide*, 239.

47. Ibid.

48. Kenneth J. Heineman, *God Is a Conservative: Religion, Politics, and Morality in Contemporary America* (New York: New York University Press, 1998), 161–62.

49. Guth et al., *The Bully Pulpit*, 166. Another interesting finding here is that significant levels of support for Dobson's emphases were found among somewhat less conservative clergy as well. Obviously, the fear for one's children's future permeates a much larger swath of the population than the religious right.

50. Frederick Clarkson, *Eternal Hostility: The Struggle Between Theocracy and Democracy* (Monroe, ME: Common Courage Press, 1997), viii.

51. Ibid., 39.

52. Robertson, *The Turning Tide*, 233.

53. Pat Robertson, *The New World Order* (Dallas: Word Publishing, 1991), 250.

54. Heineman, *God Is a Conservative*, 100.

55. See Michelle Fine, Lois Weis, Linda C. Powell, and L. Mun Wong, eds., *Off White* (New York: Routledge, 1997); Richard Dyer, *White* (New York: Routledge, 1997); and Michael W. Apple, "The Absent Presence of Race in Educational Reform," *Race, Ethnicity, and Education* 2 (March 1999): 9–16.

56. Watson, *The Christian Coalition*, 171.

57. Robertson, *The Turning Tide*, 144. Robertson also makes reference to the suffering of the Jews and draws parallels between the oppression of Jews under the Nazis and the contemporary experiences of evangelicals. Yet he often has anti-Semitic subtexts within his own writings.

58. Ralph Reed, "Putting a Friendly Face on the Pro-family Movement," *Christianity Today*, April 1993, 28.

59. Heineman, *God Is a Conservative*, 146.

60. Watson, *The Christian Coalition*, 59.

61. Ibid., 63.

62. Ibid., 64.

63. Ibid.

64. Ibid., 64–65.

65. Pat Robertson, *The Secret Kingdom,* 2d ed. (Dallas: Word Publishing, 1992), 60.

66. Watson, *The Christian Coalition,* 175.

67. See Benedict Anderson, *Imagined Communities* (New York: Verso, 1991).

68. Raymond Williams, *Marxism and Literature* (New York: Oxford University Press, 1977). In some ways this is similar to Bourdieu's concept of habitus. See Pierre Bourdieu, *Distinction* (Cambridge: Harvard University Press, 1984).

69. Kintz, *Between Jesus and the Market,* 3.

70. Ibid., 6.

71. Elaine Pagels, *The Origins of Satan* (New York: Random House, 1995), 181. See also Michael O'Leary, *Arguing the Apocalypse* (New York: Oxford University Press, 1994).

72. Kintz, *Between Jesus and the Market,* 9.

73. Ibid., 18.

74. Ibid., 30.

75. Watson, *The Christian Coalition,* 77.

76. Diamond, *Spiritual Warfare,* 104–5.

77. Beverly LaHaye, "Women Restoring Righteousness," in *Judgement at the Gate: A Call to Awaken the Church,* ed. Richie Martin (Westchester, IL: Crossway Books, 1986), 35, 38.

78. Kintz, *Between Jesus and the Market,* 37.

79. Ibid.

80. Julie Kristeva, "Women's Time," *Signs* 7 (autumn 1981): 13–35.

81. Kintz, *Between Jesus and the Market,* 39–40.

82. Ibid., 41.

83. Connie Marshner, *Can Motherhood Survive?* (Brentwood, IN: Wolgemuth & Hyatt, 1990), 2.

84. Robertson, *The New World Order,* 241. See also, Kintz, *Between Jesus and the Market,* 43.

85. Kintz, *Between Jesus and the Market,* 219.

86. Michael Novak, *This Hemisphere of Liberty* (Washington: American Enterprise Institute, 1992), 33.

87. Michael Novak, *Toward a Theology of the Corporation* (Washington, DC: American Enterprise Institute, 1981), 34.

88. Kintz, *Between Jesus and the Market,* 44.

89. As I argue in *Cultural Politics and Education,* having paid work is the identificatory sign of full citizenship in this society, unless one is a white mother. See Michael W. Apple, *Cultural Politics and Education* (New York: Teachers College Press, 1996).

90. Ibid., 99.

91. Diamond, *Spiritual Warfare,* 102.

92. Ibid., 103.

93. Kintz, *Between Jesus and the Market,* 22.

94. Allen Hertzke, *Echoes of Discontent* (Washington, DC: Congressional Quarterly Press, 1992), xv.

95. Kintz, *Between Jesus and the Market,* 185–86.

96. Michelle LeDoeuff, *Hipparchia's Choice* (Cambridge: Blackwell, 1991), 313.

97. Kintz, *Between Jesus and the Market,* 271.

98. Dean Kelly, *Why Conservative Churches Are Growing* (New York: Harper & Row, 1972).

99. Ibid., 85.

100. Ibid., 87.

101. Christian Smith, *American Evangelicalism,* 89.

102. Ibid., 91.

103. Bourdieu, *Distinction.* See also Smith, *American Evangelicalism,* 96–97.

104. Smith, *American Evangelicalism,* 121.

105. I have devoted a good deal of time to specifically arguing against the conceptual and political uses of ideas such as false consciousness. See, for example, Michael W. Apple, *Education and Power,* 2d ed. (New York: Routledge, 1995) and Michael W. Apple, *Official Knowledge,* 2d ed. (New York: Routledge, 2000).

106. Smith, *American Evangelicalism,* 117.

107. Ibid., 103.

108. Ibid., 104.

109. Watson, *The Christian Coalition,* 146.

110. See, for example, Peter McLaren, *Revolutionary Multiculturalism* (Boulder: Westview, 1997).

111. Watson, *The Christian Coalition,* 148.

112. Smith, *American Evangelicalism,* 100.

113. Ibid.

114. Watson, *The Christian Coalition,* 38.

115. For a close up portrayal of the people involved in such racist and militia groups, see Raphael Ezekiel, *The Racist Mind* (New York: Penguin, 1995).

116. Clarkson, *Eternal Hostility,* 78–79.

117. Ibid., 78. Among the most important figures in this movement are the following: Rousas John Rushdoony, author of the defining text, *The Institutes of Biblical Law* (Phillipsburgh, NJ: Presbyterian and Reformed Publishing, 1973); Gary North of the Institute for Christian Economics; and Gary De Mar, president of the Reconstructionist publishing house American Vision, which publishes books primarily for use in Christian schools and for home schoolers. Rushdoony is one of the guiding ideological forces behind the ultrarightist U.S. Taxpayers Party and is on the board of Howard Phillips' Conservative Caucus. The hidden connections between rightist political mobilizations around taxes and unquestioned support of privatization on the one hand and far-right religious groups is important.

118. Clarkson, *Eternal Hostility,* 8.

119. Ibid., 17.

120. Ibid., 119.

121. See Robert Therburn, *The Children Trap: Biblical Principles for Education* (Fort Worth, TX: Dominion Press and Thomas Nelson Publishers, 1986), 171–72.

122. Christopher Klicka, *The Right Choice: The Incredible Failure of Public Education and the Rising Hope of Home Schooling* (Gresham, OR: Noble Publishing Associates, 1992), 109.

123. See, for example, Watson, *The Christian Coalition,* 109–19.

124. Ibid., 37.

125. Ibid., 112.

126. See Bruce Barron, *Heaven on Earth? The Social and Political Agendas of Dominion Theology* (Grand Rapids, MI: Zondervan, 1992), 144–46.

127. Robertson, *The New Millennium,* 64.

128. Watson, *The Christian Coalition,* 121.

Chapter 6

1. It is important that we remember that public schools were and are a victory. They constituted a gain for the majority of people who were denied access to advancement and to valued cultural capital in a stratified society. This is not to claim that the public school did not and does not have differential effects. Indeed, I have devoted many books to uncovering the connections between formal education and the re-creation of inequalities. It is to say that public schooling is a site of conflict, but one that also has been a site of major victories by popular groups. Thus, conservatives would not be so angry at schools if public schools had not had a number of progressive tendencies cemented in them. For more on the victories as well as defeats, see William Reese, *Power and the Promise of School Reform* (New York: Routledge, 1986). On the ways in which many people continued to struggle over the content and processes of schooling, even when they partly lost, see Kenneth Teitelbaum, *Schooling for Good Rebels* (New York: Teachers College Press, 1996).

2. For further information on the National Home Education Research Institute and on its data on home schooling, see the following Web site: http://www.nheri.org.

3. In the United States—unlike, say, England—the term "public" schooling refers only to those schools that are organized, funded, and controlled by the state. All other schools are considered "private" or "religious." Different linguistic meanings provide important insights into the ways language is mobilized in historical conflicts. See Raymond Williams, *Keywords* (New York: Oxford University Press, 1985).

4. See Michael W. Apple, *Cultural Politics and Education* (New York: Teachers College Press, 1996) and Nancy Fraser, *Justice Interruptus* (New York: Routledge, 1997).

5. See, for example, Michael W. Apple and James A. Beane, eds., *Democratic Schools* (Alexandria, VA: Association for Supervision and Curriculum De-

velopment, 1995) and Michael W. Apple and James A. Beane, eds., *Democratic Schools: Lessons from the Chalk Face* (Buckingham, England: Open University Press, 1999).

6. See Fritz Detwiler, *Standing on the Premises of God* (New York: New York University Press, 1999) and Brian Ray, *Home Schooling on the Threshold* (Salem, OR: National Home Education Research Institute, 1999).

7. Detwiler, *Standing on the Premises of God* and Linda Kintz, *Between Jesus and the Market* (Durham, NC: Duke University Press, 1997). In part, the attractiveness of home schooling among religiously motivated parents is also due to a structural difference between schools in the United States and those in many other nations. Historically, although at times mythical, the separation between state-supported schooling and an officially defined state religion has been a distinctive feature of education here. Thus, the absence of particular kinds of religious instruction in schools has been a source of tension among many groups and has generated even more antischool sentiment. See Warren Nord, *Religion and American Education* (Chapel Hill: University of North Carolina Press, 1995). The idea that there has always been a religious substratum—largely white and "mainstream" Protestant—has been advanced in interesting ways in Randall Collins, *The Credential Society* (New York: Academic Press, 1979).

8. Elaine Pagels, *The Origin of Satan* (New York: Random House, 1995).

9. Ibid., 49.

10. Quoted in Kintz, *Between Jesus and the Market,* 80.

11. See William Greider, *One World, Ready or Not* (New York: Simon & Schuster, 1997).

12. I am thinking here of Channel One, the for-profit commercial television show that is in an increasingly large percentage of our middle and secondary schools. In this "reform," students are sold as a captive audience to corporations intent on marketing their products to our children in schools. See Michael W. Apple, *Official Knowledge,* 2d ed. (New York: Routledge, 2000) and Alex Molnar, *Giving Kids the Business* (Boulder: Westview Press, 1996).

13. Of course, the very distinction between "public" and "private" spheres has strong connections to the history of patriarchal assumptions. See Nancy Fraser, *Unruly Practices* (Minneapolis: University of Minnesota Press, 1989).

14. Kintz, *Between Jesus and the Market,* 97.

15. This is a *particular* construction of the family. As Coontz has shown in her history of the family in the United States, it has had a very varied form, with the nuclear family that is so important to conservative formulations merely being one of many. See Stephanie Coontz, *The Way We Never Were* (New York: Basic Books, 1992).

16. Kintz, *Between Jesus and the Market,* 107.

17. Ibid.

18. Ibid., 108.

19. Of course, it is important to realize that there may be good reasons for some groups to engage in cocooning. Take the example of indigenous or colonized groups. Given the destruction of cultures (and bodies) of oppressed peoples, it is clear that for many of them a form of cocooning is one of the only ways in which cultures and languages can be preserved. Since dominant groups already have cultural and economic power, the relative lack of such power by oppressed peoples creates protective needs. Thus, in cases such as this, cocooning may have a more positive valance.

20. Andrew Shapiro, "The Net That Binds," *The Nation,* 21 June 1999, 168.

21. Ibid.

22. Kintz, *Between Jesus and the Market,* 168.

23. Ibid., 186.

24. Christian Smith, *American Evangelicalism* (Chicago: University of Chicago Press, 1998).

25. John Clarke and Janet Newman, *The Managerial State* (Thousand Oaks, CA: Sage, 1997).

26. Ibid., 5–7.

27. Ibid., 8.

28. See Apple, *Official Knowledge,* especially Chapter 2.

29. For a much less stereotypical picture, one that shows the complexities and struggles of poor and working-class people, see Michelle Fine and Lois Weis, *The Unknown City* (Boston: Beacon Press, 1998).

30. Clarke and Newman, *The Managerial State,* 15.

31. For parts of how this has affected debates over schooling and the curriculum, see Joan Delfattore, *What Johnny Shouldn't Read* (New Haven, CT: Yale University Press, 1992).

32. Antiteacher discourse has a long history, especially in the United States. It was often employed to legitimate centralized and standardized curricula and centralizing decision making about textbooks within the state. See, for example, my discussion of the growth of state textbook adoption policies in Apple, *Official Knowledge.*

33. Apple, *Cultural Politics and Education,* 68–90.

34. A number of highly publicized shootings in schools have occurred in the past few years in the United States. The most well known occurred in Columbine High School in a relatively affluent community in Colorado in which two alienated students killed a teacher and twelve other students and also planted pipe bombs throughout the building. This followed upon other shootings in suburban schools. In a recent instance in a suburban but much less affluent community in Michigan, a six-year-old boy killed a six-year-old girl classmate after an altercation on the playground. The threat of violence is now seen as a very real possibility in schools throughout the United States. It is crucial to understand that violence, both symbolic and material, is wreaked on communities, especially poor ones, *every day.* When families and entire communities are destroyed by job loss, the lack of health care and decent housing, poor or nonexistent child care, and so on, this society is apt to ignore it until what is officially labeled as violence erupts. Millions of more lives are affected by these "unofficial" forms of violence, but because it has somehow become "naturalized," we as a society seem unwilling to deal with it in any serious and long-term way.

35. For a discussion of the larger issues surrounding technology and the contradictions embodied in it, see Hank Bromley and Michael W. Apple, eds., *Education/Technology/Power* (Albany: State University of New York Press, 1998).

36. These changing demographic characteristics are dealt with in more detail in Smith, *American Evangelicalism.*

37. This and other similar material can be found at the following Web site address for The Teaching Home. See <http://www.teachinghome.com/qa/why/htm>.

38. For more on the vision of gender relations underpinning the home, see Kintz, *Between Jesus and the Market.*

39. Class dynamics within the state are quite complicated. See Pierre Bourdieu, *The State Nobility* (Stanford: Stanford University Press, 1996). On the gender specificities within the state and its policies, see Madeleine Arnot, Miriam David, and Gaby Weiner, *Closing the Gender Gap* (Cambridge: Polity Press, 1999) and Suzanne Franzway, Diane Court, and R. W. Connell, *Staking a Claim: Feminism, Bureaucracy, and the State* (Boston: Allen & Unwin, 1989).

40. Fraser, *Justice Interruptus,* 13.

41. Ibid., 14.

42. See Geoff Whitty, Sally Power, and David Halpin, *Devolution and Choice in Education* (Philadelphia: Open University Press, 1998).

43. Apple, *Cultural Politics and Education.*

44. See Whitty, Power, and Halpin, *Devolution and Choice in Education* and Hugh Lauder and David Hughes, *Trading in Futures* (Philadelphia: Open University Press, 1999).

45. Amy Stuart Wells, personal communication. For more on the ways charter schools have provided such mechanisms, see Amy Stuart Wells, *Beyond the Rhetoric of Charter School Reform* (Los Angeles: Graduate School of Education and Information Studies, UCLA, 1999).

46. See Moshe Re'em, *Young Minds in Motion: Teaching and Learning About Difference in Formal and Non-formal Settings,* unpublished doctoral dissertation, University of Wisconsin, Madison, 1998, for an interesting analysis of some of this content.

47. I have gone into considerably more detail on these points in Apple, *Cultural Politics and Education* and Michael W. Apple, *Power, Meaning, and Identity* (New York: Peter Lang, 1999).

48. See, for example, Apple and Beane, *Democratic Schools.*

49. Reese, *Power and the Promise of School Reform* and David Hogan, "Education and Class Formation," in *Cultural and Economic Reproduction in Education,* ed. Michael W. Apple (Boston: Routledge, 1982), 32–78.

50. As I pointed out earlier, one of the best places to turn for an understanding of the more progressive movements surrounding education and social

justice in public schools in the United States is the fast-growing newspaper *Rethinking Schools*. It represents one of the most articulate outlets for critical discussions of educational policy and practice in the country and brings together multiple activist voices: teachers, community activists, parents, academics, students, and others. Once again, it can be contacted at *Rethinking Schools,* 1001 E. Keefe Avenue, Milwaukee, WI 53212, USA or via its Web site at <www.rethinkingschools.org>. See also the British journal *Education and Social Justice*.

51. For more on this, see Michael W. Apple, *Education and Power,* 2d ed. (New York: Routledge, 1995).

52. Raymond Williams, *Resources of Hope* (New York: Verso, 1989), 322.

Chapter 7

1. Michael W. Apple, *Teachers and Texts: A Political Economy of Class and Gender Relations in Education* (New York: Routledge, 1988).

2. Cameron McCarthy, unpublished lecture given at the International Sociology of Education Conference, University of Sheffield, Sheffield, England, January 2000.

3. Tim LaHaye and Jerry B. Jenkins, *The Indwelling* (New York: Tyndale, 2000). Tim LaHaye is the husband of Beverly LaHaye. As I noted in previous chapters, they are both deeply involved in ultraconservative political and cultural causes.

4. Of course, people read all kinds of fiction and are not compelled to follow its precepts. Thus, people can read hard-boiled detective novels in which women and men detectives often engage in violent acts of retribution. This does not necessarily mean that the readers are in favor of such acts. The politics of pleasure follows its own relatively autonomous logic. Most people engage in what have been called "guilty pleasures" and reading books like *The Indwelling* may fall under that category for many readers. However, the fact that it is a national best-seller still has considerable importance.

5. The parallels between this position and standpoint epistemology should be obvious. However, this claim has a long history that goes back many years before the development of even more nuanced positions within feminist discourse. See Sandra Harding, *Whose Science? Whose Knowledge? Thinking from*

Women's Lives (Ithaca: Cornell University Press, 1991) and Gyorgy Lukacs, *History and Class Consciousness* (Cambridge: MIT Press, 1971).

6. Jose Segarra and Ricardo Dobles, eds., *Learning as a Political Act: Struggles for Learning and Learning from Struggles* (Cambridge: Harvard Educational Review Reprint Series No. 33, 1999), xiii.

7. E. D. Hirsch Jr., *The Schools We Need and Why We Don't Have Them* (New York: Doubleday, 1996). See also the powerful criticism of Hirsch in Kristen Buras, "Questioning Core Assumptions: A Critical Reading and Response to E. D. Hirsch, *The Schools We Need and Why We Don't Have Them,*" *Harvard Educational Review* 69 (spring 1999): 67–93.

8. Michael W. Apple, *Cultural Politics and Education* (New York: Teachers College Press, 1996).

9. Of course, in actuality the content and form of curricula and teaching have always been political issues. See Michael W. Apple, *Ideology and Curriculum,* 2d ed.(New York: Routledge, 1990). On some of the recent curriculum struggles in England and Wales, see Richard Hatcher and Ken Jones, eds., *Education After the Conservatives* (Stoke-on Trent, England: Trentham Books, 1996).

10. Jo Boaler, *Experiencing School Mathematics* (Philadelphia: Open University Press, 1998).

11. In Basil Bernstein's terminology, we could say the curriculum and teaching in this instance were strongly classified and strongly framed. See Basil Bernstein, *Class, Codes, and Control, Volume 3,* 2d ed. (London: Routledge, 1977).

12. The focus on keeping youth "under control" is connected to a long history of the fear of youth and of seeing them as constantly in need of regulation. For an insightful discussion of this history, see Nancy Lesko, *Act Your Age!* (New York: Routledge, 2001).

13. See Alex Molnar, Philip Smith, John Zahorik, Amanda Palmer, Anke Halbach, and Karen Ehrle, "Evaluating the SAGE Program," *Educational Evaluation and Policy Analysis* 21 (summer 1999): 165–77. See also Alex Molnar, *Vouchers, Class Size Reduction, and Student Achievement* (Bloomington, IN: Phi Delta Kappa Education Foundation, 2000).

14. Linda Tuhiwai Smith, *Decolonizing Methodologies* (New York: Zed Books, 1999). See also Andrew Gitlin, ed., *Power and Method* (New York: Routledge, 1994).

15. A large amount of data are synthesized in Apple, *Cultural Politics and Education,* 68–90.

16. See, for example, Michael W. Apple, *Power, Meaning, and Identity* (New York: Peter Lang, 1999). The debate over class analysis and over how it might be done can be found in Erik Olin Wright, ed., *The Debate on Classes* (New York: Verso, 1989) and Erik Olin Wright, *Class Counts: Comparative Studies in Class Analysis* (New York : Cambridge University Press, 1997).

17. Michael Omi and Howard Winant, *Racial Formation in the United States* (New York: Routledge, 1994), 158–59.

18. Ibid., 159.

19. I am thinking of Richard Herrnstein and Charles Murray's *The Bell Curve* (New York: Free Press, 1994).

20. See Daniel Liston, *Capitalist Schools* (New York: Routledge, 1988).

21. See, for example, Stephen Jay Gould, *The Mismeasure of Man* (New York: W. W. Norton, 1981) and Donna Harraway, *Primate Visions* (New York: Routledge, 1989).

22. Sally Tomlinson, "New Inequalities: Educational Markets and Ethnic Minorities," paper presented at the symposium on Racism and Reform in the United Kingdom at the annual meeting of the American Educational Research Association, San Diego, April 1998.

23. See, for example, the provoucher arguments advanced by Gary Rosen where he argues that vouchers are the only way African-Americans can have the possibility of a "real" education. See Gary Rosen, "Are School Vouchers Un-American?" *Commentary* 109 (February 2000): 26–31.

24. Linda McNeil, *Contradictions of School Reform* (New York: Routledge, 2000).

25. Charles Gallagher, "White Reconstruction in the University," *Socialist Review* 94, nos. 1 and 2 (1995): 194.

26. Richard Dyer, *White* (New York: Routledge, 1997), 19.

27. There is a vast literature here. See, for example, Omi and Winant, *Racial Formation in the United States;* Cameron McCarthy and Warren

Crichlow, eds., *Race, Identity, and Representation in Education* (New York: Routledge, 1994); William Tate, "Critical Race Theory and Education," in *Review of Research in Education, Volume 22,* ed. Michael W. Apple (Washington, DC: American Educational Research Association, 1997), 195–247; Michelle Fine, Lois Weis, Linda Powell, and L. Mun Wong, eds., *Off White* (New York: Routledge, 1997); and Cameron McCarthy, *The Uses of Culture* (New York: Routledge, 1998), to name just a few.

28. Dyer, *White,* 1.

29. Ibid., 2.

30. Ibid., 47.

31. Ibid., 4.

32. Joan Scott, " Multiculturalism and the Politics of Identity," in *The Identity in Question,* ed. John Rajchman (New York: Routledge, 1995), 11.

33. See Joe Kincheloe and Shirley Steinberg, eds., *White Reign: Deploying Whiteness in America* (New York: St. Martin's Press, 1998).

34. Michael W. Apple, *Official Knowledge,* 2d ed. (New York: Routledge, 2000).

35. Steven Selden, *Inheriting Shame* (New York: Teachers College Press, 1999).

36. Rosen, "Are School Vouchers Un-American?" An edited version of my response, along with many others that were critical of Rosen's position, was published in the journal in the next issue. See Michael W. Apple, "Response to Gary Rosen," *Commentary* 109 (June 2000): 20.

37. For example, in one of the "teach-ins" in which I participated in preparation for the anti-WTO mobilizations in Seattle and Washington, DC, very few people had thought about the integration of Spanish language newspapers, television, radio, and Web sites in building support for the movement. Yet these are among the fastest-growing media in the United States, and they reach an audience that is suffering deeply from the effects of globalization and economic exploitation.

38. For analyses of the unequal ways the media are now controlled and for proposals to reconstruct these processes, see Robert McChesney, Ellen Meiksins Wood, and John Bellamy Foster, eds., *Capitalism and the Information Age* (New York: Monthly Review Press, 1998). See also Douglas Kellner,

Media Culture (New York: Routledge, 1995). A useful guide on how to employ talk radio for progressive purposes is Ellen Ratner, *101 Ways to Get Your Progressive Issues on Talk Radio* (Washington, DC: National Press Books, 1997). Discussions of the roles that "public intellectuals" can play here have been varied. Among the more interesting recent discussions is Pierre Bourdieu, *Acts of Resistance* (Cambridge: Polity Press, 1998). Talk radio is not alone here, of course. Once again, creative uses of the World Wide Web can be very useful. The Institute for Public Accuracy, for example, acts as a central link to a large number of progressive reports, media, and activists. Its Web site is institute@igc.org.

39. This is described in Porto Alegre City Secretariat of Education, "Cycles of Formation: Politic-Pedagogical Proposal for the Citizen's School," *Cadernos Pedagogicos* 9 (April 1999): 1–111.

40. Diane Elson, "Socializing Markets, Not Market Socialism," in *Necessary and Unnecessary Utopias,* ed. Leo Panitch and Colin Leys (New York: Monthly Review Press, 1999), 67–85. Elson's entire essay on the criteria that should be used to socialize markets is very thoughtful.

41. See, for example, the discussion in Lesko, *Act Your Age!*

42. Material on this can be gotten from the International Research Institute on Maori and Indigenous Education at the University of Auckland, Auckland, New Zealand.

43. Ruth Coniff, "Left-Right Romance," *The Progressive,* May 2000, 12–15.

44. Ibid., 13.

45. See Apple, *Official Knowledge,* 89–112.

46. Coniff, "Left-Right Romance," 13.

47. For an interesting discussion of these and other issues, see Amy Stuart Wells, Alejandra Lopez, Janelle Scoot, and Jennifer Holme, "Charter Schools as Postmodern Paradox: Rethinking Social Stratification in an Age of Deregulated Choice," *Harvard Educational Review* 69 (summer 1999): 172–204. Recent research on the ways charter schools and "reforms" surrounding school finance have functioned in Arizona, for instance, should make us extremely wary of the connections between rhetoric and reality. See, for example, Michele Moses, "The Arizona Tax Credit and Hidden Considerations of Justice," paper presented at the annual meeting of the American Educational Research As-

sociation, New Orleans, April 2000 and Glen Y. Wilson, "Effects on Funding Equity of Arizona Tax Law," paper presented at the annual meeting of the American Educational Research Association, New Orleans, 2000.

48. See the interesting arguments in Jonathan Schorr, "Giving Charter Schools a Chance," *The Nation,* 5 June 2000, 19–23. I am still not totally convinced that Shorr's arguments in support of the progressive possibilities of charter schools can overcome the conservative context in which charter schools are actually situated. However, Shorr's points need to be taken seriously and should not be rejected out of hand.

49. Michael W. Apple and James A. Beane, eds., *Democratic Schools* (Alexandria, VA: Association for Supervision and Curriculum Development, 1995) and Michael W. Apple and James A. Beane, eds., *Democratic Schools: Lessons from the Chalk Face* (Buckingham, England: Open University Press, 1998). The book has been translated into multiple languages including Spanish, Portuguese, and Japanese and has served as a focal point for more democratic practices in many nations.

50. See Larry Rosenstock and Adria Steinberg, "Beyond the Shop: Reinventing Vocational Education," in Apple and Beane, *Democratic Schools,* 41–57.

51. See, for example, Deborah Meier, Theodore Sizer, Linda Nathan, and Abigail Thernstrom, *Will Standards Save Public Education?* (Boston: Beacon Press, 2000) and David Levine, Robert Lowe, Bob Peterson, and Rita Tenorio, eds., *Rethinking Schools : An Agenda for Change* (New York : New Press, 1995). See also Robert Lowe and Barbara Miner, eds., *Selling Out Our Schools : Vouchers, Markets, and the Future of Public Education* (Milwaukee, WI : Rethinking Schools, 1996) and Robert Lowe and Barbara Miner, eds., *False Choices : Why School Vouchers Threaten Our Children's Future* (Milwaukee, WI: Rethinking Schools, 1992).

52. For an account of these practices, see Apple and Beane, *Democratic Schools* and Gloria Ladson-Billings, *The Dreamkeepers* (San Francisco: Jossey-Bass, 1994). See also Meier, et al. *Will Standards Save American Education?*

53. Leo Panitch and Colin Leys, "Preface," in *Necessary and Unnecessary Utopias,* ed. Leo Panitch and Colin Leys (New York: Monthly Review Press, 1999), vii.

54. Ibid., viii.

Bibliography

Aasen, Petter. "What Happened to Social Democratic Progressivism in Scandinavia?: Restructuring Education in Sweden and Norway." Unpublished paper, Department of Education, Norwegian University of Science and Technology, Trondheim, Norway, 1998.

Acker, Sandra. "Gender and Teachers' Work." In *Review of Research in Education Volume 21,* ed. Michael W. Apple, 99–162. Washington, DC: American Educational Research Association, 1995.

Anderson, Benedict. *Imagined Communities.* New York: Verso, 1991.

Anyon, Jean. *Ghetto Schooling: A Political Economy of Urban Educational Reform.* New York: Teachers College Press, 1997.

Apple, Michael W. *Teachers and Texts: A Political Economy of Class and Gender Relations in Education.* New York: Routledge, 1988.

———. *Ideology and Curriculum,* 2d ed. New York: Routledge, 1990.

———. *Education and Power,* 2d ed. New York: Routledge, 1995.

———. *Cultural Politics and Education.* New York: Teachers College Press, 1996.

———. *Power, Meaning and Identity.* New York: Peter Lang, 1999.

———. "The Absent Presence of Race in Educational Reform." *Race, Ethnicity, and Education* 2 (March 1999): 9–16.

———. *Official Knowledge: Democratic Education in a Conservative Age,* 2d ed. New York: Routledge, 2000.

———. "Are School Vouchers the Answer: A Response to Gary Rosen." *Commentary* 109 (June 2000): 20.

Apple, Michael W., ed. *Cultural and Economic Reproduction in Education*. Boston: Routledge, 1982.

Apple, Michael W., and James A. Beane, eds. *Democratic Schools*. Alexandria, VA: Association for Supervision and Curriculum Development, 1995.

———. *Democratic Schools: Lessons from the Chalk Face*. Buckingham, England: Open University Press, 1999.

Arnot, Madeleine. "Schooling for Social Justice." Unpublished paper, Department of Education, University of Cambridge, 1990.

Arnot, Madeleine, Miriam David, and Gaby Weiner. *Closing the Gender Gap*. Cambridge: Polity Press, 1999.

Ball, Stephen. *Education Reform: A Critical and Post-Structural Approach*. Buckingham, England: Open University Press, 1994.

Ball, Stephen, Richard Bowe, and Sharon Gewirtz. "Market Forces and Parental Choice." In *Educational Reform and Its Consequences*, ed. Sally Tomlinson, 13–25. London: IPPR/Rivers Oram Press, 1994.

Barron, Bruce. *Heaven on Earth? The Social and Political Agendas of Dominion Theology*. Grand Rapids, MI: Zondervan, 1992.

Beckford, James A. *Religion and Advanced Industrial Society*. New York: Routledge, 1989.

Belluck, Pam. "Board for Kansas Deletes Evolution from the Curriculum." *The New York Times, 12* August 1999, A1–A13.

Bennett, William. *Our Children and Our Country*. New York: Simon & Schuster, 1988.

———. *The Book of Virtues*. New York: Simon & Schuster, 1994.

Bennett, William, Chester E. Finn Jr., and John T. E. Cribb Jr. *The Educated Child*. New York: Free Press, 1999.

Berke, Richard. "Conservatives Look for Believers Amid G.O.P. Presidential Field." *The New York Times*, 4 February 1999, A19.

Bernstein, Basil. *Class, Codes, and Control, Volume 3*, 2d ed. London: Routledge, 1977.

———. *The Structuring of Pedagogic Discourse*. New York: Routledge, 1990.

———. *Pedagogy, Symbolic Control, and Identity*. Bristol, PA: Taylor & Francis, 1996.

Boaler, Jo, *Experiencing School Mathematics*. Philadelphia: Open University Press, 1998.

Bourdieu, Pierre, *Distinction*. Cambridge: Harvard University Press, 1984.

———. *Homo Economicus*. Stanford: Stanford University Press, 1988.

———. *The State Nobility*. Stanford: Stanford University Press, 1996.

———. *Acts of Resistance*. Cambridge: Polity Press, 1998

Bowles, Samuel, and Herbert Gintis. *Schooling in Capitalist America*. New York: Basic Books, 1976.

———. *Democracy and Capitalism*. New York: Basic Books, 1986.

Brine, Jacky. *Under-Educating Women: Globalizing Inequality*. Philadelphia: Open University Press, 1999.

Bromley, Hank, and Michael W. Apple, eds. *Education/Technology/Power*. Albany: State University of New York Press, 1998.

Brooks, David. *Bobos in Paradise*. New York: Simon & Schuster, 2000.

Brown, Phillip. "Cultural Capital and Social Exclusion." In *Education: Culture, Economy, and Society*, ed. A. H. Halsey, Hugh Lauder, Phil Brown, and Amy Stuart Wells, 736–49. New York: Oxford University Press, 1997.

Buras, Kristen L. "Questioning Core Assumptions: A Critical Reading of and Response to E. D. Hirsch's *The Schools We Need and Why We Don't Have Them.*" *Harvard Educational Review* 69 (spring 1999): 67–93.

Carlson, Dennis, and Michael W. Apple. "Critical Educational Theory in Unsettling Times." In *Power/Knowledge/Pedagogy*, ed. Dennis Carlson and Michael W. Apple, 1–38. Boulder: Westview Press, 1998.

Carlson, Dennis, and Michael W. Apple, eds. *Power/Knowledge/Pedagogy*. Boulder: Westview Press, 1998.

Cho, Misook K., and Michael W. Apple. "Schooling, Work, and Subjectivity." *British Journal of Sociology of Education* 19 (summer 1998): 269–90.

Chomsky, Noam. *Profit Over People: Neoliberalism and the Global Order*. New York: Seven Stories Press, 1999.

Chubb, John, and Terry Moe. *Politics, Markets, and America's Schools.* Washington, DC: The Brookings Institution, 1990.

Clarke, John, and Janet Newman. *The Managerial State.* Thousand Oaks, CA: Sage, 1997.

Clarkson, Frederick. *Eternal Hostility: The Struggle Between Theocracy and Democracy.* Monroe, ME: Common Courage Press, 1997.

Clinton, Catherine. *The Plantation Mistress: Woman's World in the Old South.* New York: Pantheon Books, 1982.

Cole, Mike, ed. *Bowles and Gintis Revisited.* New York: Falmer Press, 1988.

Coles, Gerald. *Reading Lessons: The Debate Over Literacy.* New York: Hill & Wang, 1998.

Collins, Randall. *The Credential Society.* New York: Academic Press, 1979.

Coniff, Ruth. "Left–Right Romance." *The Progressive* (May 2000): 12–15.

Cook, Christopher. "Temps Demand a New Deal," *The Nation*, 27 March 2000, 13–19.

Coontz, Stephanie. *The Way We Never Were.* New York: Basic Books, 1992.

Cornbleth, Catherine, and Dexter Waugh. *The Great Speckled Bird.* New York: St. Martin's Press, 1995.

Cott, Nancy, ed. *Roots of Bitterness: Documents of the Social History of Women.* New York: E. P. Dutton, 1972.

Dale, Roger. *The State and Education Policy.* Philadelphia: Open University Press, 1989.

———. "The Thatcherite Project in Education: The Case of the City Technology Colleges." *Critical Social Policy* 9 (winter 1989/1990): 4–19.

Delfattore, Joan. *What Johnny Shouldn't Read.* New Haven, CT: Yale University Press, 1992.

Detwiler, Fritz. *Standing on the Premises of God.* New York: New York University Press, 1999.

Diamond, Sara. *Spiritual Warfare: The Politics of the Christian Right.* Boston: South End Press, 1989.

Douglas, Mary. *Purity and Danger: An Analysis of Concepts of Pollution and Taboo.* London: Routledge and Kegan Paul, 1966.

Duneier, Mitchell. *Sidewalk.* New York: Farrar, Straus & Giroux, 1999.

Dyer, Richard. *White.* New York: Routledge, 1997.

Elson, Diane. "Socializing Markets, Not Market Socialism." In *Necessary and Unnecessary Utopias,* ed. Leo Panitch and Colin Leys, 67–85. New York: Monthly Review Press, 1999.

Engel, Michael. *The Struggle for Control of Public Education.* Philadelphia: Temple University Press, 1999.

Epstein, Debbie, and Richard Johnson. *Schooling Sexualities.* Philadelphia: Open University Press, 1998.

Evans, John, and Dawn Penney. "The Politics of Pedagogy: Making a National Curriculum in Physical Education." *Journal of Education Policy* 10 (January 1995): 27–44.

Ezekiel, Raphael. *The Racist Mind: Portraits of American Neo-Nazis and Klansmen.* New York: Penguin, 1995.

Fine, Michelle, and Lois Weis. *The Unknown City: Lives of Poor and Working Class Young Adults.* Boston: Beacon Press, 1998.

Fine, Michelle, Lois Weis, Linda Powell, and L. Mun Wong, eds. *Off White: Readings on Race, Power, and Society.* New York: Routledge, 1997.

Foner, Eric. *The Story of American Freedom.* New York: Norton, 1998.

Foucault, Michel. "The Subject and Power." In *Michel Foucault: Beyond Structuralism and Hermeneutics,* ed. Herbert Dreyfus and Paul Rabinow, 208–26. Chicago: University of Chicago Press, 1982.

Franzway, Suzanne, Diane Court, and R. W. Connell. *Staking a Claim: Feminism, Bureaucracy, and the State.* Boston: Allen & Unwin, 1989.

Fraser, Nancy. *Unruly Practices: Power, Discourse, and Gender in Contemporary Social Theory.* Minneapolis: University of Minnesota Press, 1989.

———. *Justice Interruptus: Critical Reflections on the "Postsocialist" Condition.* New York: Routledge, 1997.

Fraser, Nancy, and Linda Gordon. "A Genealogy of Dependency." *Signs* 19 (winter 1994): 309–36.

Fuller, Bruce, Elizabeth Burr, Luis Huerta, Susan Puryear, and Edward Wexler. *School Choice: Abundant Hopes, Scarce Evidence of Results.* Berkeley and Stanford: University of California, Berkeley and Stanford University, Policy Analysis for California Education, 1999.

Gallagher, Charles. "White Reconstruction in the University." *Socialist Review* 24, nos. 1 and 2 (1995): 165–87.

Gee, James P., Glynda Hull, and Colin Lankshear. *The New Work Order: Behind the Language of the New Capitalism.* Boulder: Westview Press, 1996.

Gewirtz, Sharon, Stephen Ball, and Richard Bowe. *Markets, Choice, and Equity in Education.* Philadelphia: Open University Press, 1995.

Gillborn, David. "Racism and Reform." *British Educational Research Journal* 23 (June 1997): 345–60.

———. "Race, Nation, and Education." Unpublished paper, Institute of Education, University of London, 1997.

Gillborn, David, and Debbie Youdell. *Rationing Education: Policy, Practice, Reform, and Equity.* Philadelphia: Open University Press, 2000.

Gipps, Caroline, and Patricia Murphy. *A Fair Test?: Assessment, Achievement and Equity.* Philadelphia, Open University Press, 1994.

Giroux, Henry. *Border Crossings: Cultural Workers and the Politics of Education.* New York: Routledge, 1992.

Gitlin, Andrew, ed. *Power and Method.* New York: Routledge, 1994.

Goodstein, Laurie. "Coalition's Woes May Hinder Goals of Christian Right." *The New York Times,* 2 August 1999, A1.

Gould, Steven J. *The Mismeasure of Man.* New York: Norton, 1981.

Greider, William. *One World, Ready or Not.* New York: Simon & Schuster, 1997.

Guth, James L., John C. Green, Corwin E. Smidt, Lyman A. Kellstedt, and Margaret Poloma. *The Bully Pulpit: The Politics of Protestant Clergy.* Lawrence, KS: The University of Kansas Press, 1997.

Hall, Stuart. "The Problem of Ideology: Marxism Without Guarantees." In *Stuart Hall: Critical Dialogues in Cultural Studies,* ed. David Morley and Kuan-Hsing Chen, 25–46. New York: Routledge, 1996.

Hall, Stuart, and Lawrence Grossberg. "On Postmodernism and Articulation: An Interview with Stuart Hall." In *Stuart Hall: Critical Dialogues in Cultural Studies,* ed. David Morley and Kuan-Hsing Chen, 131–50. New York: Routledge, 1996.

Haraway, Donna. *Primate Visions: Gender, Race, and Nature in the World of Modern Science.* New York: Routledge, 1989.

Harding, Sandra G. *Whose Science? Whose Knowledge?: Thinking from Women's Lives.* Ithaca, NY: Cornell University Press, 1991.

Hartocollis, Anemona. "Math Teachers Back Return of Education to Basic Skills." *The New York Times,* 15 April 2000, A16.

Hatcher, Richard, and Ken Jones, eds. *Education After the Conservatives.* Stoke-on-Trent, England: Trentham Books, 1996.

Heineman, Kenneth J. *God Is a Conservative: Religion, Politics, and Morality in Contemporary America.* New York: New York University Press, 1998.

Henig, Jeffrey R. *Rethinking School Choice: Limits of a Market Metaphor.* Princeton, NJ: Princeton University Press, 1994.

Herrnstein, Richard, and Charles Murray. *The Bell Curve: Intelligence and Class Structure in American Life.* New York: Free Press, 1994.

Hertzke, Allen D. *Echoes of Discontent: Jesse Jackson, Pat Robertson, and the Resurgence of Populism.* Washington, DC: Congressional Quarterly Press, 1992.

Heyrman, Christine L. *Southern Cross: The Beginnings of the Bible Belt.* New York: Knopf, 1997.

Hirsch, E. D. Jr. *The Schools We Need and Why We Don't Have Them.* New York: Doubleday, 1996.

Hobsbawm, Eric. *The Age of Extremes: A History of the World, 1914–1991.* New York: Pantheon, 1994.

Hogan, David. "Education and Class Formation." In *Cultural and Economic Reproduction in Education,* ed. Michael W. Apple, 32–78. Boston: Routledge, 1982.

Honderich, Ted. *Conservatism.* Boulder: Westview Press, 1990.

House, Ernest. *Schools for Sale.* New York: Teachers College Press, 1998.

Hunter, Allen. *Children in the Service of Conservatism: Parent-Child Relations in the New Right's Pro-Family Rhetoric.* Madison, WI: University of Wisconsin, Institute for Legal Studies, 1988.

Kao, Grace, Marta Tienda, and Barbara Schneider. "Racial and Ethnic Variation in Academic Performance." In *Research in Sociology of Education and Socialization, Volume 11,* ed. Aaron Pallas, 263–97. Greenwich, CT: JAI Press, 1996.

Kearns, David T., and James Harvey. *A Legacy of Learning: Your Stake in Standards and New Kinds of Public Schools.* Washington, DC: The Brookings Institution, 2000.

Kelley, Dean M. *Why Conservative Churches Are Growing: A Study in Sociology of Religion.* New York: Harper & Row, 1972.

Kellner, Douglas. *Media Culture.* New York: Routledge, 1995.

Kessler-Harris, Alice. *Out to Work: A History of Wage-Earning Women in the United States.* New York: Oxford University Press, 1982.

Kincheloe, Joe L., and Shirley R. Steinberg, eds. *White Reign: Deploying Whiteness in America.* New York: St. Martin's Press, 1998.

Kincheloe, Joe L., Shirley R. Steinberg, and Aaron D. Greeson, eds. *Measured Lies: The Bell Curve Examined.* New York: St. Martin's Press, 1996.

Kintz, Linda. *Between Jesus and the Market: The Emotions That Matter in Right-Wing America.* Durham, NC: Duke University Press, 1997.

Klatch, Rebecca E. *Women of the New Right.* Philadelphia: Temple University Press, 1987.

Klicka, Christopher. *The Right Choice: The Incredible Failure of Public Education and the Rising Hope of Home Schooling.* Gresham, OR: Noble Publishing Associates, 1992.

Kliebard, Herbert M. *The Struggle for the American Curriculum,* 2d ed. New York: Routledge, 1995.

———. *Schooled to Work.* New York: Teachers College Press, 1999.

Kristeva, Julie. "Women's Times." *Signs* 7 (autumn 1981): 13–35.

Ladson-Billings, Gloria. *The Dreamkeepers: Successful Teachers of African American Children.* San Francisco: Jossey-Bass, 1994.

LaHaye, Beverly. "Women Restoring Righteousness." In *Judgement at the Gate: A Call to Awake the Church,* ed. Richie Martin, 34–42. Westchester, IL: Crossway Books, 1986.

LaHaye, Tim, and Jerry B. Jenkins. *The Indwelling.* New York: Tyndale, 2000.

Larrain, Jorge. "Stuart Hall and the Marxist Concept of Ideology." In *Stuart Hall: Critical Dialogues in Cultural Studies,* ed. David Morley and Kuan-Hsing Chen, 47–70. New York: Routledge, 1996.

Larson, Edward. *Trial and Error: The American Controversy Over Creation and Evolution.* New York: Oxford University Press, 1989.

———. *Summer of the Gods: The Scopes Trial and America's Continuing Debate Over Science and Religion.* New York: Basic Books, 1997.

Lauder, Hugh, and David Hughes. *Trading in Futures: Why Markets in Education Don't Work.* Philadelphia: Open University Press, 1999.

LeDoeuff, Michèle. *Hipparchia's Choice: An Essay Concerning Women, Philosophy, etc.* Cambridge, MA: Basil Blackwell, 1991.

Lee, Stacy. *Unraveling the Model-Minority Stereotype.* New York: Teachers College Press, 1996.

Lesko, Nancy. *Act Your Age!* New York: Routledge, 2001.

Levine, David, Robert Lowe, Bob Peterson, and Rita Tenorio, eds. *Rethinking Schools: An Agenda for Change.* New York: New Press, 1995.

Levine, Lawrence W. *The Opening of the American Mind: Canon, Culture, and History.* Boston: Beacon Press, 1996.

Linn, Robert L. "Assessment and Accountability." *Educational Researcher* 29 (March 2000): 4–16.

Liston, Daniel. *Capitalist Schools.* New York: Routledge, 1988.

Loewen, James W. *Lies My Teacher Told Me: Everything Your American History Textbook Got Wrong.* New York: New Press, 1995.

Lowe, Robert, and Barbara Miner, eds. *False Choices: Why School Vouchers Threaten Our Children's Future.* Milwaukee, WI: Rethinking Schools, 1992.

———. *Selling Out Our Schools: Vouchers, Markets, and the Future of Public Education.* Milwaukee, WI: Rethinking Schools, 1996.

Lukas, Gyorgy, *History and Class Consciousness.* Cambridge: MIT Press, 1971.

Luke, Alan. "Series Editor's Introduction" to Jay Lemke, *Textual Politics.* Bristol, PA: Taylor & Francis, 1995.

Marsden, George. *Understanding Fundamentalism and Evangelicalism.* Grand Rapids, MI: Eerdmans, 1991.

Marshner, Connie. *Can Motherhood Survive?* Brentwood, IN: Wolge-muth & Hyatt, 1990.

Marx, Karl, and Friedrich Engels. "Manifesto of the Communist Party." In *Marx and Angels: Basic Writings on Politics and Philosophy,* ed. Lewis S. Feuer, 1–41.. New York: Anchor Books, 1959.

McCarthy, Cameron. *The Uses of Culture.* New York: Routledge, 1998.

———. Unpublished lecture at the International Sociology of Educa-tion Conference, University of Sheffield, Sheffield, England, Janu-ary 2000.

McCarthy, Cameron, and Warren Crichlow, eds. *Race, Identity, and Rep-resentation in Education.* New York: Routledge, 1994.

McChesney, Robert. "Introduction" to Noam Chomsky, *Profit Over Peo-ple: Neoliberalism and the Global Order,* 7–16. New York: Seven Sto-ries Press, 1999.

McChesney, Robert, Ellen M. Wood, and John Bellamy Foster, eds. *Capitalism and the Information Age.* New York: Monthly Review Press, 1998.

McCulloch, Gary. "Privatizing the Past? History and Education Policy in the 1990s." *British Journal of Educational Studies* 45 (March 1997): 69–82.

McLaren, Peter. *Revolutionary Multiculturalism: Pedagogies of Dissent for the New Millennium.* Boulder: Westview Press, 1997.

McNeil, Linda. *Contradictions of School Reform: Educational Costs of Standardization.* New York: Routledge, 2000.

Meier, Deborah, Theodore Sizer, Linda Nathan, and Abigail Thern-strom. *Will Standards Save Public Education?* Boston: Beacon Press, 2000.

Menter, Ian, Yolanda Muschamp, Peter Nicholl, Jenny Ozga, and An-drew Pollard. *Work and Identity in the Primary School.* Philadelphia: Open University Press, 1997.

Middleton, Sue. *Disciplining Sexualities.* New York: Teachers College Press, 1998.

Mills, Charles W. *The Racial Contract.* Ithaca: Cornell University Press, 1997.

Molnar, Alex. *Giving Kids the Business: The Commercialization of America's Schools.* Boulder: Westview Press, 1996.

———. *Vouchers, Class Size Reduction, and Student Achievement.* Bloomington, IN: Phi Delta Kappan Education Foundation, 2000.

Molnar, Alex, Philip Smith, John Zahorik, Amanda Palmer, Anke Halbach, and Karen Ehrle. "Evaluating the SAGE Program." *Educational Evaluation and Policy Analysis* 21 (summer 1999): 165–77.

Moses, Michele, S. "The Arizona Tax Credit and Hidden Considerations of Justice." Unpublished paper presented at the annual meeting of the American Educational Research Association, New Orleans, April 2000.

Nord, Warren A. *Religion and American Education: Rethinking a National Dilemma.* Chapel Hill: University of North Carolina Press, 1995.

Novak, Michael. *Toward a Theology of the Corporation.* Washington, DC: American Enterprise Institute, 1990.

———. *This Hemisphere of Liberty: A Philosophy of the Americas.* Washington, DC: American Enterprise Institute, 1992.

Numbers, Ronald L. *The Creationists.* New York: Alfred A Knopf, 1992.

———. *Darwinism Comes to America.* Cambridge: Harvard University Press, 1998.

———. "Creationists and Their Critics in Australia." Unpublished paper, Department of the History of Medicine, University of Wisconsin, Madison.

Numbers, Ronald L. and John Stenhouse. "Antievolutionism in the Antipodes: From Protesting Evolution to Promoting Creationism in New Zealand." *British Journal for the History of Science*, in press.

Oakes, Jeannie. "Can Tracking Research Inform Practice?" *Educational Researcher* 21 (March 1992): 12–21.

Oakes, Jeannie, Karen H. Quartz, Steve Ryan, and Martin Lipton. *Becoming Good American Schools: The Struggle for Civic Virtue in Education Reform.* San Francisco: Jossey-Bass, 2000.

Oakes, Jeannie, Amy Stuart Wells, Makeba Jones, and Amanda Datnow. "Detracking: The Social Construction of Ability, Cultural Politics, and Resistence to Reform." *Teachers College Record* 98 (spring 1997): 482–510.

O'Cadiz, Maria del Pilar, Pia L. Wong, and Carlos A. Torres. *Education and Democracy: Paulo Freire, Social Movements, and Educational Reform in Sao Paulo.* Boulder: Westview Press, 1998.

Ohanian, Susan. *One Size Fits Few: The Folly of Educational Standards.* Portsmouth, NH: Heinemann, 1999.

O'Hear, Philip. "An Alternative National Curriculum." In *Educational Reform and Its Consequences,* ed. Sally Tomlinson, 55–72. London: IPPR/Rivers Oram Press, 1994.

O'Leary, Stephen D. *Arguing the Apocalypse: A Theory of Millennial Rhetoric.* New York: Oxford University Press, 1994.

Olssen, Mark. "In Defense of the Welfare State and of Publicly Provided Education." *Journal of Educational Policy* 11 (May 1996): 337–62.

Omi, Michael, and Howard Winant. *Racial Formation in the United States: From the 1960s to the 1990s,* 2d ed. New York: Routledge, 1994.

Opdycke, Sandra. *No One Was Turned Away.* New York: Oxford University Press, 1999.

Pagels, Elaine. *The Origin of Satan.* New York: Random House, 1995.

Panitch, Leo, and Colin Leys. "Preface." In *Necessary and Unnecessary Utopias,* ed. Leo Panitch and Colin Leys, vii–xi. New York: Monthly Review Press, 1999.

Pink, William, and George Noblit, eds. *Continuity and Contradiction: The Futures of the Sociology of Education.* Cresskill, NJ: Hampton Press, 1995.

Podheretz, Norman. *My Love Affair with America: The Cautionary Tale of a Cheerful Conservative.* New York: Free Press, 2000.

Porto Alegre City Secretariat of Education. "Cycles of Formation: Politic-Pedagogical Proposal for the Citizen's School." *Cadernos Pedagogicos* 9 (April 1999): 1–111.

Power, Sally, David Halpin, and John Fitz. "Underpinning Choice and Diversity." In *Educational Reform and Its Consequences,* ed. Sally Tomlinson, 26–40. London: IPPR/Rivers Oram Press, 1994.

Provenzo, Eugene F. Jr. *Religious Fundamentalism and American Education: The Battle for the Public Schools.* Albany: State University of New York Press, 1990.

Ranson, Stewart. "Theorizing Education Policy." *Journal of Education Policy* 10 (July 1995): 427–48.

Ratner, Ellen. *101 Ways to Get Your Progressive Issues on Talk Radio.* Washington, DC: National Press Books, 1997.

Ravitch, Diane. *National Standards in American Education: A Citizen's Guide.* Washington, DC: The Brookings Institution, 1995.

Ray, Brian. *Home Schooling on the Threshold.* Salem, OR: National Home Education Research Institute, 1999.

Reed, Ralph. "Putting a Friendly Face on the Pro-Family Movement." *Christianity Today,* April 1993, 28.

———. *Politically Incorrect.* Dallas: Word Publishing, 1994.

———. *After The Revolution: How the Christian Coalition Is Impacting America.* Dallas: Word Publishing, 1996.

Re'em, Moshe. "Young Minds in Motion: Teaching and Learning About Difference in Formal and Non-formal Settings." Unpublished doctoral dissertation, University of Wisconsin, Madison, 1998.

Reese, William. *Power and the Promise of School Reform: Grassroots Movements During the Progressive Era.* Boston: Routledge and Kegan Paul, 1986.

Robertson, Pat. *The Secret Kingdom.* Nashville, TN: Thomas Nelson Publishers, 1982.

———. *The New Millennium.* Dallas: Word Publishing, 1990.

———. *The New World Order.* Dallas: Word Publishing, 1991.

———. *The Turning Tide.* Dallas: Word Publishing, 1993.

———. "Law Must Embrace Morality," *Christian American* 6 (April 1995): 16–17.

Robertson, Susan L. *A Class Act: Changing Teachers' Work, the State, and Globalization.* New York: Falmer Press, 2000

Rorty, Richard. *Achieving Our Country: Leftist Thought in Twentieth Century America.* Cambridge: Harvard University Press, 1998.

Rosen, Gary. "Are School Vouchers Un-American?" *Commentary* 109 (February 2000): 26–31.

Rosenstock, Larry, and Adria Steinberg. "Beyond the Shop: Reinventing Vocational Education." In *Democratic Schools,* ed. Michael Apple and James Beane, 41–57. Alexandria, VA: Association for Supervision and Curriculum Development, 1995.

Rury, John, and Jeffrey Mirel, "The Political Economy of Urban Education." In *Review of Research in Education, Volume 22,* ed. Michael W. Apple, 49–110. Washington, DC: American Educational Research Association, 1997.

Rushdoony, Rousas John. *The Institutes of Biblical Law.* Phillipsburgh, NJ: Presbyterian and Reformed Publishing, 1973.

Schlafly, Phyllis. "Fact and Fiction About Censorship." Washington, DC: National Defense Committee, National Society, Daughters of the American Revolution, 1984.

Schorr, Jonathan. "Giving Charter Schools a Chance." *The Nation,* 5 June 2000, 19–23.

Scott, Joan. "Multiculturalism and the Politics of Identity." In *The Identity in Question,* ed. John Rajchman, 3–12. New York: Routledge, 1995.

Seddon, Terri. "Markets and the English." *British Journal of Sociology of Education* 18 (June 1997): 165–85.

Segarra, Jose, and Ricardo Dobles, eds. *Learning as a Political Act: Struggles for Learning and Learning from Struggles.* Cambridge: Harvard Educational Review Reprint Series No. 33, 1999.

Selden, Steven. *Inheriting Shame: The Story of Eugenics and Racism in America.* New York: Teachers College Press, 1999.

Shapiro, Andrew L. "The Net That Binds." *The Nation,* 21 June 1999, 11–15.

Slack, Jennifer D. "The Theory and Method of Articulation in Cultural Studies." In *Stuart Hall: Critical Dialogues in Cultural Studies,* ed. David Morley and Kuan-Hsing Chen, 112–27. New York: Routledge, 1996.

Slaughter, Sheila, and Larry L. Leslie. *Academic Capitalism.* Baltimore: The Johns Hopkins University Press, 1997.

Smith, Adam. *The Wealth of Nations.* Oxford: Clarendon Press, 1976.

Smith, Christian. *American Evangelicalism: Embattled and Thriving.* Chicago: University of Chicago Press, 1998.

Smith, Gregory A. *Public Schools That Work: Creating Community.* New York: Routledge, 1993.

Smith, Kevin B., and Kenneth J. Meier, eds. *The Case Against School Choice: Politics, Markets, and Fools.* Armonk, NY: M. E. Sharpe, 1995.

Smith, Linda Tuhiwai, *Decolonizing Methodologies.* New York: Zed Books, 1999.

Smith, Mary Lee, Walter Heinecke, and Audrey Noble, "Assessment Policy and Political Spectacle," *Teachers College Record* 101 (winter 1999): 157–91.

Smith-Rosenberg, Carol. *Disorderly Conduct: Visions of Gender in Victorian America.* New York: Oxford University Press, 1985.

Steinberg, Jacques. "Blue Books Closed, Students Boycott Standardized Tests." *The New York Times,* 13 April 2000, A1–A22.

Stearns, David, and James Harvey. *A Legacy of Learning: Your Stake in Standards and New Kinds of Public Schools.* Washington, DC: The Brookings Institution, 2000.

Swartz, David. *Culture and Power: The Sociology of Pierre Bourdieu.* Chicago: University of Chicago Press, 1997.

Tate, William. "Critical Race Theory and Education." In *Review of Research in Education Volume 22,* ed. Michael W. Apple, 195–247. Washington, DC: American Educational Research Association, 1997.

Teitelbaum, Kenneth. *Schooling for Good Rebels.* New York: Teachers College Press, 1996.

Therburn, Robert. *The Children Trap: Biblical Principles for Education.* Fort Worth, TX: Dominion Press and Thomas Nelson, 1986.

Tomlinson, Sally. "New Inequalities: Educational Markets and Ethnic Minorities." Unpublished paper presented at the symposium on Racism and Reform in the United Kingdom at the annual meeting of the American Educational Research Association, San Diego, April 1998.

Tomlinson, Sally, ed. *Educational Reform and Its Consequences.* London: IPPR/Rivers Oram Press, 1994.

Van Vught, Johannes. *Democratic Organizations for Social Change: Latin American Christian Base Communities and Literacy Campaigns.* New York: Bergin & Garvey, 1991.

Wacquant, Loic. "Foreword" to Pierre Bourdieu, *The State Nobility*, ix–xxii. Stanford: Stanford University Press, 1996.

Watson, Justin. *The Christian Coalition: Dreams of Restoration, Demands for Recognition.* New York: St Martin's Press, 1997.

Wells, Amy S. *Time to Choose: America at the Crossroads of School Choice Policy.* New York: Hill & Wang, 1993.

———. *Beyond the Rhetoric of Charter School Reform.* Los Angeles: University of California at Los Angeles, Graduate School of Education and Information Studies, 1999.

Wells, Amy S., Alejandra Lopez, Janelle Scott, and Jennifer Holme. "Charter Schools as Postmodern Paradox: Rethinking Social Stratification in an Age of Deregulated School Choice." *Harvard Educational Review* 69 (summer 1999): 172–204.

West, Cornel. *Prophesy Deliverance!: An Afro-American Revolutionary Christianity.* Philadelphia: Westminster Press, 1982.

———. *Race Matters.* New York: Vintage Books, 1994.

Wheen, Francis. *Karl Marx: A Life.* New York: Norton, 1999.

White, Geoffrey, ed. *Campus, Inc.* New York: Prometheus Books, 2000.

Whitty, Geoff. "Sociology and the Problem of Radical Educational Change." In *Educability, Schools, and Ideology*, ed. Michael Flude and John Ahier, 112–37. London: Halstead Press, 1974.

———. "Creating Quasi-Markets in Education." In *Review of Research in Education, Volume 22*, ed. Michael W. Apple, 3–47. Washington, DC: American Educational Research Association, 1997.

Whitty, Geoff, Tony Edwards, and Sharon Gewirtz. *Specialization and Choice in Urban Education.* London: Routledge, 1993.

Whitty, Geoff, Sally Power, and David Halpin. *Devolution and Choice in Education: The School, the State, and the Market.* Philadelphia: Open University Press, 1998.

Williams, Raymond. *Marxism and Literature.* New York: Oxford University Press, 1977.

————. *Keywords: A Vocabulary of Culture and Society.* New York: Oxford University Press, 1985.

————. *Resources of Hope: Culture, Democracy, Socialism.* New York: Verso, 1989.

Wilson, Glen Y. "Effects on Funding Equity of the Arizona Tax Credit Law." Paper presented at the annual meeting of the American Educational Research Association, New Orleans, April 2000.

Witte, John F. *The Market Approach to Education: An Analysis of America's First Voucher Program.* Princeton, NJ: Princeton University Press, 2000.

Wong, Ting-Hong, and Michael W. Apple. "Rethinking the Education/State Formation Connection." Unpublished paper.

Wright, Erik O. *Classes.* New York: Verso, 1985.

————. *Class Counts: Comparative Studies in Class Analysis.* New York: Cambridge University Press, 1997.

Wright, Erik O., ed. *The Debate on Classes.* New York: Verso, 1998.

Wyatt, Edward, "Investors See Room for Profit in the Demand for Education." *The New York Times,* 4 November 1999, A-1.

Zinn, Howard. *The Zinn Reader: Writings on Disobedience and Democracy.* New York: Seven Stories Press, 1997.

————. *A People's History of the United States.* New York: HarperCollins, 1999.

————. *The Future of History: Interviews with David Barsamian.* Monroe, ME: Common Courage Press, 1999.

Index